Making
the Gospel
Plain

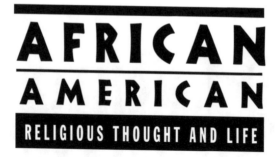

AFRICAN
AMERICAN
RELIGIOUS THOUGHT AND LIFE

This series provides opportunity for African American scholars from a wide variety of fields in religion to develop their insights into religious discourse on issues that affect African American intellectual, social, cultural, and community life. The series focuses on topics, figures, problems, and cultural expressions in the study of African American religion that are often neglected by publishing programs centered on African American theology. The AARTL program of publications will bridge theological reflection on African American religious experience and the critical, methodological interests of African American religious studies.

SERIES EDITORS

ANTHONY B. PINN, Macalester College, St. Paul, Minnesota
VICTOR ANDERSON, Vanderbilt University, Nashville, Tennessee

Making the Gospel Plain

THE WRITINGS OF BISHOP REVERDY C. RANSOM

Edited by Anthony B. Pinn

TRINITY PRESS INTERNATIONAL
Harrisburg, Pennsylvania

Trinity Press International, P.O. Box 1321, Harrisburg, PA 17105
Trinity Press International is a division of the Morehouse Group.

Library of Congress Cataloging-in-Publication Data

Ransom, Reverdy C. (Reverdy Cassius), 1861-1959.
    Making the gospel plain : the writings of Bishop Reverdy C.
Ransom / edited by Anthony B. Pinn.
        p.   cm. – (African American religious thought and life)
    Includes bibliographical references and index.
    ISBN 1-56338-264-4 (pbk. : alk. paper)
    1. Afro-Americans – Religion. 2. Afro-Americans – Civil rights.
I. Pinn, Anthony B.   II. Title.   III. Series.
BX8449.R35 A25 1999
287'.8 – dc21   99-13076

Printed in the United States of America

99   00   01   02   03   04   10 9   8   7   6   5   4   3   2   1

To
the Unnamed Ancestors
and
Raymond W. Pinn Sr.
(1928–1998)

As an orator, Bishop Ransom has few equals. His addresses are not mere outbursts of eloquence, but show the conviction of the man as to the claims of the Negro to recognition in this country and the procedure to be followed in reaching this end. He has, therefore, taken the advanced position of espousing forward-looking movements securing to the Negro the rights which have been denied him by the reactionaries now in control of the State and Federal governments.

— CARTER WOODSON
Negro Orators and Their Orations

Millions of us here have courage without fear. And shall firmly stand to support the foundation upon which this nation was established, and upon which it stands today. It remains the brightest hope for all Americans regardless of race, creed, or color. If we could ascend from the depths of slavery from which we came to the place we occupy today, we can also achieve the goals of brotherhood and peace for which we strive.

— REVERDY C. RANSOM
Letter written on behalf of W. E. B. Du Bois to the National Council of the Arts, Sciences and Professions

Contents

Part Two
ARTICLES AND PAMPHLETS

Part Three
BOOK CHAPTERS

Acknowledgments

Although my name is on the cover of this volume, many persons helped to bring it to completion, among them Harold Rast, Laura Barrett, and others from Trinity Press International. Mary Byers and John Eagleson did a fine job of turning the manuscript into a polished text. I must also extend my thanks to those at Payne Theological Seminary, Wilberforce University, Howard University, and the Schomburg Center for Research in Black Culture who assisted me with the securing of documents for this volume. I would also like to thank Dr. Paulette Coleman, Dr. Ricky Spain, and Dr. A. Lee Henderson for their cooperation. I must also thank Mrs. Ruth L. Ransom and her son, Louis A. Ransom, Jr., for their kindness. The librarians at Macalester College also went above and beyond the call of duty in tolerating my tardy return of resources and urgent request for additional materials. Barbara Wells-Howe scanned several documents and, by so doing, saved me a great deal of time. Also at Macalester, I must thank my research assistants: Gregory Colleton, Leif Johnson, Gretchen Rohr, and Mary Kate Little. Two very good friends in New York City — Benjamin Valentin and Eli Valentin — helped secure documents and "lighten up" tense situations, taking time from their own work to help me with mine. I would like to thank my mother, the Reverend Anne H. Pinn, for reading this text with enthusiasm and helping with this project in numerous ways. I would also like to thank Joyce Pinn for reading and commenting on this manuscript. I also owe a huge debt of gratitude to my companion, Cheryl Johnson, for her good spirit, sense of humor, patience, and encouragement.

Thanks to all.

Chronology

January 4, 1861	Born in Flushing, Ohio, to Harriet Ransom; biological father unknown; stepfather is George Warner Ransom.
1865	Moves to Washington, Ohio.
1869	Moves with parents to Cambridge, Ohio.
1881	Marries Leanna Watkins; son George Ransom born.
1881	Enters Wilberforce University and joins the church.
1882–83	Accepts "call" to preach while studying at Oberlin College; returns to Wilberforce the following year.
1883	Is licensed to preach.
1885	Joins the Ohio Annual Conference of the A.M.E. Church
1886	Divorces Leanna Watkins.
1886	Graduates from Wilberforce University; during senior year he pastors in Selma, Ohio.
1886–90	Pastors mission churches in Pennsylvania in the Pittsburgh Conference, having been transferred from the Ohio Conference. In Pennsylvania he is ordained a deacon in the A.M.E. Church.
1887	Marries Emma S. Connor, of Selma, Ohio; from this marriage is born Reverdy C. Ransom, Jr.

Based on Calvin Morris's chronology in *Reverdy C. Ransom: Black Advocate of the Social Gospel*; David Wills, "Reverdy C. Ransom: The Making of an A.M.E. Bishop"; and archival findings.

1888	Is ordained an elder in the A.M.E. Church; works as associate editor of the *Afro-American Spokesman* newspaper.
1890–96	Pastors in Ohio: North Street in Springfield and St. John's in Cleveland. Develops a regional reputation. Friendships with figures such as Dunbar continue to grow. He also starts St. James Church as a mission. He develops the first Men's Club during this period.
1894	Organizes first Deaconess Board. Some scholars list the date as 1893; Ransom indicates 1894.
1896	Publicly endorses socialism in an *A.M.E. Church Review* article.
1896–1900	Pastors Bethel Church in Chicago. Develops the Men's Sunday Club and other social gospel church organizations. Becomes acquainted with figures such as Jane Addams, Ida B. Wells-Barnett, and Fannie Barrier Williams. His sense of the social gospel is further developed through these and other contacts.
1898	Joins reactivated Afro-American Council. His disagreement with Booker T. Washington becomes public.
1901	A.M.E. Church representative to the Ecumenical Conference of Methodism in London, Ontario (Toronto, 1911; London, 1921; Springfield, Mass., 1947).
1903	Campaigns against numbers racketeers in Chicago.
1900–1904	Organizes and pastors the Institutional Church and Social Settlement House in Chicago, the first effort of its kind in the A.M.E. Church. He begins to develop a national reputation.
1904	Helps mediate stockyard strike in Chicago.
1904–7	Pastors in Massachusetts: New Bedford for one year and Charles Street Church in Boston.

1905	Participates in the development of the Niagara Movement.
1907	Helps Tammany Hall win mayoral race in New York based upon the Democrats' willingness to incorporate blacks into the political structures.
1907–12	Pastors Bethel Church in New York City.
1909	Participates in the founding of the NAACP.
1912–24	Serves as editor of the *A.M.E. Church Review.*
1913	Founds Church of Simon of Cyrene in New York City.
1918	Unsuccessfully runs for Congress.
1924–52	Is elected forty-eighth bishop in the A.M.E. Church.
1932–48	Chairs the Wilberforce University Board of Trustees.
1934	Founds the Fraternal Council of Negro Churches, a national organization of clergy for the purpose of supporting the objectives of African Americans.
1940	Is appointed first African American member of Ohio Board of Parole; gives the opening prayer at Democratic National Convention.
1941	Wife, Emma Ransom, dies. Named by President Roosevelt to the Volunteer Participation Committee in the Office of Civil Defense.
1943	Marries Georgia Myrtle Teal.
1948–56	Serves as A.M.E. church historiographer.
1950	Is honored in Flushing, Ohio, with a marble plaque in a park near his home.
1952	Retires from active service as a bishop.
April 22, 1959	Dies in Wilberforce, Ohio.
1979	Is named to Guernsey County (Ohio) Hall of Fame.

A Tribute to
Reverdy Cassius Ransom

W. E. B. Du Bois

"Frederick Douglass" by Paul Laurence Dunbar is one of the price-less gems of poetry by the "Poet Laureate" of America. It was written in honor of the precious memory of the great former slave, abolitionist, and orator of fame. It is prized highly by the Reverend James C. Dixon of Detroit, and often we have para-phrased it in dedicatory terms of Reverdy Cassius Ransom. Now the Centenarian has crossed the frontier of time, and in his honor we substitute his name for that of Douglass. Without being sac-rilegious or plagiaristic we present it in prosaic form instead of poetry:

A hush is over all the teeming lists, And there is a pause, a breath-space in the strife; A spirit brave has passed be-yond the mists And vapors that obscure the sun of life. And Ethiopia, with bosom torn, Laments the passing of her no-blest born. She weeps for him a mother's burning tears — She loved him with a mother's deepest love. He was her cham-pion thro' direful years, And held her weal all other ends above. When bondage held her bleeding in the dust, He raised her up and whispered, "Hope and Trust."

For her his voice, a fearless clarion rung That broke in warn-ing on the ears of men; For her the strong bow of his power he stung, And sent arrows to the very den Where grim op-pression held his bloody place And gloated o'er the mis'ries of a race. And he was no soft-tongued apologist; He spoke straightforward, fearlessly uncowed; The sunlight of his truth dispelled the mist, And set in bold relief each dark hued

First published in *A.M.E. Church Review*, April–June 1959. Reprinted by permis-sion of the *A.M.E. Church Review*.

cloud; To sin and crime he gave their proper hue, And hurled at evil what was evil's due. Through good and ill report he cleaved his way Right upward, with his face set toward the heights, Nor feared to face the foeman's dread array, — The lash of scorn, the sting of petty spites. He dared the lightning in the lightning's track, And answered thunder with his thunder back. When men maligned him, and their torrent wrath Infurious imprecations o'er him broke, He kept his counsel as he kept his path; 'Twas for his race, not for himself he spoke. He knew the import of his Master's call, And felt himself too mighty to be small. No miser in the good he held was he, — His kindness followed his horizon's rim. His heart, his talents, and his hands were free To all who truly needed aught of him. Where poverty and ignorance were rife, He gave his bounty as he gave his life. The place and cause that first aroused his might Still proved its power until his latest day. In Freedom's list and for the aid of Right. Still in the foremost rank he waged the fray; Wrong lived; his occupation was not gone. He died in action with his armor on! We weep for him, but we have touched his hand. And felt the magic of his presence nigh. The current that he sent throughout the land, The kindling spirit of his battle-cry. O'er all that holds us we shall triumph yet, And place our banner where his hopes were set! Oh, Reverdy Cassius Ransom, thou hast passed beyond the shore, But still thy voice is ringing o'er the gale! Thou'st taught thy race how high her hopes may soar, And bade her seek the heights, nor faint, nor fail. She will not fail, she heeds thy stirring cry, She knows thy guardian spirit will be nigh, And rising from beneath the chast'ning rod, She stretches out her bleeding hands to God.

As Dunbar knew Douglass and admired him, Ransom knew Dunbar, and encouraged him who had been inspired by the muses to write gems of poetry. [Ransom's] funeral service was held in the Jones Auditorium, Shorter Hall, at Wilberforce, Tuesday, 11:00 A.M., April 28 [1959]. Most of the bishops, general officers, a large number of ministers and laymen from over the Connection honored "The Sage of Tawawa Chimney Corner" by their presence. They listened to a most impressive and heart-stirring eulogy delivered by Dr. Joseph Gomez, bishop of the Fourth Episcopal District, a spiritual son and heir of the decedent. The presiding officer was Bishop Frank Madison Reid, president of the Council of Bishops.

We lean upon the immortal Dunbar, for words are inadequate to express desired appreciation of Reverdy Cassius Ransom — preacher par excellence, orator in the category of Demosthenes Chrysostom, T. M. D. Ward, and B. W. Arnett; founder and builder of churches, literary genius, author of many books and pamphlets; twelve years editor of the *A.M.E. Church Review,* and twenty-eight years a Bishop. He has erected a monument in the history of African Methodism, America, and the world which shall last throughout time and eternity. His decrease has left a vacancy which only time can fill.

In 1906 Bishop Ransom spoke at Harpers Ferry on John Brown. It was the second meeting of the Niagara Movement and that speech more than any single event stirred the great meeting. It led through its inspiration and eloquence to the eventual founding of the National Association for the Advancement of Colored People, and twenty-five years of work for Negro equality and freedom....

Editor's Introduction

Context

Questions concerning the nature and manifestations of leadership in African American communities are not new. However, prior to what Gayraud Wilmore labels the deradicalization of black churches,[1] many of these questions were addressed through attention to leadership in the form of black churches and their central figures. During this period, the church played a strong and undeniable role in the total life of African American communities, providing spiritual uplift and insightful action with respect to the material concerns of their congregations and beyond. According to C. Eric Lincoln and Lawrence H. Mamiya:

> The black Church has no challenger as the cultural womb of the black community. Not only did it give birth to new institutions such as schools, banks, insurance companies, and low income housing, it also provided an academy and an arena for political activities, and it nurtured young talent for musical, dramatic, and artistic development.[2]

The inspiration for and the stature of this black church tradition are forever connected to figures such as Richard Allen, Maria Stewart, and Henry M. Turner and their biting jeremiads in response to U.S. hypocrisy. These Christian activists, and others unnamed, mark the best of the church's interaction with the basic issues of life. However, the legacy they created by bringing the church and social concerns together did not remain intact or unmarred. Changing sociopolitical and economic realities during the early twentieth century pushed the black church tradition to the point of rupture. In response, this tradition in large part adopted an uncharacteristically parochial posture. With the growing otherworldly

1. See Gayraud Wilmore, *Black Religion and Black Radicalism: An Interpretation of the Religious History of African-American People,* 2d ed. (Anchor Press/ Doubleday, 1972; Maryknoll, N.Y.: Orbis Books, 1983).
2. C. Eric Lincoln and Lawrence H. Mamiya, *The Black Church in the African American Experience* (Durham: Duke University Press, 1990), 8.

and defensive stance of many black churches emerging during the period of the Great Migration, the assumed role of the church in providing leadership for the larger African American community was brought into question.

In spite of the general deradicalization of black churches and the consequential lack of leadership coming from black churches, some clergy nevertheless strove to maintain the black church's commitment to the full — spiritual and physical — liberation of the African American community. One such figure was Reverdy Cassius Ransom.

Ransom and Praxis

From Ransom's perspective, to be Christlike required a concern for the condition of African Americans, and the gospel had to be applied to this because religion should affect the depth of being and radiate outward in transformed attitudes and behaviors. The abuse faced by African Americans contradicted the recorded aims and goals of the United States. Yet, Ransom felt that the Christian faith, when lived, could promote healing and the transformation of society. The Christian faith provided the final outcome, the development of the Kingdom of God that social Christianity addresses through the concretization of democracy and equality. The otherworldly thrust is thus lost on Ransom, and the benefits of the gospel and Christian conduct are felt in a qualitative change in human life in this world. He espouses this opinion early in his ministry. In this way, Ransom merged worlds and brought to his Christian commitment a full range of resources that gave little attention to distinctions between "sacred" and "secular." The full range of human needs made such distinctions useless, particularly in light of God's desire to dwell where humans suffered most; Ransom gave little of this attention, however, to foreign mission efforts within the church as advocated by Bishop Henry Turner. Yet, he did give some attention to rethinking the place of women in the black church through attempts to provide for a fuller inclusion of their talents and abilities.

Ransom's contribution to African American Christianity as a social force was based upon his awareness of the complexity of the African American community and its various career-related layers. Ministry must recognize and respond to the various professional and economic levels of African American communities. For example, many ministers in New York failed to take seriously the needs of African American entertainers because of strict moral codes against dancing, acting, and so on. Ransom would not abide by moral codes that denied those in need the opportunity for fulfillment:

> It used to be a common practice among our ministers to preach against attending theaters or participating in dancing. Thousands of Negro actors and musicians were thus left unshepherded so far as the ministrations of the clergy was concerned. . . . I sought these people, cultivated their acquaintance and friendship, often visited them when they were sick and always stood ready to respond to cause whenever requested.[3]

Ransom was concerned with the progress of African Americans, but he was not a nationalist in the worst sense — he did not have a preoccupation with race that did not allow for social interaction between peoples of differing backgrounds. Hence, race was important but as a marker that allowed for unique contributions to human civilization and for the mosaic-like nature of the human family. Each member of this mosaic was considered important, vital, and indispensable. U.S. democracy, in theory, is premised upon this idea. However, social conditions, according to Ransom, would not change unless the existing form of government also changed.[4] Ransom came to understand as early as 1897 that socialism entailed the full enactment of democracy and equality. He understood that the sense of full humanity and community espoused in socialism was the only way of providing the type of "level playing field" necessary for the development of the United States in keeping with its ideals and desires outlined in its early documents. Socialism provided, in essence, the societal blueprint for the world community rhetorically addressed in his liberal theology. In this way, African Americans could obtain the political, social, economic, industrial, and educational advantages their efforts merited. Ransom's interest in socialism was in keeping with his commitment to the social gospel and the social gospelers who influenced his thought. In addition to this influence, Ransom's analysis of the United States and its problems points to the type of sociological work pioneered by figures such as W. E. B. Du Bois.

---

3. Reverdy C. Ransom, *The Pilgrim of Harriet Ransom's Son* (Nashville: A.M.E. Sunday School Union, 1949), 207.
4. Ibid., 184.

Readers should also be sensitive to the influence of pragmatism within Ransom's thought, easily accessed with respect to Ransom's commitment to the force of human power and action to transform the world, as well as his explicit response to the problem of evil. Interaction with Du Bois, revolving around the Niagara Movement, would undoubtedly have exposed Ransom to Du Bois's version of pragmatism, learned from William James and others during Du Bois's years at Harvard University.[5] Furthermore, auxiliary organizations at Bethel Church in Chicago, the development of the Institutional Church and Social Settlement House, also in Chicago, the creation of the Church of Simon of Cyrene in New York City, and the development of the Fraternal Council of Negro Churches formed in 1934 mark Ransom's ministry as a unique combination of the social gospel, socialism, radical love, and humanitarianism that modeled the best of a Bishop Henry Turner's race consciousness and praxis without the extremist tendencies, and the political activity of a Paul Robeson without the isolation from church structures.

These efforts continued during Ransom's years as a bishop and, after his retirement from the bishopric, as historian of the A.M.E. Church. Even at an advanced age, Ransom continued to provide vision and guidance for the A.M.E. Church through, for example, the creation of the "African Methodist Social Creed," which addressed the church's necessary response to issues such as the dignity of all human beings, the destructive nature of prejudice, religious freedom, and mutually beneficial bargaining between employees and employers. This statement, to be read to all congregations, was undertaken because "more than one million members of our communion look to their church for moral and social, as well as spiritual guidance in this time of confusion, aggression and fear."[6] With his retirement, Ransom continued in Tawawa "Chimney Corner," his home in Wilberforce, Ohio, to push the church toward

---

5. For a discussion of Du Bois the pragmatist, as well as the importance of theodicy or the problem of evil in pragmatic thought, see Cornel West, *The American Evasion of Philosophy: A Genealogy of Pragmatism* (Madison: University of Wisconsin Press, 1989) and *Prophetic Thought in Postmodern Times* (Monroe, Maine: Common Courage Press, 1993), esp. pt. 1, chaps. 2–3. For a discussion of pragmatism as a challenge to African American religion and religious thought, see Cornel West, *Prophesy Deliverance: An Afro-American Revolutionary Christianity* (Philadelphia: Westminster Press, 1982), chaps. 4–5.

6. Quoted in Donald Drewett's "Ransom on Race and Racism: The Racial and Social Thought of Reverdy Cassius Ransom — Preacher, Editor, and Bishop in the African Methodist Episcopal Church, 1861–1959," Ph.D. dissertation, Drew University, 1988, 495.

the completion of its obligations and responsibilities. Ransom died on April 22, 1959.

Rationale for This Volume

If Ransom's influence had died with him, there would be no need for this volume. But the careful observer of African American religious history and thought must note that through Ransom's pioneering work with the social gospel black churches found a map for making inroads into the modern scope of human need and potential. This, combined with the need for a much fuller and more textual understanding of African American religious history as a way to contextualize and understand current religious trends in African American communities, makes this collection of Ransom's writings an essential tool.

I first became familiar with Reverdy C. Ransom while working on my dissertation. Looking through materials in an attempt to reconstruct African American theology and praxis as they developed during the early twentieth century, I came across several of Ransom's pamphlets. Looking for additional writings by him was a difficult process, and I was surprised by the difficulty in securing more than just the random document. It seemed to me that Ransom's church work marked a major contribution to African American religious history and life, and consequently deserved more sustained attention. Almost three years after publishing my dissertation, I have finally turned my attention to this project. My goal is to provide additional information concerning the manner in which the social gospel and other representations of liberal thought, as well as the black church tradition, have informed the efforts of African Americans to transform society. It points to the rich and layered nature of this religious tradition. Furthermore, for those who seek to trace the major trends in African American Christianity, this volume provides a bridge between the radical activity of the early black church under figures such as Richard Allen and Henry McNeal Turner and the work of Adam Clayton Powell, Jr., Martin L. King, Jr., and Jesse Jackson among other contemporary examples. It demonstrates, in this way, a strand of "prophetic Christianity," to use Cornel West's phrase, that is usually ignored from 1915 (with the death of Turner) to 1955 (with the emergence of Martin L. King, Jr.). In the words of Randall Burkett, Ransom is a figure whose life and work can provide "a much fairer view of the richness of black religious life in the second quarter of the twentieth century."[7] His visionary thought offers a great gift and tool for the construction of more responsive and flexible church structures and an "earthier" theology, fitted for the needs of the contemporary scene. I must also say that we can learn from Ransom's mistakes. For example, the sexism (e.g., cult of true womanhood) that marked his historical moment and some of his work should motivate readers to move beyond sexist practices and attitudes in contemporary churches.

The writings of historically significant figures provide an invaluable resource for those who are interested in understanding the development of ideas and actions. This is no less true for those interested in understanding the rich religious tradition of African Americans. Over the past ten years, the collected writings of Maria Stewart, Ida B. Wells-Barnett, and others highlight the rich history of African American religious thought. However, the small number of such projects also marks tremendous need. That is to say, there are valuable materials that are still lost to the public; only those who have access to private collections and the manuscript rooms of select libraries can benefit. In addition, many volumes exist which explore the nature and development of African American religion. Several of these give some treatment to particular figures. However, with respect to Reverdy Ransom, little substantive attention exists outside the writings of Calvin Morris ("Reverdy Ransom, the Social Gospel and Race," 1984, and *Reverdy Ransom: Black Advocate of the Social Gospel,* 1990), David Wills (e.g., "Reverdy C. Ransom: The Making of an A.M.E. Bishop," 1978), and Donald Drewett's dissertation ("Ransom on Race and Racism: The Racial and Social Thought of Reverdy Cassius Ransom, Preacher, Editor and Bishop in the African Methodist Episcopal Church, 1861–1959"). These documents, while informative, are secondary treatments.[8]

---

7. Randall Burkett, "The Baptist Church in the Years of Crisis: J. C. Austin and Pilgrim Baptist Church, 1926–1950," 151. In *African-American Christianity: Essays in History,* ed. Paul E. Johnson (Berkeley: University of California Press, 1994).

8. Readers who are unfamiliar with some of the historical moments and figures mentioned by Ransom throughout his writings should see, for example, the following texts: James Brewer Stewart, *Holy Warriors: The Abolitionists and American Slavery,* rev. ed. (New York: Hill and Wang, 1976, 1996); Reginald Horsman, *Race and Manifest Destiny: The Origins of American Racial Anglo-Saxonism* (Cambridge, Mass.: Harvard University Press, 1981); James Oliver Horton and Lois E. Horton, *In Hope of Liberty: Culture, Community and Protest among Northern Free Blacks, 1700–1860* (New York: Oxford University Press, 1997); Leon F. Litwack, *Trouble in Mind: Black Southerners in the Age of Jim Crow* (New York:

Structure

The reader will note that several of these secondary documents are included in this volume in order to provide contextual information for Ransom's writings. Including these documents, I believe, is ultimately more useful than an introduction to Ransom's life and work based strictly on the editor's interests and disciplinary limitations. I made an effort to provide contextual information that gave attention to both descriptive and interpretative discussions of Ransom. The essays included are an essay by the editor outlining Ransom's theology and those who influenced his thought, as well as a historical essay written by David Wills which outlines Ransom's ministry during his highly active and developmental years. Although not included here because of space limitations, both Morris's treatment of Ransom's social Christianity and Drewett's dissertation would be of interest to readers. I believe that these secondary treatments are also valuable because they make explanatory footnotes within the various primary documents unnecessary. By presenting these studies, the editor seeks to provide context and background for Ransom's work that explain the full scope of his life.

After these essays the volume is divided according to type of document rather than thematically: Sermons and Speeches; Articles and Pamphlets; and Book Chapters. Arranging the documents by class allows for the maintenance of a "natural" progression with respect to the issues Ransom addresses. It gives attention to issues and problems as Ransom did, without an artificial sense of consistency or variety. Where possible, documents within the three sections are also arranged by date. With these documents there is overlap along thematic lines as well as presentation. However, because Ransom's writings mirror the times and the same issues continued to appear during his lifetime, it is only natural that his writings will approach these same themes. In addition, an attempt has been made to limit the number of materials that already appear in collections. However, it is impossible to completely avoid this overlap. Finally, introductory comments accompany each document.

Travel accounts and accounts of official denominational functions are omitted here because I do not believe they are the best way of knowing Ransom's thought and praxis. If the growth and development of the A.M.E. Church as a denomination were the

Alfred A. Knopf, 1998); Paula Giddings, *When and Where I Enter* (New York: Bantam Books, 1985).

emphasis of this volume, as opposed to my concern with the development of a particular figure, such travel and conference accounts would have been included. In addition, Ransom wrote editorials during his editorship of the *A.M.E. Church Review*. But because this same information is available in a more substantive form through the various articles and other documents, I have decided to exclude these editorials with few exceptions.

The final component of this volume is a bibliography that provides a list of documents housed in the major archival collections as well as newspapers carrying articles by Ransom and texts by Ransom not housed in archive collection. The bibliography also includes useful secondary treatments of Ransom's life and work.

The selection of documents for this volume is informed by my own archival work and conversations with those who also have an interest in Ransom. I do not claim to provide a complete set of writings by and about Ransom. Some will undoubtedly question the "essential" nature of some pieces. Nevertheless, I sought to publish some of what I consider his more substantive and important pieces that highlight his thought and praxis and point to his significance for students of American religion. It is my assumption that, with his writings available, the next step is an intellectual biography of Ransom and his work, but I will leave that to other scholars.

I am aware of the manner in which the personal agenda of an editor can influence the presentation of materials. I worked with this awareness and tried to avoid this problem as best as possible. Regardless of my efforts, it is unlikely that the editor is completely removed from this project and the presentation of Ransom's voice. Where I have fallen short in my efforts, I encourage other scholars to correct through additional study.

Reverdy C. Ransom:
The Making of an A.M.E. Bishop

David Wills

Reverdy Cassius Ransom (1861–1959) was one of the most important black churchmen of the first half of this century. Within the A.M.E. Church, he can justly be classed with Richard Allen, Daniel Alexander Payne, and Henry McNeal Turner as among the church's greatest bishops. Outside the church, he was for decades an eloquent and influential spokesman for racial justice. Yet Ransom has received very little scholarly attention. Not only is there no full-length study of his career, but apart from a few pages in S. P. Fullinwider's *The Mind and Mood of Black America* there is not a single published interpretation of his work. Such a lapse in scholarly attention clearly needs correction.[1]

Ideally, that correction should take the form of a book-length account of Ransom's long and productive life. A southwestern Ohio boyhood lasting from the eve of the Civil War through the end of Reconstruction; five troubled college years at Wilberforce and Oberlin; twenty-six years as the increasingly prominent pastor of A.M.E. congregations in Pennsylvania, Ohio, Illinois, Massachusetts, and New York, and as an influential member of such racial protest groups as the Afro-American Council and the Niagara Movement; twelve years as editor of the *A.M.E. Review;*

First published in Richard Newman and Randall K. Burkett, editors, *Black Apostles: Afro-American Clergy Confront the Twentieth Century* (Boston: G. K. Hall, 1978). Reprinted by permission of Macmillan and Company.

1. S. P. Fullinwider, *The Mind and Mood of Black America: 20th Century Thought* (Homewood, Ill.: Dorsey Press, 1969), 41–47. There are also important general comments on Ransom in August Meier, *Negro Thought in America, 1880–1915: Racial Ideologies in the Age of Booker T. Washington* (Ann Arbor: University of Michigan Press, 1963), 180, 182, 185, 220–21, 229–33. Richard R. Wright, Jr., *The Bishops of the African Methodist Episcopal Church* (Nashville: A.M.E. Sunday School Union, 1963), 287–92, contains the best biographical synopsis.

twenty-four years as the leading bishop of a denomination struggling to overcome severe internal divisions and to adjust to a
reduced role in black American life; and seven years as a retired
observer of the desegregation struggle of the 1950s — Ransom's
life is clearly rich enough to sustain such a lengthy account.

The present essay, however, attempts no such ambitious task.
It is, rather, quite limited both in the period it emphasizes and the
topics it most fully treats. More is said here about Ransom's youth,
education, and early years in the pastorate than about his later career as editor and bishop. Greater attention is given to his place
within the A.M.E. tradition than to his role in black protest movements. The controlling purpose of the essay is to trace through
the personal experiences, ecclesiastical developments, and public
affairs of those earlier years — the emergence of the distinctive
style of churchmanship which Ransom brought with him to the
bishopric in 1924. The rest of the story, hopefully, will be told
elsewhere.[2]

"Harriet Ransom's son," as Reverdy termed himself in the title
of his autobiography, was born on January 4, 1861, in the village
of Flushing, Ohio.[3] His mother, a woman of "light bronze complexion, with clearly cut features, high cheek bones and a straight,
well-formed nose," was the daughter of an Indian father and an
ex-slave mother. She was also, by her son's account, the dominant
influence of his childhood and youth. She selected from the black
and white worlds around her those ideas and values which seemed
most commendable and impressed them upon young Reverdy with
all the forcefulness that a strong and independent woman could
muster. Her place in the title of his life story was earned, not
merely honorary.

At birth, Reverdy was a frail child, whose appearance gave no
hint of the long life that was to follow. He also had red hair and
no admitted father, two facts possibly related to one another. His

---

2. Two doctoral dissertations on Ransom are currently in progress: Donald A.
Drewett, "Ransom and Race: A Social, Political, and Ecclesiastical Study, 1861–
1959" (Drew University), and Frank E. Moorer, "Reverdy C. Ransom and the
Transformation of the A.M.E. Church, 1860–1950" (Johns Hopkins). I have also
discussed Ransom's economic ethics in an unpublished essay, "The Meaning of
Racial Justice and the Limits of American Liberalism," 32–38.

3. Except where otherwise indicated, the factual information and direct quotations contained in the following account of Ransom's childhood and youth are
drawn from his autobiography, *The Pilgrimage of Harriet Ransom's Son* (Nashville:
Sunday School Union, 1949), 15–27. His birthdate is supplied by Wright, *Bishops,*
287.

first two names were bestowed upon him, curiously enough, by Congressman John A. Bingham, who paid five dollars in gold for the privilege of naming his new Constituent after two politicians, Reverdy Johnson of Maryland and Cassius M. Clay of Kentucky.[4] He also at some point gained a surname from George Warner Ransom, the "silent, taciturn man" who eventually married Reverdy's mother and became, by his "son's" account, "a father to me for more than fifty years." By temperament and affection, however, young Reverdy remained "Harriet Ransom's son."[5]

For the first four years of his life — the Civil War years — mother and son lived with Harriet's mother, Lucinda, in whose two-room log house Reverdy had been born. Lucinda was a brown-skinned woman from Virginia, who always impressed her grandson with her "exceptionally bright mind." Like a considerable number of other blacks in southeastern Ohio, she had been settled in the area (along with some relatives) by her former master.[6] She owned, in addition to the house, a plot of land that Reverdy, at least, regarded as "sizable." She was also literate, having learned to read in Virginia.

For some reason, perhaps having to do with her relationship with George Ransom, Harriet in 1865 left her mother's home and took Reverdy with her to Washington, Ohio, a slightly larger town a few miles to the west, in Guernsey County. There she boarded her son with George's parents, Louis and Betsy Ransom, who owned a

---

4. Bingham (1815–1900), who served in every Congress save one between 1854 and 1873, was a resident of nearby Cadiz, Ohio. He later played an important role in the impeachment proceedings against Andrew Johnson. Reverdy Johnson (1796–1876), a well-known constitutional lawyer active in politics as a Whig and then as a War Democrat, served twice in the United States Senate. A gradual emancipationist, he argued the pro-slavery side in the Dred Scott case, was prominent in the abortive Washington peace conference of 1861, and later was one of President Johnson's main senatorial defenders. Cassius Marcellus Clay (1810–1903), an anti-slavery Kentucky Whig and Republican, was prominently mentioned for the vice-presidency in 1860. Thomas D. McCormick, "John Armor Bingham"; E. Merton Coulter, "Cassius Marcellus Clay," and Mary W. Williams, "Reverdy Johnson," in *Dictionary of American Biography*, ed. Allen Johnson and Dumas Malone (New York: Scribner's, 1928+), 11, 277–78; IV, 169–70; X, 112–41.

5. Wright, *Bishops,* 287, identifies George Ransom as Reverdy's father. I have concluded otherwise strictly from a reading of Ransom's autobiography. The phrasing of Reverdy's initial allusion to him, and the declaration that he knew "nothing" of his "paternal forbearers," seem to me to indicate that George Ransom was actually his stepfather. I have not, however, been able to confirm this interpretation by any other documentary evidence, so it must be accepted with considerable caution.

6. On the general pattern of antebellum black settlement in Ohio, see David A. Gerber, *Black Ohio and the Color Line* (Urbana: University of Illinois Press, 1976), 14–24.

farm on the outskirts of town. She herself worked in Washington as a domestic servant. At night, Reverdy would join her, sleeping on a pallet in the cold, unheated attic of one of the homes in which his mother worked. Reverdy cared neither for the sleeping nor the eating arrangements. The attic was uncomfortable and the Ransoms, with a large family of their own to care for, seemed to him short on both food and affection for their boarder. He especially did not get along with George's sister, who persisted in calling him "that little red haired devil."

Both the Ransoms and his mother's employers, however, made a mark on his life as lasting as these memories of childhood deprivation. The Ransoms were regular attendees of the local African Methodist Episcopal church, and they trained the children, Reverdy included, to emulate their piety. (They also were confirmed whiskey drinkers who shared their toddies with the children, a practice which also may have influenced Reverdy's later habits.) His mother's employers, mostly affluent, pro-slavery, northern Democrats, were influential in a more indirect but no less important way. According to Reverdy, their "speech, manners and ideals" in rearing their own children were observed and emulated by his mother, who became, in the eyes of Reverdy's playmates, bent on turning her son into a " 'white folks' nigger.' " Most especially, convinced that ignorance lay at the heart of black America's problems, she became determined that her son go to college.

The prospects for this were not encouraging. Reverdy began his education in Washington at a black school which met in the local A.M.E. church. Apparently it offered little beyond instruction in literacy. When Ransom and his parents moved eight miles west to Cambridge in 1869, he was able to attend the town's somewhat more advanced black public school (which also met in the local A.M.E. church). But by the time he was thirteen, he had exhausted the education available from this "noisy undisciplined ungraded" school and its white teachers. Harriet Ransom then took her son to the principal of the Cambridge Public School and requested that he be admitted to the white school, but they were met with a firm refusal. (She also took him at some point to the white Presbyterian church's Sunday School. There, the teacher to whom he was assigned burst into tears, which probably ended that experiment as well.) Undaunted, Reverdy's mother pieced together a more advanced education for him by taking in the washing of several white families in exchange for their instructing her son in various subjects. Meanwhile, Reverdy himself did janitorial work in a shoe store in order to receive algebra lessons from its owner. Later on, after working in a brickyard, a barber shop, a saloon, and a bank, he secured a position as house-boy in the bank cashier's home. This post, he later recalled, both expanded the horizon of his readings and gave him the opportunity to "absorb...and assimilate...the best in these people and their friends who came and went."

The friends who came and went in these white homes were, indeed, sometimes national celebrities to whom a black boy in small-town Ohio would not ordinarily be exposed. Ransom recalled, for example, that Henry Wadsworth Longfellow, visiting in a home his mother was working in, had come around and paid a call at the Ransoms' home, too. Yet most of the impressive out-of-town visitors who attracted young Reverdy's interest were not white poets or politicians who might happen to take a momentary interest in a bright, red-haired black boy. They were, rather, black community leaders, particularly A.M.E. churchmen, who passed through Cambridge frequently and were no doubt well acquainted with some of the local African Methodists. The church's leading bishop, Daniel Alexander Payne, had his headquarters across the state at Wilberforce University, but traveling widely in the pursuit of his episcopal duties, he must have passed through Cambridge often, for the town lay on the old National Road at an important railroad junction.[7] Ransom also recalled, among others, the visits of Benjamin Arnett, an Ohio A.M.E. pastor and politically active Republican, and Henry McNeal Turner, the church's fiery Georgian leader, whose duties as manager of the A.M.E. Book Concern took him after 1876 on nationwide travels. Each of these men proved important to Ransom's future.[8]

One immediate mark of their influence was Ransom's decision to make Wilberforce University the goal of his educational efforts. The A.M.E. school was in many ways a synthesis of the white and black influences that Harriet Ransom had tried to cultivate in her son's life. In curricular content, in the moral standards it sought to inculcate, and in the evangelical Protestantism it confessed, Wilberforce was very much in tune with the ethos that reigned in "the best white homes" in Cambridge. But it was also a black institution firmly committed to equal rights for

---

7. Henry Howe, *Historical Collections of Ohio*, I, Ohio Centennial ed. (Cincinnati: C. J. Krehbiel, Printer and Binders, 1900), 728–30.

8. Ransom, *Pilgrimage*, 23, also mentions the visits to Cambridge of Richard T. Greener, Francis E. W. Harper, and John G. Mitchell — all prominent blacks and members of the A.M.E. Church.

black Americans. That must have mattered to Harriet Ransom, for Reverdy remembered that, of all his relatives, it was she who most bristled and spoke back when taunted with racial insults. Wilberforce, then, must have seemed a fitting culmination for her son's education.

At the last minute, however, Harriet Ransom's goal for her son almost went unachieved. Everything seemed in order for Reverdy to enroll in Wilberforce in the fall of 1881. He had completed his preparation by taking a summer normal school course and then teaching two short terms in a county school. The necessary funds had somehow been put away. Then, late in the winter before Reverdy's planned departure, he decided he was ready for marriage. The object of his affections was Leanna Watkins, a "comely" teenager whose "correctness of life and conduct" seemed to Reverdy to set her apart from the "community of free morals" in which they both lived. They were married in mid-February and immediately thereafter Leanna became pregnant. She herself had long since quit school to enter domestic service and it was readily apparent that if Reverdy undertook to support his wife and prospective child, his education must come to an end as well. Harriet Ransom, therefore, relieved her son of this responsibility. To secure additional funds, she mortgaged the house the family had acquired and, when in November Leanna gave birth to Harold George Ransom, she took her grandson into her home and reared him herself. Reverdy went to Wilberforce, after all.[9]

Wilberforce University was, in 1881, the "intellectual center of the A.M.E. Church."[10] It was also the lengthened shadow of one man, Daniel Alexander Payne. By then seventy, the church's senior bishop had been associated with the school since 1856, when it was first launched by the Cincinnati Conference of the Methodist Episcopal Church, North. In 1863, having arranged for the school's purchase by the A.M.E. Church, he had become the first black president of the first black-controlled college in America. He retired from this post in 1876, but remained a resident of "Tawawa Springs" and a major influence in the life of the school.

Payne was, moreover, the single most important figure in the

---

9. The records of the Probate Division, Court of Common Pleas, Guernsey County, Cambridge, Ohio, show that the marriage occurred on February 17, 1881, and that Harold George Ransom was born on November 4, 1881. Reverdy and Leanna were divorced on February 3, 1886. Ransom later described this marriage as a "youthful folly."

10. Wright, *Bishops*, 81.

A.M.E. Church as a whole.[11] Elected to the bishopric in 1852, he had soon become and long remained the dominant influence among the handful of bishops who ran the church. An intense, rigidly self-disciplined, bookish man, Payne had tried for years — especially through the church's educational program — to reshape African Methodism in his own ascetic image. Theologically, he was a strict biblicist who admired the Princeton scholastic Charles Hodge above all other American theologians. He also was convinced that the Bible, properly read, taught one to respect authority and restrain contention in the conduct of church business, to worship "in a rational manner," and to adhere strictly to an ascetic code of personal conduct. He therefore fought vigorously throughout his career against those in the church who seemed to him to lack proper respect for church law and episcopal authority, who engaged in such "heathenish" worship practices as the "ring shout" or insisted on singing the spirituals ("cornfield ditties"), and who violated or refused to enforce the church's strict moral disciplinary rules. Not surprisingly, some of these people fought back, and the result was a half-century struggle between Payne and his adversaries that at times sharply polarized the church.

In the antebellum period, when the restrictive laws of the southern states generally excluded the A.M.E. Church from slave territory, the line of cleavage seemed roughly to follow the major class division of northern black communities. Payne spoke from the point of view of a relatively affluent black elite strongly imbued with the middle-class ethos of white America, while his opponents were more likely to view things from the vantage point of more impoverished blacks with closer ties to Afro-American folk culture. As a result of the church's rapid explosion in the south during the

---

11. The standard accounts of Payne's life and influence are his own autobiography, *Recollections of Seventy Years* (Nashville: A.M.E. Sunday School Union, 1888; reprint ed., New York: Arno Press and the New York Times, 1969), and Josephus R. Coan, *Daniel Alexander Payne: Christian Educator* (Philadelphia: A.M.E. Book Concern, 1935). These have been supplemented recently by two doctoral dissertations: Charles Denmore Killian, "Bishop Daniel A. Payne: Black Spokesman for Reform" (Ph.D. dissertation, Indiana University, 1971), and Arthur Paul Stokes, "Daniel Alexander Payne: Churchman and Educator" (Ph.D. dissertation, Ohio State University, 1973). My own interpretation of Payne is more fully developed and documented in "Aspects of Social Thought in the African Methodist Episcopal Church, 1884–1910" (Ph.D. dissertation, Harvard University, 1975), chap. 1 and passim; "The Meaning of Racial Justice and the Limits of American Liberalism" (unpublished essay), 19–26; and "Daniel Alexander Payne in Charleston, 1811–1835" (unpublished essay).

Reconstruction period, however, the controversy increasingly came to have a geographical cast. Payne now represented a beleaguered northern leadership elite struggling to maintain its control of an overwhelmingly southern church, while his most visible opponents were younger southern churchmen. Naturally, there were many exceptions to and variations on this pattern. Payne's northern opposition did not disappear, he had imitators as well as enemies in the south, and the play of personal idiosyncrasies made for curious alliances on any given issue. But there was in the church a general sense that a division was there and that it ran roughly along sectional lines.

There was also a sense that the south was on the offensive and gradually gaining in power. At the General Conference of 1880, the south had elected two bishops — Richard H. Cain and Henry McNeal Turner — over the opposition of Bishop Payne. In the early 1880s, moreover, the southern Annual Conferences launched a series of educational ventures that created unprecedented competition for Wilberforce. The South Carolina Conference led the way in 1880 by reorganizing Payne Institute as Allen University and locating it at Columbia. The next year, the North Georgia Conference took initial steps to organize Morris Brown College (it opened in Atlanta in 1885), while Paul Quinn College was established at Waco, Texas. Edward Waters College was launched in Jacksonville, Florida, in 1883. There was also already an A.M.E. school, Western University, in Quindaro, Kansas, which had evolved from the earlier efforts of a white Presbyterian minister, and several more A.M.E. schools were to follow in the latter half of the decade. In a way, of course, these schools demonstrated the hold of Payne's educational concerns on the southern wing of the church. He was, however, not pleased. He feared that the rapid creation of new schools would divide the church's already meager resources and undermine the quest for excellence at Wilberforce itself. He therefore issued increasingly strident warnings against the effort to build up more than one college at a time.[12]

Whatever Payne's worries about this southern threat to the church in general and Wilberforce in particular, the college itself

---

12. Charles Spencer Smith, *A History of the African Methodist Episcopal Church...from 1856 to 1922* (Philadelphia: Book Concern of the A.M.E. Church, 1922; reprint ed., New York: Johnson Reprint Corporation, 1968), 351–69; Daniel A. Payne, "Some Thoughts about the Past, Present and Future of the African M.E. Church," *A.M.E. Church Review* 1 (July 1884): 5–8; Reverdy C. Ransom, editor, *Response of Bishop Payne to Rev. R. C. Ransom, B.D.* (n.p., 1890).

seemed perfectly to exemplify — within the limits imposed by its small budget — the kind of African Methodism the old bishop was so determined to create.[13] The emerging theological liberalism of the time had not made a dent in the school's orthodoxy. Though it regularly culminated in an annual revival in which students might even "fall down in the classroom and plead with the Lord to pardon their sins," the extensive worship life of the college (two required services daily, six days a week) did not include "bush meetings," "ring shouts," or "the frenzy" in their most intense forms. Individual conduct was strictly regulated from the rising bell at 6:00 A.M. until lights out at 9:30 P.M. and the lessons of hard work and self-discipline were inculcated at every turn. There were stern prohibitions against "immoral books and papers, fire-arms, card-playing, games of chance" and unsupervised encounters between members of the opposite sex. Administrative and faculty authority to enforce these rules and generally govern the institution went unchallenged by the disrespect for authority and general boisterousness that Payne thought his southern brethren had brought to the General Conference of 1880. It was, in sum, Daniel Alexander Payne's world.

It also became, in the fall of 1881, Reverdy Ransom's world — though, finally, a world he was more "in" than "of." Especially during what seems to have been a difficult first year, Ransom struggled over the direction of his life and Wilberforce's place in it. The religious life of the school he found thoroughly congenial. "Though reared in an atmosphere of prayer by a devout Christian mother" and long familiar with the life of the A.M.E. Church, Ransom had neither been "converted" nor joined the church. Regarded by some of his friends and relatives at home as a stone-hearted reprobate, Ransom knew his problem lay not in a lack of Christian conviction but in an unwillingness "to go to the mourner's bench and kneel on the bare floor with a great crowd of singing, shouting, perspiring men and women surrounding me." At Wilberforce, he found a religious atmosphere in which submission to this sort of "spectacle" was not a required rite of passage.

---

13. The standard history of Wilberforce University is Frederick A. McGinnis, *A History and an Interpretation of Wilberforce University* (Wilberforce, Ohio: n.p., 1941). The ethos of the school's early years is best conveyed by Hallie Q. Brown, *Pen Pictures of Pioneers of Wilberforce* (Xenia, Ohio: Aldine Publishing, 1937), and, especially, Reverdy C. Ransom, *School Days at Wilberforce* (Springfield, Ohio: New Era, 1890). My own account relies heavily on the last volume, especially 20–24, 35–40, and 63–66.

Able at last to pursue his own path, Ransom struggled on his own for grace until one night, alone in his room, he experienced "one of those rapturing moments...when earth and heaven meet and blend in the happy consciousness that God has entered into our life making Himself known." In his own estimation, achieving this "knowledge of the conscious, inward presence of God was worth more to me than all other things gained during my first year at Wilberforce."[14]

Other aspects of campus life, however, he found much less satisfactory. In *School Days at Wilberforce,* published some half-dozen years after his graduation, Ransom described the carefully regulated, once-a-month socials, where men and women were allowed two carefully chaperoned hours of polite conversation, as "among the most pleasant...experience...of our college days." Writing a half-century later, however, he admitted they had been "dull and tame" affairs which he had generally avoided. Indeed preoccupied with sorting out his feelings about Leanna and their baby, Ransom must have felt remote indeed from Wilberforce's regime of highly circumspect courtships. He also, however, felt increasingly remote from his uneducated bride at home, so much so that he finally secured a divorce. The whole business, which Ransom regarded as the most painful experience of his life, clearly made his first year at Wilberforce an unhappy one.[15]

He was also discontented with the education which Wilberforce offered. Influenced, perhaps, by his mother's persistent efforts to place him in white schools or to secure white tutors for him, Ransom had come to the black college doubting that "a Faculty composed of colored men was as good as one composed of white men." Though he eventually came to greatly admire Wilberforce's small and overworked faculty and to insist that black schools could teach a lesson in self-respect that "mixed schools" could not, he was still troubled by what he later called the "cramped and narrow quality of academic life." Aware no doubt that a number of prominent blacks — including Wilberforce's own well-regarded young classicist, William Sanders Scarborough — had been educated at Oberlin College, Ransom decided that he too should avail himself of that school's "broader and more liberal educational advantages." He also hoped that he would find it easier there to

---

14. Ransom, *Pilgrimage,* 31–33.
15. Ransom, *School Days,* 65; Ransom, *Pilgrimage,* 27, 39.

make ends meet financially — another real problem for him at Wilberforce.[16]

Ransom's arrival at Oberlin in the fall of 1882 was, however, an untimely one. A free tuition scholarship and a variety of odd jobs solved his financial problems and, if one can judge by his lack of complaint, the quality of education seems to have met his expectations. He also enjoyed the friendship of his black classmates — though he had neither the money nor leisure fully to share their social life. But liberal Oberlin was in the process of adapting to the racially more conservative ethos of the early 1880s and Ransom soon found himself in the thick of a fight over segregated eating facilities. Ladies Hall, the college's main dormitory, had long had an integrated dining room. In the fall of 1882, however, pressure from white students led to the establishment there of a separate table for black women. Counter-pressure from black students and from many alumni and administrators led finally to the restoration of integrated dining, but not before Ransom had become a casualty of the battle. By his account, his organizing and addressing a protest meeting provoked the faculty to terminate his scholarship. This made his position at the college untenable. Resentful in any case of "the outward friendliness which subtly, but firmly, closed so many doors to the freedom of the larger life about us to colored students," Ransom left Oberlin and returned to Wilberforce.[17]

By now, knowing more clearly the limited character of his options and having a no doubt heightened appreciation of Wilberforce's commitment to black equality, Ransom was ready to make his peace with the A.M.E. school. He was enormously helped in this reconciliation by a change in his vocational plans. As a result of the religious deepening that had occurred during his first year at Wilberforce, and in response to what he regarded as a call "so vividly clear and impressive as to leave no doubt," Ransom had decided to enter the A.M.E. ministry. The decision had not been easy, for Ransom, since his youthful fascination with the doings of the Cambridge Court of Common Pleas, had intended to pursue a

---

16. Ransom, *School Days,* 19–20; Ransom, *Pilgrimage,* 33; Francis P. Weisenburger, "William Sanders Scarborough: Early Life and Years at Wilberforce," *Ohio History* 71 (October 1962): 203–26, 287–89.

17. W. E. Bigglestone, "Oberlin College and the Negro Student, 1865–1940," *Journal of Negro History* 55 (July 1971): 199–201, describes both the general changes of the 1880s and the Ladies Hall dining room dispute but makes no reference to Ransom. Ransom himself omitted from *School Days* all mention of his stay at Oberlin, describing it only in *Pilgrimage,* 33–34.

legal career.[18] The choice for the ministry once made, however, the advantages of Wilberforce were obvious. There he could combine his collegiate and theological education and graduate in four years. There he could also move within the circle of men important in shaping the institution he proposed to serve.

But there were still problems. As always, Ransom was short of money. Even after Harriet Ransom sold the family cow to pay his initial expenses and Reverdy secured a steady Saturday job in a Xenia barbershop, life at Wilberforce meant "often going hungry and always poorly clad." He had also somewhere acquired a taste for liberal theology, a set of ideas equated with rank heresy at Wilberforce. Keeping his forbidden views hidden from the watchful eye of the college's strictly orthodox theological instructor, T. H. Jackson, proved a difficult and painful task, and led to much brooding about whether he was truly suited for the ministry. There was also the continuing problem of Wilberforce's stilted social life — though he managed to get around this difficulty in his senior year by courting Emma S. Connor, a girl who belonged to his student charge at nearby Selma, Ohio.[19]

By June 1886, Ransom had completed his studies and was ready to graduate — an accomplishment that most of the students who enrolled in Wilberforce in those days never achieved.[20] His address at the college literary society's commencement meeting was, by one account at least, "the finest students' oration delivered at Wilberforce." On commencement day itself, moreover, Ransom was involved in a scene that the same observer thought unprecedented:

> When Mr. R. C. Ransom had concluded his oration and amid the deafening applause that followed (wrote John G. Brown in the *Christian Recorder*), his mother, who sat in the audience, forced her way to the stage and fell upon the neck of her son. Overcome with emotion, realizing the fulfillment of her prayers, she could not contain herself. Well she might rejoice with love that is a tender mother's when her mind

---

18. Ransom, *Pilgrimage,* 23, 37, 49.

19. Ransom, *Pilgrimage,* 37–40, 42. Wright, *Bishops,* 289, suggests that Emma Connor was also a "school mate" of Ransom's at Wilberforce.

20. Reverdy C. Ransom, "The Class of 1886," typescript, Reverdy C. Ransom Papers, Wilberforce University Archives, Wilberforce, Ohio, states that his graduating class consisted of eight men and one woman. He documented and criticized the tendency of many Wilberforcians not to complete their degrees in "Why This Haste?" *Christian Recorder* 28 (August 28, 1890): 1.

wandered back a few years ago when this, her only child, was a wayward lad. Now she beheld him graduating with honors. Her prayers had been answered and he who was the wayward lad stood before her prepared to go forth preaching the gospel that she had made her staff through life. Those who witnessed the scene are not likely soon to forget it.

Ransom often told his mother that "she and I had graduated together."[21]

Ransom's career in the pastorate fell into three phases. From 1886 to 1890, assigned to small, difficult parishes in western Pennsylvania, he served the typical apprenticeship of a beginning A.M.E. preacher. From 1890 to 1896, he rose to regional prominence as the pastor of two important Ohio churches, North Street Church in Springfield (1890–93) and St. John's Church, Cleveland (1893–96). From 1896, when he was assigned, at the age of thirty-five, to Bethel Church in Chicago, until 1912, when he was elected editor of the *A.M.E. Review,* Ransom achieved a church-wide reputation as the pastor of a series of important churches in Chicago, Boston, and New York. He was, then, from a relatively early age, a "successful" pastor and well-known A.M.E. churchman.

Such success was important to Ransom for he was clearly an ambitious man. When, as a theological student he became sufficiently troubled by his doctrinal doubts to question his calling, he experienced the conflict as one between honestly abandoning the ministry to "dwell in poverty obscure" or hypocritically preaching his way to "the honors the Church can give." A few years later, as a novice pastor, he became angry when he was assigned once too often to a tiny, impoverished congregation. He had willingly served for two years a circuit near Altoona, Pennsylvania, where his major charge had only thirteen members. But when Bishop Payne assigned him in 1888 to the even smaller and poorer Manchester Mission in Allegheny City (now part of Pittsburgh), Ransom at first refused to go. (Sixty years later, he was still complaining about "the theory and practice among us that a young man in the ministry, regardless of his ability and training, should be sent out to small churches and made to suffer hardship and deprivation for a few years before being given a living charge.") He was also a will-

---

21. John G. Brown, "Wilberforce University: Twenty-Third Commencement Exercises — A Brilliant Closing," *Christian Recorder* 24 (July 8, 1886): 1; Ransom, *Pilgrimage,* 41–42.

ing, if not always eager, candidate for higher church office, who did not rest content until he had won his way to the bishopric.[22]

Ambition alone, however, could scarcely have secured Ransom's rapid rise to churchly prominence. Neither could his personal charm, general administrative abilities, or exceptional oratorical skills — though all of these no doubt helped. What he needed as well were "connections," particularly among the bishops, who could so easily make or break a young pastor's career.

Here Wilberforce served Ransom well, for it placed him within the immediate circle of men highly influential in the church. Indeed, Ransom shortly found himself under the benevolent protection of Bishop Payne himself. In spite of his adamant assignment of Ransom to the obscure Manchester Mission in 1888, the old bishop clearly liked the young Wilberforcian. In 1890, telling Ransom that he was sending him to a church with "carpets on the floor, cushioned pews, stained glass windows and a marble pulpit," Payne transferred him from the Pittsburgh to the Ohio Conference and assigned him to North Street Church in Springfield. This was a congregation of several hundred members which included "a majority of the most intelligent and most prosperous colored people in Springfield." In 1893, after carefully checking beforehand to make sure that the thin young pastor considered himself hardy enough to face the city's winters, Payne moved Ransom to the equally prestigious St. John's Church in Cleveland. Shortly thereafter, Payne died at the advanced age of eighty-two. He had, however, already brought Ransom to a position of considerable regional prominence within the church.[23]

The old bishop's favoring of Ransom is not hard to understand, for Ransom clearly had begun his career as a loyal member of the Payne wing of the A.M.E. Church. Through his education at Wilberforce, he had not only become personally acquainted with Payne, but was identified as well with the institution that, above all else, embodied Payne's vision of the church. This was an important identification, for Wilberforce and its place in the church were in those years matters of considerable churchwide controversy. On the very day that Ransom graduated, the denomination's weekly newspaper, the *Christian Recorder*, carried a long article attacking the existing financial arrangements by which Wilberforce

---

22. Ransom, *Pilgrimage*, 38–39, 43–47, 50, 261–64.
23. Ransom, *Pilgrimage*, 55, 57, 65; Gerber, *Black Ohio*, 144–46. Payne died on November 29, 1893.

received support from the whole church while the other A.M.E. schools were financed on a regional basis. Benjamin F. Lee, a former president of Wilberforce and now editor of the *Recorder,* tried to meet this attack by explaining that the denomination must concentrate its resources on its oldest school because "we can make Wilberforce a great college sooner than we can any other." But such attacks persisted and Wilberforce was clearly on the defensive — as was evidenced by Lee's own concession that the shift in membership perhaps required that "We should concentrate just as strongly on establishing one great university in the South, perhaps in Atlanta." Still, he warned, "two respectable universities are all we should be able to build up."[24]

Ransom, as a Wilberforcian, would presumably have been more or less identified with the ideals and interest of his alma mater even had he not actively worked to underscore the association. The identification must therefore have been all the greater when, from an early point in his ministry, he energetically espoused Wilberforce's cause. In 1890, he published a vigorous plea for the concentration of the church's institutional resources on Wilberforce, warning that equal support for the many "so-called colleges being set up in nearly every one of the episcopal districts" would lead to a pointless dissipation of A.M.E. efforts. (This piece caught the eye of Bishop Payne, who published a reply in which he gently chided Ransom for not sufficiently praising the school's present strengths but generally agreed with his "just and timely" assessment of the school's needs.) Ransom also made it clear in *School Days at Wilberforce,* published shortly thereafter, that he regarded the college and its community as the pinnacle of black America's highest educational and cultural achievement. Wilberforce, he declared, "has gathered around itself a community as intelligent, refined and Christian as can be found anywhere in our land." He also openly acknowledged that his book had been written precisely to quicken support for the school.[25]

---

24. A. J. Kershaw, "The A.M.E. Church — Its Educational Department: No. 6," *Christian Recorder* 24 (June 17, 1886): 1; Benjamin F. Lee, "Our Schools — Their Location," *Christian Recorder* 24 (June 24, 1886): 2.

25. R. C. Ransom, ed., *Response of Bishop Payne to Rev. R. C. Ransom, B.D.,* 1, 2 (unnumbered); Ransom, *School Days,* 8 and preface (unnumbered). In introducing Payne's reply, Ransom indicates that the article which occasioned it had appeared in the *Christian Recorder* during September 1890, but I have been unable to locate it there. Presumably it appeared in another periodical or at a considerably earlier or later date.

Ransom identified himself, moreover, not only with the institution and its needs but also with the general ethos of "colored Christian civilization" that was associated with it — particularly as it applied to the ministry. His first article in the *Christian Recorder,* published in the fall of 1886, was an apology on behalf of the educated and morally disciplined minister. Acknowledging that sometimes a minister seemed "too cultured for his flock," he insisted that the gap be closed by an elevation of the congregation's tastes. He also sharply criticized those clergymen whose ministries seemed to have the opposite effect:

> Many preachers [he complained], by the manner in which they associate with their members, and in the community generally, are imparting to the people a false education on the subject of ministerial culture and decorum. When a man follows who has proper ideas concerning preaching and pastoral work, one who uses the pastoral visits as a means of spiritual instruction, one who prays from hour to hour, instead of feasting and joking from hour to hour, one who spends his otherwise unemployed time in study and with his family, instead of loafing around barber shops and the like — he is often styled "stuck up" or as being unsociable.

To get to the root of the problem, he called, in another *Christian Recorder* article, for conference examining committees to be stricter in applying the educational tests for admission into the A.M.E. ministry. "No amount of sympathy," he insisted, "should be sufficient to pass a man who has not made proficiency in his studies." His views also caught the attention of Daniel Alexander Payne, who was happy to count Ransom as a new recruit in his battle against "ignorance." At a meeting of the North Ohio Conference, for example, Payne put Ransom on an examining committee with explicit instructions to block a rumored effort to deny ordination to Oscar J. W. Scott, a young Ohio Wesleyan graduate. "I need more men like you and Reverend Scott," he told Ransom, "because we have so few educated men in the ranks of our ministry." It is evident, then, why Payne liked Ransom and so quickly advanced him to large and prestigious churches.[26]

What is not so clear is whether Ransom himself deliberately exaggerated his conformity to Payne's ideals in order to secure

26. Reverdy C. Ransom, "Too Cultured for His Flock," *Christian Recorder* 24 (November 18, 1886): 2; Reverdy C. Ransom, "Annual Conference," *Christian Recorder* 26 (September 27, 1888): 4; Ransom, *Pilgrimage,* 65–66.

advancement. It has already been noted that Ransom's post-graduation enthusiasm for Wilberforce masked misgivings about the school which he only acknowledged much later. More striking is Ransom's April 1890 assault on C. S. Smith of the A.M.E. Sunday School Union for using a revised version of the Apostles' Creed in the agency's literature. Although, according to his autobiography, he had himself abandoned as a college student the doctrine of the Trinity ("as it was usually taught"), he assailed Smith for changes that were more verbal than substantive. He hinted that Smith had eliminated the phrase "He descended into hell" because he did not believe it and lamented the fact that "in the publications of the Sunday School Union this important link in the golden chain of faith is broken." He warned that "those who have rejected the statement of doctrine contained in the Apostles' Creed have ultimately drifted into mysticism and pantheism" and cited with approval A. A. Hodge's declaration that creedal revision amounted to a "dreadful violation" of Christian solidarity. He also took time to discuss the historic importance of the Nicene and Athanasian Creeds. If he had wanted to please Payne, he could scarcely have found a more effective way to do so than by this spirited defense of a learned orthodoxy.[27]

It is also possible, however, that Ransom had not by this time really made peace with himself about his own deviations from Payne's version of African Methodism. At Wilberforce, his struggle with his own heresy had been a private one, for he had found there "no sympathetic human counsellors" with whom to share his views.[28] Since the beliefs he developed were therefore lacking in public acknowledgment and support, they may have been quite unstable, and he may well at times have genuinely adhered to the orthodoxy he at other moments only pretended. Indeed, it is conceivable that by attacking Smith he was unconsciously trying to silence his own doubts — to appease the Payne within as much as to please the bishop without. The same might be said of his exaggerated enthusiasm for Wilberforce and his general effort energetically to align himself with the Payne wing of the church.

In the long run, however, neither calculation nor conscience could disguise the fact that Ransom simply was not cast from the same mold as his patriarchal sponsor. Differences of temper-

27. Reverdy C. Ransom, "Dr. C. S. Smith's Version of the Apostles' Creed," *Christian Recorder* 28 (April 24, 1890): 1; Ransom, *Pilgrimage*, 38.
28. Ransom, *Pilgrimage*, 38.

ament, background, and generation, obscured by their common immersion in the Wilberforce ambience of the late 1880s and early 1890s, increasingly came to the fore after Payne's death. Gradually, Ransom developed his own perspective on the nature and task of African Methodism. His mature views were identical neither with Payne's nor with those of that disparate group of southern church-men whom Payne counted as his opponents. They were rather a blending of the two, a synthesis shaped by his own experience and organized around his own special concerns. This is evident in a number of areas.

For one thing, Ransom did not share Payne's view that the church must strictly enforce an ascetic morality — not even in the early years of his ministry. When, for example, the young, unwed church organist at Manchester Mission became pregnant during Ransom's pastorate there, he refused the demands of the congre-gation's officers that she be brought to trial and expelled from membership. "Now that she is in this trouble and disgrace," he insisted, "she needs us. We must not cast her out." No doubt, Ran-som's leniency for those who in one way or another departed from the church's teaching about sex and marriage in part reflected a personal sympathy based on his own experience. But it also seems to have been based on a deliberate shift of emphasis from "law" to "gospel." Speaking of a very different and much later case in which he also declined for the sake of mercy to carry out the requirements of the Book of Discipline, Ransom remarked: "I knew in my heart of hearts that a sinner like me could not refuse to give that which he hopes to receive when he comes at last to stand before the Judge of all the earth." Nevertheless, conventional Methodist morality as such was not directly challenged by Ransom. He was careful to see that the wayward organist eventually married the father of her child. He was also, by this time, a respectable family man himself, having married Emma Connor, in 1887. (During their two years in Allegheny City, their family grew as Reverdy C. Ransom, Jr., their only child, was born, and Harold George Ransom, Reverdy's older son, came to live with them.) Even in the area of "temper-ance," moreover, Ransom never presented his own noncompliance with the ethic of abstinence, which became increasingly notorious in his later years, as anything other than a sinful (but presumably forgivable) failing.[29]

---

29. Ransom, *Pilgrimage*, 45, 47–50, 290–91, 304. Ransom's marriage to Emma Connor, who proved to be an exceptionally effective minister's wife, lasted until

Ransom was similarly more flexible and tolerant than Payne in his attitude toward black folk worship practices — without becoming a practitioner or partisan of the "ring shout." He was enough the Wilberforcian that one of his earliest parishioners was moved to refer to his sermons as "gospel lectures," but when a visiting Kentucky revivalist greatly stirred his Springfield congregation, Ransom tried the next week to imitate the musical cadences of the revivalist's delivery. (Another parishioner chided the experiment by telling him that such preaching, coming from him, sounded "ridiculous.") He had no sympathy, moreover, for the Cleveland parishioner who reported that "she had outgrown the old-fashioned and sometimes noisy manner of worship in St. John" and was going to become a Congregationalist. And when he later served, in New Bedford, Massachusetts, a congregation that seemed ignorant of and uninterested in "Negro spirituals and other forms of religious expression so characteristic of the Negro Church," he judged "their mode of worship...rather cold and formal." Still, worship in one of Ransom's more typical churches would have been readily distinguishable from the practices of the storefront or "bush meeting."[30]

Ransom was also more an ecclesiastical democrat (and politician) than Payne, though he remained, on the whole, more an enemy than a friend of "lawlessness." He shared enough of Payne's commitment to parliamentary decorum and the rule of law to respond with disgust when, as a first-time delegate to the General Conference of 1896, he witnessed the general tumult, electoral corruption, and even physical violence that had become typical of these assemblies. Yet Ransom's reverence for episcopal authority never matched Payne's. In 1888, when Payne refused to change his assignment of Ransom to Manchester Mission, Ransom submitted. But in 1904, when Bishop C. T. Shaffer seemed bent on banishing him from Chicago to the hinterlands of Indiana, Ransom simply left the bishop's jurisdiction and went, without the proper transfer papers, to New England, where he knew he would be more favorably treated. He was also, throughout his career, generally sympathetic toward efforts to democratize church life and he had an undeniable taste for church politics.[31]

---

her death in 1941. Two years thereafter, Ransom married Georgia Myrtle Teal, the Dean of Women at Wilberforce University. Wright, *Bishops,* 291–92.

30. Ransom, *Pilgrimage,* 53, 58, 72, 143.

31. Ransom, *Pilgrimage,* 75–76, 135, 267–70; George A. Singleton, *The Romance of African Methodism* (New York: Exposition Press, 1952), 162–69.

In sum, while Ransom did not altogether abandon Payne's strictly ordered vision of what African Methodism should be, he greatly softened its rather authoritarian and even repressive cast. Where Payne had sought to conquer and rule the passions that informed "heresy," "immorality," "heathenish worship," and "strife and contention," Ransom was willing to come to terms, to negotiate a settlement that allowed more play to individual imaginings, bodily indulgence, emotional enthusiasm, and the spirit of rebellion. This, after all, was Ransom's private sentiment — as a stern asceticism had been Payne's. Ready, apparently, to acknowledge and accept in himself both "the wayward lad" and the Wilberforce-trained preacher, Ransom could scarcely do otherwise. His private struggles thereby bore public fruit and, more and more his own man, he was increasingly able to lead.

Personal autonomy could not, however, be translated into ecclesiastical independence without considerable risk, and Ransom was therefore still dependent on episcopal sponsorship even after Payne's death and his own maturing. Fortunately, he found in Bishop Benjamin W. Arnett a man who was personally less formidable than Payne but nonetheless effective in advancing and protecting his career. Elected to the bishopric in 1888 at the age of fifty, Arnett was known for his wooden leg, his active involvement in politics, his oratorical skills, and his compilation as financial secretary of a series of important denominational reports. A resident of Wilberforce, he had employed Ransom during his student years and was therefore by the early 1890s an old friend. From Payne's death in 1893 until his own demise in 1906, Arnett was an energetic and reliable defender of Ransom's interests.[32]

In 1896, after Ransom had served at St. John's A.M.E. in Cleveland for three years, Arnett arranged to transfer him to whichever of the Church's two major Chicago congregations Ransom preferred. Choosing Bethel Church, "a well built structure with a seating capacity for about nine hundred people" and a congregation that was willing to pay him $1,800 a year, Ransom moved that October to the "big, wicked, but splendid city" of Chicago. Here, "[playing] to a crowded house" that included some

---

32. The standard biographical account of Arnett is Wright, *Bishops,* 78–82. There is also a biography, Lucretia H. Newman Coleman, *Poor Ben: A Story of Real Life* (Nashville: A.M.E. Sunday School Union, 1890), which does not, however, cover Arnett's years in the bishopric. Most helpful is Gerber, *Black Ohio,* especially 350–69 passim. Singleton, *Romance of African Methodism,* 129, reports on Ransom's having worked for Arnett at Wilberforce.

of Chicago's most prominent black families and linked through Arnett's political connections to several members of the city's white elite, Ransom achieved both considerable local prominence and a nationwide reputation among black leaders. He also developed a new style of ministry that was at once a clearer expression of his own deepest concerns and an important innovation in the urban work of the entire denomination.[33]

The change in the method of Ransom's ministry was rooted in his growing concern to bring together in the church "the Negro who is up and the Negro who is down, the Negro who is good and the Negro who is ignorant." Difficult enough in Bishop Payne's day, this task was severely complicated by the sociocultural milieu of a modern industrial city such as Chicago. There, and across the urban north, one could discern the emergence both of an "up Negro" who was increasingly critical of the black church and progressively more susceptible to an altogether secular view of life, and of a "down Negro" who was by the desperate living conditions of urban poverty separated ever more sharply from the world of black respectability. Sympathetic to the currents of thought which were influencing the disaffected elite and bound by the memories of his own economic struggles to the life of the black poor, Ransom sought to overcome this growing fragmentation:

> The methods which he employed in this enterprise were partially an adaptation of the newer patterns of urban church work recently developed among white Protestants. Ida B. Wells-Barnett, the well-known anti-lynching crusader and one of Ransom's Chicago parishioners, reported enthusiastically to the *Christian Recorder* early in 1900 that Ransom had "emerged and broadened the church horizon" in part by creating at Bethel a series of "auxiliary movements." The most prominent of these [she wrote] was "The Men's Sunday Club," an organization which has gathered young men off the streets and out of saloons...together with the best representatives of our professional and business manhood every Sunday afternoon for intellectual culture....[Another] child of Rev. Ransom's brain...is..."The Woman's Conference" which purposes to do the same thing for women. The in-

---

33. Ransom, *Pilgrimage*, 81–82; Reverdy C. Ransom to George A. Myers, October 17, 1896, Box 2, George A. Myers Papers, Ohio Historical Society, Columbus, Ohio; Allan H. Spear, *Black Chicago: The Making of a Negro Ghetto, 1890–1920* (Chicago: University of Chicago Press, 1967), 63, 91–93.

dustrial school for children, The Twentieth Century Club, a
literary organization, and a kindergarten were all fostered by
this pastor and his church. In like manner have the physical necessities of, not Bethel Church alone, but whoever in
the church district needed it, been looked after. Rev. Ransom distracted that part of the city . . . and created an order of
deaconesses, twelve women, who cover that district seeking
strangers, visiting the sick, and feeding, clothing and making
warm the poor and needy.[34]

Ransom himself, however, was apparently less satisfied than
Mrs. Wells-Barnett with the impact of all these "auxiliaries,"
for he became persuaded that what was needed was an entirely
new organization. Securing the assistance of Bishop Arnett, who
used his influence as president of the Church's Financial Board to
obtain denominational funds to support Ransom's new venture,
Ransom left Bethel in 1900 to launch the Institutional Church and
Settlement House.[35]

Located in what had at one time been known as "the Railroad Chapel" ("a magnificent stone and brick . . . building . . . , with
an auditorium holding nearly two thousand persons . . . , the finest
pipe organ, save one, in Chicago . . . [and] rooms up and down
stairs for almost any imaginable purpose"), the "only colored Social Settlement in the world" was modeled after Jane Addams's
Hull House and Graham Taylor's Chicago Commons. Its program
included a day care center, a kindergarten, boys' and girls' clubs,
a mothers' club, music classes, sewing classes, cooking classes, an
employment bureau, a penny savings bank, and a public forum.
On its staff, among others, were two later prominent University
of Chicago students, Monroe Work, who ran the boys' club, and
Richard R. Wright, Jr., who served for a year as the assistant
pastor. The Institutional Church and Settlement House attracted
favorable comment in the Chicago press and served as a model for
similar A.M.E. efforts elsewhere. Already by Christmas 1902, the
Christian Recorder was declaring it a successful experiment.[36]

---

34. Ransom, *Pilgrimage*, 82–83, 230; the quotation is from *Pilgrimage*. See also
Spear, *Black Chicago*, 91–97.

35. Alfreda M. Duster, editor, *Crusade for Justice: The Autobiography of Ida B.
Wells* (Chicago: University of Chicago Press, 1970), 297; Ida B. Wells-Barnett,
"Rev. R. C. Ransom, B.D.," *Christian Recorder* 47 (January 25, 1900): 1; Ransom,
Pilgrimage, 103.

36. Thomas W. Henderson, "Manager's Weekly Letter: A Visit to Chicago,"
Christian Recorder 47 (March 15, 1900): 3; Reverdy C. Ransom, "The Institutional

Ransom did not, however, rely solely on these innovations in church organization and programming to achieve the results he was seeking. He also took a leading part in a number of wider efforts to promote the general welfare of Chicago's black community. Early in his ministry at Bethel, he disregarded the raised eyebrows of some of his parishioners and worked with black saloon keeper Robert T. Motts to defeat a city alderman who refused to arrange for the paving of Dearborn Street. In 1903, as pastor of the Institutional Church, he launched a major campaign against the South Side's numbers racketeers, during which the church was dynamited and his own life threatened. The following year, 1904, he became actively involved in efforts to mediate the violent stockyards strike, which pitted hundreds of imported black strikebreakers against the largely white ethnic union workforce in a confrontation that created tension all over the city. Not surprisingly, he soon became, according to Ida B. Wells-Barnett, "the best known colored preacher Chicago has ever had."[37]

He meanwhile became active in racial advancement efforts at the national level. In this — especially to the extent that it involved him in electoral politics — he followed the example and benefited from the sponsorship of Benjamin Arnett. Bishop Payne had early decided to forgo abolitionist lecturing and political involvement in order to concentrate his energies entirely on the church, but Arnett had chosen a different course. Active in racial advancement organizations and Republican politics from the beginning of his ministry, he had served a term in the Ohio legislature (1885–87) and introduced one of the bills that ended school segregation in the state. He had also carefully cultivated William McKinley, Ohio's governor from 1892 to 1896, and Mark Hanna, his political manager. After McKinley's election to the White House, he became perhaps his most influential Afro-American adviser. All this clearly was to Ransom's advantage when he sought to widen the scope of his own activities.[38]

Church and Social Settlement," *Christian Recorder* 48 (November 29, 1900): 1; Reverdy C. Ransom, "The Institutional Church," *Christian Recorder* 48 (March 7, 1901): 1; Ransom, *Pilgrimage,* 103–10; Spear, *Black Chicago,* 95–96; Richard R. Wright, *Eighty-Seven Years behind the Black Curtain: An Autobiography* (Philadelphia: Rare Book, 965), 94–96; "St. Paul Social Settlement," *Christian Recorder* 50 (December 25, 1902): 2.

37. Ransom, *Pilgrimage,* 83–84, 113–14, 117–35; Spear, *Black Chicago,* 36–39, 63; Wells-Barnett, "Rev. R. C. Ransom, B.D.," 1.

38. Payne, *Recollections,* 66–68; Gerber, *Black Ohio,* 350–64; Meier, *Negro Thought,* 57.

Ransom had also developed political ties of his own. Among the members of his Cleveland congregation was George A. Myers, owner of the elite Hollenden House barbershop and wielder of significant influence in Ohio Republican circles. Also on good terms with Mark Hanna, whom he both barbered and supported politically, Myers along with Arnett arranged for Ransom himself to become at least casually acquainted with the Cleveland kingmaker. Myers helped Ransom secure $500 from Hanna to help pay off the mortgage at St. John's Church, while Ransom himself was subsequently able to talk Hanna into contributing $800 toward the rebuilding of Bishop Arnett's fire-damaged Wilberforce home. When Ransom moved to Chicago, moreover, he was linked through Bethel Church member Ida Wells-Barnett to Ferdinand Barnett, who ran the Afro-American Bureau for the Republican National Committee in both the 1896 and 1900 campaigns. He was, then, well placed to pursue a career of mounting political influence.[39]

The nature of Ransom's interest in politics differed, however, from that of Arnett, Myers, or Barnett. These men were all enormously interested in patronage. On the basis of his good service in 1896, Barnett angled for a presidential appointment and then secured in Illinois a position as assistant state's attorney, a post he held for a decade. Myers, though declining Hanna's offer of a position for himself, tried very hard, albeit unsuccessfully, to secure appropriate places in the McKinley administration for his friends and political allies. Similarly, but more successfully, Arnett worked to secure appointments both for two of his sons and for a variety of other political and ecclesiastical allies. Ransom, however, was at this time uninterested either in personal office holding or political empire-building. When Hanna offered him a position as army chaplain (a prestigious post for a black cleric) he turned it down, and there is no record of his having tried systematically to influence the appointments of others. His concern seems to have been

---

39. Felix James, "The Civic and Political Activities of George A. Myers," *Journal of Negro History* 58 (April 1973), 166–78; Gerber, *Black Ohio*, 345–70; Ransom, *Pilgrimage*, 68–71; Reverdy C. Ransom to George A. Myers, October 17, 1896, October 28, 1896, December 15, 1896, January 9, 1897, January 13, 1897, January 26, 1897, February 18, 1897, March 3, 1897, George A. Myers Papers, Ohio Historical Society, Columbus, Ohio. Ransom's correspondence with Myers suggests that he was something of a mediator between Myers and Arnett, who though allies, were also rivals for influence with Hanna and McKinley.

more exclusively focused on securing the election of candidates sympathetic to the interests of black America.[40]

Ransom also seems to have differed from these men in being too independent and outspoken to have easily played the role of a powerseeking party regular. He especially differed from Arnett, whose continuing political influence depended heavily on his partisan reliability and discreet silences. When, for example, McKinley was sharply criticized by many black leaders for his failure to condemn the Wilmington, North Carolina, race riot in November 1898, Arnett not only failed to join the criticism but was later discovered to have recommended to McKinley the policy of silence. Ransom during this same period publicly warned that the failure to check such mob outrages would eventually drive blacks to defend themselves with dynamite. He also privately called upon the president to "give more attentive ear to the great mass of people who are Republicans from principle and who seek no office, rather than its professional champions in church and state."[41]

Given these limitations in his taste for partisan politics, it is not surprising that Ransom found racial protest organizations an important vehicle for his own efforts to secure racial justice. When the Afro-American Council was revived in 1898, he quickly became an active member. Perhaps through the influence of Ida Wells-Barnett, a veteran of the old Afro-American League who was elected secretary of the new Council at its first meeting, the group's second meeting was convened at Ransom's church in Chicago. More prominent as host than he otherwise might have been, Ransom emerged from the session as the eighth of the Council's nine vice-presidents.[42]

He also emerged from the meeting, however, as the center of a storm of controversy over the Council's relation to Booker T. Washington. Washington, in bad repute with some of the Coun-

---

40. Ransom to Myers, February 18, 1897, March 3, 1897; Spear, *Black Chicago*, 60–61; Gerber, *Black Ohio*, 345–70; Ransom, *Pilgrimage*, 66–67. Ransom recalled that Hanna's offer came during his last year in Cleveland, but since McKinley was not elected to the presidency until after Ransom had moved to Chicago, the offer may, in fact, have come later.

41. Gerber, *Black Ohio*, 353, 361–62; Willard B. Gatewood, Jr., *Black Americans and the White Man's Burden, 1893–1903* (Urbana: University of Illinois Press, 1975), 253–54; Reverdy C. Ransom, "Chicago Paragraphs," *Christian Recorder* 47 (July 6, 1899): 1; Reverdy C. Ransom to John P. Green, June 27, 1899, William McKinley Papers, Manuscripts Division, Library of Congress, Washington, D.C.

42. *Autobiography of Ida B. Wells*, 254–56, 262; *Chicago Inter-Ocean*, August 20, 1899, clipping, Container 1031, 102–3, Booker T. Washington Papers, Manuscripts Division, Library of Congress, Washington, D.C.

cil's members over his failure forcefully to condemn the Sam Hose lynching of a few months earlier, had decided prudently to avoid the annual meeting even though he would be in Chicago during its sessions. His absence itself proved a further irritant, especially after he summoned the Council's president, A.M.E. Zion Bishop Alexander Walters, to meet with him privately in his hotel room. When Mrs. Washington requested toward the end of the meeting that her name also be removed from the program, that proved the last straw — at least to Ransom. Having already blocked in committee a resolution to endorse Washington, he now publicly rebuked the Tuskeegean for his absence and moved that he be removed from the Council's list of members. Accounts of the proceedings vary, but according to one newspaper, Ransom made his attack in these stinging words:

> I know of no man who has received more advertising from his connection with the Negro race than has Booker T. Washington. He has posed as the leader of the colored people and the Moses who was to lead his people out of the wilderness. Yet he has hung around the outskirts of this council casting aspersions and contempt on its proceedings. He has refused to come inside. He sat in his room at the Palmer House and sent for our president to wait upon him. No such man ought to claim to be our leader. We want the country to know he is nothing to us. We hold him in contempt. He is trying to hold us in line. From his room in the Palmer House, he says "Sh! Sh!," but he's afraid to come in. I move that Mr. Washington's name be stricken from the roll.

With cries of "traitor," "trimmer," and "coward" arising from the floor, the motion went down to tumultuous defeat. More conservative members of the Council soon rallied their troops and rushed through the closing session a ringing endorsement of Washington. Early press reports, however, carried the mistaken news that the Council had repudiated Washington, and even when, amidst a shower of editorial condemnation of Ransom, the truth emerged, "the Wizard" was not pleased.[43]

---

43. Louis Harlan, *Booker T. Washington: The Making of a Black Leader, 1856–1901* (New York: Oxford University Press, 1972), 263–66; Theophile T. Allain to Booker T. Washington, August 20, 1899, Container 161, and *Minneapolis Times,* August 22, 1899, clipping, Container 1031, 128, Booker T. Washington Papers, Manuscripts Division, Library of Congress, Washington, D.C. Allain's letter and some of the other correspondence pertaining to this episode have been published

Under considerable pressure from all sides (Du Bois, for example, who was there, referred to his remarks as "ill-timed and foolish"), Ransom backed down. In a letter to the *Chicago Inter-Ocean*, published less than a week after the meeting, he admitted that his attack on Washington might have been "unwise." He also sought to excuse himself by explaining that he had meant Washington no harm but simply felt that if Washington had wished to influence the Council's deliberations he should have directly participated in its meetings. After all, he concluded weakly, "We needed the help of our best and wisest minds." A few days later, in replying privately to an "earnest letter" from Washington himself, Ransom blamed the whole affair on the misrepresentation of Washington's "overzealous...friends and admirers." He assured him that "I regard your career as one of the most fruitful and remarkable of any man of our race, and your work as the most influential and helpful of any that is being done for the great mass of our people who, if they rise at all, must do so through habits of industry, frugality, character and thrift." To clinch the matter, he wrote Washington again two weeks later requesting a copy of the latest Tuskeegee Conference program for use in preparing a forthcoming *A.M.E. Review* article on "what the wisest and best among us are doing in the direction of mapping out a program for the race." Washington apparently obliged, and when the article appeared the following April it listed the Tuskeegee program ahead of those devised by the National Association of Colored Women, the Afro-American Council, and the Hampton Conference, and came no closer to a criticism of Washington than the observation that his program made "no reference...to political action, which has been thought for so long by many to be the lever by which the race would be lifted to the enjoyment of its rights." He did not even attempt, moreover, to fight the ensuing Bookerite takeover of the Afro-American Council. Convinced that the Chicago delegations' expenses for the 1900 Indianapolis meeting were paid in full, through Bishop Arnett, by Mark Hanna and the Republican National Committee, Ransom concluded that the Council

---

in Louis R. Harlan and Raymond W. Smock, editors, *The Booker T. Washington Papers* (hereafter *BTW Papers*), vol. 5, 1899–1900 (Urbana: University of Illinois Press, 1976), 175–206. Ransom's only mention of this episode in his autobiography (*Pilgrimage,* 83) is an account mistakenly associated with the Council's 1900 Indianapolis meeting. He recalled Washington's coming late one night to summon Bishop Walters, who was Ransom's houseguest, for a sidewalk lecture on the need to restrain the Council.

was "useless as a weapon [for] political and social justice" and withdrew.[44]

Ransom's retreat before Washington and resignation from the Council were, however, less indicative of the long-range direction of his ministry than was his initial attempt to participate in the group and press it toward militancy. The Sunday after the "Boston riot" of July 30, 1903, in which William Monroe Trotter and several other black Bostonians directly challenged Washington at a crowded public meeting, Ransom declared from his pulpit that for all his virtues,

> Mr. Washington...does not believe as his people believe, and in promulgating his propaganda of surrender of rights he does not represent his people. The revolt at Boston was the first that has reached the public. There would be others if Mr. Washington did not control the strong papers conducted by colored men....I...insist that a colored man should have the right to vote, to own his own home, to transact his business, have a fair trial if he commits a crime, just as a white man does, and that he should be deprived of none of these. These are the things the colored people stand for and they will not countenance any surrender.

When the militant challenge to Washington took organizational form two years later in the Niagara Movement, Ransom soon became an active participant — an involvement facilitated by his move to Boston in the summer of 1905. That winter, William Monroe Trotter invited him to deliver the main address at the New England Suffrage League's celebration of the Garrison centennial, and Ransom responded with an oration that an enthusiastic W. E. B. Du Bois wrote from Atlanta to praise as a "splendid speech...[,] worthy of our best traditions." Afforded a similar opportunity at the August 1906 Harpers Ferry meeting of the Niagara

---

44. *Chicago Inter-Ocean*, August 20, 1899; Reverdy C. Ransom, letter to the editor, *Chicago Inter-Ocean*, August 25, 1899, 6, as cited in Harlan and Brock, *BTW Papers*, vol. 5, 187; Reverdy C. Ransom to Booker T. Washington, August 31, 1899, and September 12, 1899, Container 160, Booker T. Washington Papers, Manuscripts Division, Library of Congress, Washington, D.C.; Reverdy C. Ransom, "A Programme for the Negro," *A.M.E. Review* 16 (April 1900): 423–30; Ransom, *Pilgrimage*, 84–85. Sadie Harlan, to whom, along with Louis M. Harlan, I am indebted for assistance in locating A.M.E. materials in the Booker T. Washington Papers, reports that the letter from Washington to which Ransom alludes in his own letter of August 31, 1899, is not contained in this collection.

Movement, Ransom created one of the most memorable moments in that organization's brief history:

> Mr. Ransom [delivered] the most eloquent address the writer has ever listened to [wrote J. Max Barber in *The Voice of the Negro*]. He spoke of "The Spirit of John Brown," and before he was through speaking everybody in the house must have felt that John Brown's spirit was with us. Men and women who had attended the New England anti-slavery meetings fifty years ago said that they had witnessed nothing like the enthusiasm in that meeting since the dark days of slavery. Women wept, men shouted and waved bats and handkerchiefs and everybody was moved.

Other such oratorical triumphs followed, and Ransom broadened his organizational participation to include the Constitution League and, later, the NAACP, as well as a number of more ephemeral organizations. In the division of the times between Bookerites and anti-Bookerites, there was no mistaking where Ransom finally stood.[45]

Not surprisingly, this increasingly forthright militancy, combined with his continued churchly success, gradually earned for Ransom a number of ecclesiastical adversaries. After 1900 his career within the church became increasingly vulnerable to the machinations of these opponents. At that year's General Conference, Bishop Arnett — who remained Ransom's protector in spite of their political disagreements — was reassigned to another episcopal district, and Ransom's area came under the jurisdiction of Bishop Abram Grant. Grant was not only the closest A.M.E. ally of Booker T. Washington, but also an apparent good friend of Archibald Carey, Ransom's chief Chicago rival. A well-educated Georgian then serving as pastor of Quinn Chapel, Carey, along

---

45. Stephen R. Fox, *The Guardian at Boston: William Monroe Trotter* (New York: Atheneum, 1970), 49–54, 97–100; Reverdy C. Ransom, sermon of August 2, 1903, the Institutional Church and Settlement House, Chicago, as quoted in *Literary Digest* 27 (1903): 188; Ransom, *Pilgrimage*, 148–71, 196–97, 219, 221; "William Lloyd Garrison: The Centennial Oration Delivered . . . in Faneuil Hall, Boston, December 11, 1905," and "The Spirit of John Brown: Before Second Annual Meeting of the Niagara Movement, Harpers Ferry, West Va., August 17, 1906," in Reverdy C. Ransom, *The Spirit of Freedom and Justice* (Nashville: A.M.E. Sunday School Union, 1926), 5–14, 16–25; W. E. B. Du Bois to Reverdy C. Ransom, January 20, 1906, Reverdy C. Ransom Papers, Payne Seminary Archives, Wilberforce, Ohio; J. Max Barber, *Voice of the Negro* 3 (October 1906): 403; Meier, *Negro Thought*, 182; Nancy J. Weiss, *The National Urban League, 1910–1940* (New York: Oxford University Press, 1974), 26.

with A. L. Murray, the new pastor of Bethel Church, persuaded Bishop Grant to forbid Ransom to preach at the Institutional Church on Sunday mornings. This ban lasted only until Henry McNeal Turner, as senior bishop of the church, overruled Grant and ordered Ransom to preach, but Carey's opposition continued to plague Ransom throughout his Chicago pastorate. Finally, in 1904, when C. T. Shaffer replaced Grant as presiding bishop over the Chicago area, rumors began to reach Ransom that he would soon be sent from the city to serve as a presiding elder (regional superintendent) in Indiana. Unable to negotiate a more satisfactory transfer with Bishop Shaffer, Ransom resigned his position at the Institutional Church and, in effect, walked out of the Illinois Conference.[46]

Arnett, then presiding over the New England area, took Ransom in and temporarily assigned him to a church in New Bedford, Massachusetts. He had, indeed, been at work for some time trying to rescue Ransom from his Chicago troubles. In 1901, he had tried to secure Ransom an appointment to Metropolitan A.M.E. Church in Washington, D.C., one of the denomination's most prestigious congregations. Though not within his own jurisdiction, the church was within the domain of another Wilberforcian friend of Ransom's, Bishop Benjamin F. Lee, and Arnett apparently tried to arrange the transfer through the Bishops Council. Local opponents, however, including John Wesley Cromwell, the historian and A.M.E. layman, protested that they "did not want Ransom with all his eloquence," and, Arnett's personal pleadings notwithstanding, "the game was blocked." In 1905, however, Arnett was able to offer Ransom a good appointment within his own jurisdiction as pastor of the Charles Street A.M.E. Church in Boston. Grumbling at the initial salary (which was only two-thirds of what he'd made when starting at Bethel twelve years before) but no doubt pleased to be assigned to the center of northern black radicalism, Ransom

---

46. Ransom, *Pilgrimage*, 88, 95–96, 111, 115, 135; Wright, *Bishops*, 191–94 (on Grant), 127–29 (on Carey), and 301–3 (on Shaffer); Harlan, *Booker T. Washington*, 206, 225; correspondence between Grant and Washington, particularly in Containers 31, 41, 45, 50, 51, Booker T. Washington Papers, Manuscripts Division, Library of Congress, Washington, D.C.; *Autobiography of Ida B. Wells*, 191–92, 294, 297–98, 361, 393. On Carey, who eventually became a highly influential figure in Chicago politics, see also Spear, *Black Chicago*, 64–65, 84–85, 95–96, 113, 118, 124, 187, and Harold F. Gosnell, *Negro Politicians: The Rise of Negro Politics in Chicago* (Chicago: University of Chicago Press, 1935), 39, 49–51, 55–56, 58, 73, 98–99, 199–251, 275, 320.

surely thanked Arnett for the transfer. It was, however, the bishop's last favor to Ransom, for in October 1906, Arnett died.[47]

After Arnett's death, Ransom was on his own in the A.M.E. Church. No more would his career be looked after by a powerful episcopal sponsor. The negative effects of this were already evident in the spring of 1907. Henry McNeal Turner — who, as senior bishop, temporarily assumed some of Arnett's responsibilities — wrote to Ransom "private, private, private" about the possibility of transferring him to New York. Though, as his earlier helpfulness in Chicago suggests, Turner had generally been cordial to Ransom, he now presumably knew that Ransom did not wish to leave Boston and nevertheless proposed to move him for reasons of his own. Ransom, at least, regarded Turner's warm correspondence on the matter ("I wish I could make you President of Morris Brown College") as a rather disingenuous attempt to humor him into leaving town peacefully. Acquiescing, Ransom went quietly, though "with reluctance and with [a] heavy heart" to serve Bethel A.M.E. Church in New York City.[48]

If Turner's reappointment of Ransom indicated his vulnerability, however, the manner in which it was done suggested that the forty-six-year-old Boston preacher had become a formidable power within the church in his own right. Ransom himself recalled years later that his transfer "created quite a sensation, not only in my own church, but in church circles throughout the city of Boston." It was, presumably, a respect for Ransom's ability to mobilize such support on behalf of his continued appointment to the Charles Street Church that prompted Turner so carefully to secure Ransom's consent beforehand. Sending a liaison to New York's large and prestigious Bethel Church also showed more respect for Ransom's talent — and influence — than Bishop Shaffer's earlier plan to pack him off to Indiana. In New York, Ransom was able both to pursue his concern for an effective urban ministry and to participate actively in black politics and protest organizations. He was also able to maintain a position of high visibility in the life of the denomination as a whole.[49]

His effectiveness in this regard was evidenced by his election in

---

47. Ransom, *Pilgrimage,* 143, 148–52; John W. Cromwell to F. H. M. Murray, April 3, 1915, Freeman Henry Morris Murray Papers, The Moorland-Spingarn Research Center, Howard University, Washington, D.C. I am indebted to Randall K. Burkett for calling my attention to this letter.

48. Ransom, *Pilgrimage,* 199–201.

49. Ransom, *Pilgrimage,* 201–25.

1912 to the editorship of the *A.M.E. Review*. This victory, which permanently established Ransom as an independent power within the church, came after at least two unsuccessful attempts at church-wide office. In 1900, when *Recorder* editor H. T. Johnson was rumored to be due for elevation to the bishopric, Ransom was mentioned as a possible successor. But Johnson's campaign for higher office failed and he did not vacate the editorship. Nine years later, when the position finally did open, it was filled not by Ransom, but by his former junior colleague at the Institutional Church, Richard R. Wright, Jr. In the middle of the following quadrennial, however, H. T. Kealing, editor since 1896 of the *A.M.E. Review*, resigned his post, turning the magazine over temporarily to C. V. Roman, and at the General Conference of 1912, Ransom defeated Roman for the editorship. He was reelected in 1916 and 1920.[50]

In that it freed him from direct dependence on the bishops and made him instead responsible only to the General Conference for the retention of his post, Ransom's election to the editorship marked a major departure from his ministerial past. Yet, in the substance of his daily work, it represented a far less sharp break from his years in the pastorate than did his subsequent election to the bishopric. Largely this was due to Ransom's own initiative. Convinced that the editorship of the *Review* was not really a full-time job, Ransom started on his own the Church of Simon of Cyrene, a mission church intended to serve the " 'bad Negroes'...the Negroes of the slums." Since Benjamin W. Arnett, who had succeeded Ransom as pastor of Bethel Church, successfully insisted that Ransom not take any of Bethel's members with him, the new congregation was never very large. But it afforded Ransom an outlet for his pastoral energies and served as a reminder to the church at large of the type of ministry he wished African Methodists to undertake. Meanwhile, his editorial work allowed him to continue in print the political commentary and protest against racism that had previously found its way into his sermons and orations.[51]

Whatever the satisfactions of life as a part-time pastor and editor, Ransom was willing to abandon them for the bishopric. Politically, the editorship allowed Ransom to develop personal ties with western and southern church leaders, whom he had not much

---

50. (H. T. Johnson), "Editorial; Catch 'Ear and Hold' Ear," *Christian Recorder* 47 (September 2, 1899): 2; Ida B. Wells-Barnett, "Rev. R. C. Ransom, B.D.," *Christian Recorder* 47 (January 25, 1900): 1; Wright, *Bishops*, 372; Ransom, *Pilgrimage*, 226–27.

51. Ransom, *Pilgrimage*, 227–57.

known as a Midwestern and northeastern pastor. By 1920, he had sufficiently overcome southern resistance ("sectionalism," he called it) to make a strong showing at the St. Louis General Conference, losing, he claimed, only because the clerk deliberately stopped reading his name. Four years later, working closely with fellow candidates John A. Gregg, the president of Wilberforce University, and A. J. Gaines, the southern-born leader of the Baltimore Conference, Ransom — at the age of sixty-three — succeeded. "God has answered my prayer," said the aged Harriet Ransom: "He let his glory shine about [you]."[52]

As bishop, however, Ransom had more to do than rest on his laurels. The church which had elected him bishop was confronted both by an increasingly inhospitable milieu without and deepening divisions within.[53] Urban, industrial America had never been as susceptible to the dominance of evangelical Protestantism as its small-town, agricultural predecessor, and as the Great Migration increasingly carried blacks from the latter realm to the former, black churchmen more and more experienced the same frustrations that had earlier beset their white brethren. Able to retain their hold on the middling groups within the urban black community, but unable to embrace the ghetto masses or shape the thinking of the cultural elite, the mainline black churches found it increasingly difficult to speak for black America as a whole. Of no church was this more true than the African Methodist. As late as 1903, W. E. B. Du Bois could justly describe the A.M.E. Church as "probably...the greatest voluntary organization of Negroes in the world,"[54] but by 1924 such claims were scarcely more plausible than the parallel claims that Wilberforce was "the Black Athens" and the *A.M.E. Review*, the race's leading journal. Ransom, having watched this transition occur during the years of his own ministry, understood the problem well. His own early innovations in the church's urban ministry had been intended precisely to overcome African Methodism's growing separation from both "the Negro who is up" and "the Negro who is

---

52. Ransom, *Pilgrimage*, 261–64; Wright, *Bishops*, 171–72 (on Gaines) and 199–202 (on Gregg).

53. The following interpretation of the situation confronting the A.M.E. Church at the time of Ransom's election to the bishopric is more filled, developed, and documented in Wills, "Aspects of Social Thought in the African Methodist Episcopal Church," 235–42. See also 42–87.

54. W. E. B. Du Bois, editor, *The Negro Church...* (Atlanta: Atlanta University Press, 1903), 123.

down," and he had been confronted firsthand, as editor of the *Review,* with the problem of reversing the declining prestige of that journal.

Ransom also knew, from his own experience, the depth of regional, class, and personal divisions within the church. His own career, after all, had at various times run afoul of southern opposition to his northernness, the resistance of middling respectables from all regions to his attempts to minister across class lines, and the personal spite of envious colleagues. He also knew the abuse of episcopal power and disregard of church law that such divisions often prompted. Even he, however, was apparently surprised by the growing tendency of the church to fragment into ecclesiastical baronies dominated by some entrenched bishop or lay reader who resisted all outside interference in his private realm. More than once in Ransom's bishopric, the integrity as well as the influence of the church was in doubt.[55]

In meeting these challenges, Ransom drew both on his own mature sense of the church's nature and purpose and on the insights and concerns of his predecessors. Symbolic of his renewed ties with the latter was his moving back to Wilberforce, where he lived beside Bishop Payne's college in Benjamin Arnett's old house.[56] Chairman of the Wilberforce Board of Trustees from 1932 to 1948, he became more deeply involved with Payne's school — and his — than he had been for decades, playing a crucial and controversial role in the final angry separation of Wilberforce and what became Central State University. (The latter was the outgrowth of the "Combined Normal and Industrial Department" which State Senator Arnett had persuaded his fellow legislators to establish at Wilberforce in the 1880s.)[57] He also became deeply involved in Ohio politics, playing for the state's Democrats something of the role that Arnett had once played for its Republicans and enjoying as a reward an appointment to the state's Board of Parole and

---

55. The major instances of such strife during these years are recounted in Ransom, *Pilgrimage,* 264–74, 303–19; and Singleton, *Romance of African Methodism,* 86–88, 162–82. Singleton's account is generally sympathetic to Ransom. For a more critical assessment of Ransom's role in one of these episodes, the "trial" of Bishop Joshua H. Jones by the General Conference of 1932, see Wright, *Eighty-Seven Years,* 219–22.

56. Ransom, *Pilgrimage,* 70, 323. The house, known as "Tawawa Chimney Corner," is still occupied by Ransom's widow.

57. Ransom, *Pilgrimage,* 277–86; Wright, *Eighty-Seven Years,* 222–23; McGinnis, *Wilberforce University,* 103–19; Gerber, *Black Ohio,* 331.

an invitation to offer the opening prayer at the 1940 Democratic National Convention.[58]

As important as he was as a living link to the past, Ransom's chief service to the church during these troubled years was offering it a way into the future. "I see little hope for the survival of the A.M.E. Church," Ransom warned the General Conference of 1936, '. . . if we do not so apply the Gospel of Christ as to make it a vital force in the life of society."[59] This, of course, was what Ransom had tried to do in his own ministry, and his work as bishop was therefore largely a matter of trying to get the church to follow his example. In this he experienced failure as often as success, and the church from whose service he retired in 1952 was no doubt not the militant and activistic community he would have wished it to be. Still, it was far better prepared for the struggles of the 1960s than it would have been without him. Watching from retirement the emergence of the southern civil rights movement in the late 1950s, he must have taken satisfaction in that.[60]

---

58. Singleton, *Romance of African Methodism,* 156; Wright, *Bishops,* 290–91; Ransom, *Pilgrimage,* 290, 294–96.

59. Reverdy C. Ransom, "The Church That Will Survive," cited in full by Singleton, *Romance of African Methodism,* 146–56. The quotation is from 152.

60. The contention of S. P. Fullinwider, *Mind and Mood,* 45, that Ransom's gospel became "increasingly . . . race centered until it was a racial Christianity he was preaching," is, in my judgment, exaggerated and misleading. Because this essay carefully examines only Ransom's earlier years and emphasizes his career within the church rather than the course of his thought, it has not been possible fully to discuss or defend this conclusion. I have, however, offered elsewhere (Wills, "The Meaning of Racial Justice and the Limits of American Liberalism," 32–38) an alternative reading of Ransom's approach to the problem of race in America. My contention there is that one finds in Ransom a rather unsystematic blending of the liberal individualism exemplified by Daniel Alexander Payne, the black nationalism expressed by Henry McNeal Turner, and the democratic socialism which Ransom seems to have become interested in on his own in the mid-1890s. Since the second strand may have been more prominent in the latter half of Ransom's life than in the first, Fullinwider's interpretation is perhaps not altogether without foundation — though even here the loaded terms in which his thesis is expressed seem to me to distort the reality of Ransom's thought. In any case, what is most distinctive and noteworthy about Ransom's social thought is not this motif but rather his early engagement with socialism and lifelong concern with the problems which arise at the intersection of race and class. Viewed from this angle, Ransom's thought is anything but the "intellectual prison" Fullinwider claims it to be.

Black Suffering
in the Twentieth Century

Anthony B. Pinn

Theodore Roosevelt seemed to be genuinely concerned with the condition of black Americans. For example, Roosevelt demonstrated interest in the needs of black Americans when he dined with Booker T. Washington in order to discuss race issues. This move shocked and angered many whites, while serving as a ray of hope for blacks. However, as John Hope Franklin points out, this optimism was short lived. Roosevelt's "friendship" was not consistent; rather, it was expressed only when politically expedient, and this inconsistency brought with it additional hardships.[1] This desire to remain a viable political figure by acquiescing to racism continued during the administrations of Presidents Taft and Wilson. Not only did these leaders submit to pressure from southern supporters, they actively contributed to segregation machinery and legislation. In effect, they decreased black Americans' life options and attempts at progress with the stroke of a pen.

The already delicate situation of African Americans made them a ready "scapegoat," a means by which to unite various factions of the estranged white community.[2] The South was socially and politically fractured by the Civil War, and logically it looked for a convenient causation. Even destitute white Americans could compare themselves to the "scapegoat" community (even middle-class blacks) and perceive advantages resulting from whiteness. If not

---

First published in Anthony B. Pinn, *Why, Lord? Suffering and Evil in Black Theology* (New York: Continuum, 1995), 57–67. Reprinted by permission of the Continuum Publishing Company.

1. John Hope Franklin, *From Slavery to Freedom: A History of Negro Americans,* 5th ed. (New York: Alfred A. Knopf, 1947, 1980), 310.
2. C. Vann Woodward, *The Strange Career of Jim Crow* (New York: Oxford University Press, 1957), 64.

politically and economically, these poor white Americans were psychologically comforted by their "status" in the "New" South.

In addition, the economic sphere was a constant source of difficulty. Due to factors such as the destruction of cotton crops by the boll weevil, many African Americans were forced off farms and into cities. The bulk of this migration took place between 1914 and 1930, spurred in part by the promise of opportunity.[3] In northern cities blacks were able to obtain industrial jobs made available, in part, by restrictions on immigration. However, it was not long before the number of people migrating far exceeded the number of available jobs. This, combined with the hostility of organized labor and the racist attitudes of employers, resulted in blacks having to take jobs which were inferior to the opportunities they expected. The problems associated with adjustment to city life and inadequate employment were heightened by the exploitation of landlords and the depression of the 1930s. To make matters worse, housing difficulties were further increased by the practice of segregation sanctioned in many areas by law. In light of the period of "calm" that preceded it, African Americans had no way of anticipating this harsh socioeconomic and political treatment. Yet, after a short period of "toleration," blacks began to face quick and rapid negation. With no interference by the North in southern affairs, the twentieth century marked persistent hostility toward black Americans.

Hatred and fear of black Americans expressed themselves in efforts to vilify them. Examples of this are readily found in pseudoscientific documents and literature. One famous author of this literature is Thomas Dixon, whose *Clansman* (1905) was the basis for the racist film *The Birth of a Nation*. Within this text, as well as in his other writings, Dixon ignored the reality of black humanity and consciousness. Instead, he created an animal-like and savage creature, one deserving contempt and destruction. This is seen, for example, in Dixon's description of a black man accused of rape:

> He had the short, heavy-set neck of the lower order of animals. His skin was coal black, his lips so thick that they curled both ways up and down with crooked blood-marks across them. His nose was flat and its enormous nostrils seemed in perpetual dilation. The sinister bead eyes, with brown splotches in their whites, were set wide apart and

---

3. Franklin, *From Slavery to Freedom* (1980), 310.

gleamed ape-like under his scant brows. His enormous cheek-
bones and jaws seemed to protrude beyond the ears and
almost hid them.[4]

Undoubtedly, this perception of black men made lynching and
other forms of destruction that much easier to exercise. Such depictions of black men as sexually aggressive beasts were often
supplemented with images of black women as sexually loose
temptresses who "forced" men (particularly white men) into un-
seemly and lustful acts. If not cast this way, black women were
presented as asexual "mammies" content to care for white families.

Pseudoscientific proscriptions reinforced negative literary depictions of African Americans. As Cornel West illustrates in *Prophesy
Deliverance,* faulty science and philosophy provided a "normative
gaze" used to define white superiority and black inferiority on
biological and physiological grounds. Through procedures made
available by pseudoscience,[5] North American scientists argued that
"Negroes" inherently lacked the biological structure necessary for
productive cohabitation with Anglo-Saxons. That is, black bodies
betrayed marked distinctions from the Greek ideal of beauty and
intelligence which marked blacks as physiologically and mentally
inferior "creatures." With the blessing of scientific and popular "proofs," the racist onslaught had "concrete" intellectual and
refined social force.

Many black Americans believed helping to secure democracy,
through service in World War I, in other parts of the world,
would result in better treatment at home. Yet, black soldiers were
subjected to verbal insults, poor housing, unhealthy working conditions, and denial of promotion. In addition, German officials
took full advantage of every opportunity to point out the dilemma
of black soldiers. Propaganda encouraged them to lay down their
weapons because

> ... they should not be deluded into thinking that they were
> fighting for humanity and democracy.... "Do you enjoy the

---

4. Thomas Dixon, *The Clansman: An Historical Romance of the Ku Klux
Klan* (1905; reprinted, Lexington: University Press of Kentucky, 1970). Cited in
Thomas F. Gossett, *Race: The History of an Idea in America* (New York: Schocken
Books, 1963, 1968), 272.

5. Examples of the pseudosciences include phrenology (the reading of skulls)
and physiognomy (the reading of faces). See Cornel West, *Prophesy Deliverance! An
Afro-American Revolutionary Christianity* (Philadelphia: Westminster Press, 1982),
57–65.

same rights as white people . . . or are you rather not treated over there as second-class citizens?"[6]

Nonetheless, black soldiers continued to fight in hopes of proving their loyalty and their merits. Regardless of their efforts, once back on American soil, it became clear that nothing had changed. As the editor of *Crisis* magazine stated, "this country of ours, despite all its better souls have done and dreamed, is yet a shameful land. It lynches. . . . It disenfranchises its own citizens. . . . We return from fighting. We return fighting."[7]

Blacks continued to have their societal activities proscribed by Jim Crow laws and U.S. Supreme Court "separate but equal" mandates. These laws made black Americans second-class citizens and placed restrictions on blacks with reference to public accommodations, transportation, restaurants, and stores.[8] It is certain that psychological belittling and physical subjugation were unavoidable for most African Americans. As David Nielson remarks,

> The color line was wavy here and there, and where ill defined, its customs were not consistent. But that a color line existed and that it affected their daily lives, all black Americans could attest to. Daily the color line served to focus the Afro-American's attention on — to make him more conscious of — cultural differences the dominant society's attitudes created.[9]

The racial environment and its various twentieth-century incarnations were not without religious consequences. The radical edge of the black church marked by Henry M. Turner (d. 1915) came to an end early in the twentieth century,[10] and in essence, black churches became "deradicalized." Damaged by war and depression, black churches tended to turn inward and address spiritual issues. Economically stable churches concentrated on becoming "mainstream" while distancing themselves from the problems ravaging the neighborhoods of less-well-off black Americans. The

6. Quoted in Franklin, *From Slavery to Freedom* (1980), 333.

7. Quoted in ibid., 345.

8. For a "tongue-in-cheek" depiction of the "layout" and arrangement of Jim Crow segregation, see Stetson Kennedy, *Jim Crow Guide to the U.S.A.: The Laws, Customs and Etiquette Governing the Conduct of Nonwhites and Other Minorities as Second-Class Citizens* (London: Lawrence and Wishart, 1959), esp. 228–300.

9. David Gord Nielson, *Black Ethos: Northern Negro Life and Thought, 1890–1930* (Westport, Conn.: Greenwood Press, 1977), 49.

10. Gayraud Wilmore, *Black Religion and Black Radicalism: An Interpretation of the Religious History of African-American People*, 2d ed. (Anchor Press/Doubleday, 1972; Maryknoll, N.Y.: Orbis Books, 1983), 135.

sociopolitical maintenance of black people, in large measure, was left to secular organizations such as the National Association for the Advancement of Colored People (NAACP). A notable exception to status quo black churches is found in the institutional churches motivated by the social gospel and headed by figures such as Rev. Reverdy Cassius Ransom.

Ransom, born January 4, 1861, in Flushing Village (Ohio),[11] was raised with the assistance of an extended family. From a young age, Ransom was told by his mother that he was to make something of himself and not be restricted by the difficulties encountered by other blacks. He was taught that white American "values" and education were necessary for success. After completing his schooling at Wilberforce University, Ransom began his service as an itinerant minister in the African Methodist Episcopal Church. His work as a "traveling" A.M.E. minister took him to several cities, including Cleveland (1893–96), Chicago (1896–1904), New Bedford, Mass. (1904), Boston (1904–7), and New York (1907–12). Within the early years of his work as a pastor, Ransom began to recognize the need for full community services:

> My first vision of the need of social services came to me as my wife and I almost daily, went through the alleys and climbed the dark stairways of the wretched tenements, or walked out on the planks to the shanty boats where our people lived on the river.[12]

He continues:

> The number of these people increased so rapidly that the colored clergymen of the city were bewildered. They were unprepared by training, experience and vision, to cope with the moral, social, and economic conditions so suddenly thrust upon them. I soon realized that the old stereotype form of church services practiced in all Negro churches fell far short of meeting the religious, moral, and social conditions that confronted them.[13]

Daily contact with those who were suffering raised questions for Ransom concerning the relationship between human suffering

---

11. For more information on his life and ministry see Reverdy C. Ransom, *The Pilgrimage of Harriet Ransom's Son* (Nashville: Sunday School Union, 1949); Calvin Morris, *Reverdy Ransom: Black Advocate of the Social Gospel* (New York: University Press of America, 1990).

12. Ransom, *Pilgrimage*, 49.

13. Ibid., 82.

and the Christian God.[14] Making use of the social gospel and its implicit liberal theology, Ransom constructed a working response.

Although the framework of social Christianity existed prior to this period, a formalized social gospel emerged in the years after the Emancipation Proclamation as a result of home mission efforts and other such activities. Tired of war and the strain upon life it creates, southern and northern religious leaders began to emphasize the Christian message's transformative influence on social existence. This work was conducted under the leadership of figures such as Strong, Gladden, and Walter Rauschenbusch.[15] Unfortunately, social gospelers, preferring to concentrate on issues of poverty,[16] spent little time applying their version of the gospel to the removal of American racism. Even those who responded to the plight of African Americans restricted their efforts to mak-

---

14. S. P. Fullinwider suggests that a more liberal theological stance during the late nineteenth and twentieth centuries resulted in clergy such as Reverdy Ransom replacing an all-powerful God with a "weak" deity who needed human assistance. This is an overstatement based on a lack of awareness of God conceptions in black religion. It is true that some black clergy suggested a coworker relationship with God; yet, they would not have considered their God "weak.' They still considered God in control of history and working out a plan. Human participation arose as a result of human freedom and consequential responsibility, not God's weakness. Nonetheless, even this freedom must fall in line with God's immanence. Fullinwider suggests that this coworker status is a type of break with black tradition, a tradition stemming back to the spirituals. My reading of this tradition suggests a counterconclusion. From the spirituals on there have been black theological opinions suggesting a copartnership with God. See S. P. Fullinwider, *The Mind and Mood of Black America: 20th Century Thought* (Homewood, Ill.: Dorsey Press, 1969), 34–46.

15. Ransom met Josiah Strong and Washington Gladden during the World Parliament of Religions and had also listened to Strong during the 1900 A.M.E. General Conference. See Calvin S. Morris, "Reverdy Ransom, the Social Gospel and Race," *A.M.E. Church Review* 102, no. 329 (January–March 1988): 27. This is reprinted from the *Journal of Religious Thought* 4, no. 1 (Spring–Summer, 1984).

16. Glenn Bucher, "Social Gospel Christianity and Racism," *Union Seminary Quarterly Review* 28, no. 1 (Fall, 1972): 146–57. In opposition to the opinion that social gospelers were not interested in race problems, Ralph E. Luker, *The Social Gospel in Black and White: American Racial Reform, 1885–1912* (Chapel Hill: University of North Carolina Press, 1982), 2, suggests a modified position. He argues that this perspective is valid only when "the social gospel is looked at from one perspective — the Schlesinger framework. Yet, if it is seen as an extension of antebellum home missions and social reform movements, one notices that social gospel leaders were conservative but not unconcerned with race issues." Furthermore, he states that the Anglo-Saxon superiority rhetoric of Strong is not race based but culture based and this position was abandoned by Strong (*Our Country* [New York: Baker & Taylor, 1891; reprinted, Cambridge: Belknap Press of Harvard University Press, 1963], 274). Nonetheless, racist remarks about blacks remained fashionable. It appears to me that the recorded remarks, however labeled, suggest a position justifying the poor treatment of blacks and a maintenance of the status quo.

ing blacks over in the image of European Americans. In fact, it
was believed by many "gospelers" that blacks could only find their
place in American society when they possessed the values, culture,
and ideas of European Americans. According to "gospelers" such
as Washington Gladden, African Americans who avoided the lure
of emigration to Africa must undergo a profound cultural, psychological, and ultimately ontological change in order to prosper.
With respect to this opinion, a sympathetic reading of Washington
Gladden asserts that

> his acceptance of segregation was not based on racism but
> on his assumption that Negroes could not exercise social
> equality fully until they achieved the standards of the white
> majority. Nevertheless, he might have neglected the plight
> of American Negroes altogether....He was a busy pastor
> with more immediate social problems to preoccupy him. His
> interest testifies to the breadth of his humanitarianism.[17]

The above apology for Gladden offered by Jacob Dorn falls short
in that it seeks to downplay, if not justify, Gladden's paternalistic
commentary regarding black Americans. The existence of strong
racist activities or overt neglect by others does not lessen or justify
the distastefulness of Gladden's presumptuous "burden;' any more
than comments to the effect of "some of my best friends are black"
soothe racial tensions and bridge culture gaps.

The acceptance of social Darwinism and cultural "norms" in
relation to African Americans is more clearly expressed in the writings of gospeler Josiah Strong. Strong, an associate of the American
Missions Association, believed that the United States was the best
of all countries populated by European blood. That is to say, the
United States, armed with the gospel and democratic ideals, had
been set apart by God for a special mission — the redemption of
the world. In a word, "to be a Christian," Strong argues, "and
an Anglo-Saxon, and an American in this generation is to stand
on the mountain-top of privilege."[18] It is in relation to this "chosen people" notion that one catches a glimpse of Strong's position
on African Americans. They, along with other less civilized groups,
prepared the way for the Anglo-Saxon.[19] True, Strong saw a com-

---

17. Jacob Henry Dorn, *Washington Gladden: Prophet of the Social Gospel*
(Columbus: Ohio State University Press, 1966), 302; in Bucher, "Social Gospel
Christianity," 1972, 150.

18. Josiah Strong, *Our Country,* xxiv.

19. Ibid., 215.

ing "brotherhood" of all human beings. Yet, for much of his life, this was based upon a Darwinian chain of events leading to the "Anglo-Saxonizing" of the world. Regarding this Strong writes:

> Thus the Finns were supplanted by the Aryan races in Europe and Asia, the Tartars by the Russians, and thus the aborigines of North America, Australia and New Zealand are not disappearing before the all-conquering Anglo-Saxons. It seems as if these inferior tribes were only precursors of a superior race.[20]

It must be noted that Strong did recognize flaws within this superior group. Nonetheless, these flaws are not fatal because of Christianity's soothing influence. Negative elements within "American" civilization do not negate the dominance of the Anglo-Saxons. Hence, the fall of "inferior races before the advancing Anglo-Saxons" is inevitable.[21]

While Ransom found the concern for the relationship between the gospel of Christ and the daily dilemmas of humans vital, he was troubled by the racist tone of Strong and other social gospelers. Nonetheless, Ransom turned this racist perspective on its head. He argued that the proper practice of Christian principles, understood through a liberal theological lens and democratic ideals, did not allow for the avoidance of hard race issues. Thereby, the social gospel and its implementation provided Ransom with the theoretical framework for an evaluation of the black existential situation.[22]

Social Christianity's commitment to meeting the full range of human needs is enacted in the creation of his Chicago Institutional Church and Social Settlement House (1900). Using the model provided by Chicago acquaintances such as Jane Addams (founder of Hull House), Ransom sought to provide material assistance and spiritual guidance: working for God is synonymous with working on behalf of humanity. Such a church "made plain the gospel" by placing the essentials of the Christian message within a contemporary and relevant language and context (e.g., the urban, industrial environment). In a *Christian Recorder* article defending this style of church, Ransom provides a clear picture of its nature and function. He is firm in his conviction that working for God is synonymous with working on behalf of humanity:

---

20. Ibid.
21. Ibid.
22. Morris, *Reverdy Ransom*, 33.

The institutional A.M.E. Church of Chicago was not born before its time. It comes to meet and serve the social condition and industrial need of the people, and to give an answer and solution to the many grave problems which confront our Christianity in the great centers of population of our people. It is not a dream spun out of the gossamer web of fancy; it is not an evasion, an abridgment, or a short cut method for the realization of Christ and the Christ life in the life of the people. It is a teaching, ministering nursing-mother, and seeks through its activities and ministrations to level the inequalities and bridge the chasms between rich and poor, the educated and the ignorant, the virtuous and the vicious....[23]

The narrowing of the economic, social, intellectual, and spiritual gap between humans serves two purposes. It, on one hand, enacts the gospel's call to unity — the manifestation of Jesus' conduct code; and secondly, it mirrors the best of the democratic principles espoused by the United States. Herein one finds Ransom's sense of collective salvation as a radical reworking of the quality and dynamics of societal life.

Like many social gospelers, Ransom recognized the manner in which industrialization, while having positive consequences, erodes the individual's ability to enjoy life. That is to say, the poor conditions faced by the "working class" are a direct result of capitalism. His desire to improve the conditions faced by workers led to the espousing of socialism as the necessary corrective for capitalism-induced misery. Casting it in terms of communal cooperation and a Christian code of ethics, Ransom and others argued that socialism allowed the unity and selfless sharing earmarking the gospel of Christ. Socialism's emphasis upon "equalizing" production and the benefits of production was in keeping with God's commitment to the downtrodden.

Much of Ransom's thought on socialism is presented in "The Negro and Socialism."[24] In this text, he argues that the nineteenth century is marked by the industrial age, complete with technological advances which put the earth's wealth at the disposal of humanity. The resulting economic windfall, in theory,

23. Reverdy C. Ransom, "The Institutional Church," *Christian Recorder,* March 7, 1901.

24. Reverdy C. Ransom, "The Negro and Socialism," in *A.M.E. Church Review* 13 (1896–97). Reprinted in Philip S. Foner, editor, *Black Socialist Preacher* (San Francisco: Synthesis Publications, 1983), 282–89.

should provide all citizens the wherewithal to secure a fulfilling
and meaningful life. However, the current economic system denies
workers access to the means and benefits of production, resulting in inequality and poverty. He argues that socialism resolves
alienation from production through the removal of greed and selfishness. One should not, according to Ransom, equate this removal
of selfishness with a rejection of individual interests nor a rejection of government. In fact, socialism places its ultimate interest in
humans over and above wealth. Nonetheless, it does not provide
complete equity in material holdings; rather, socialism encourages
mutual compassion and it

> affirms that altruism is a principle sufficient to govern the re-
> lations of men in the sense that it is opposed to individualism
> and does not regard society as composed of an army of war-
> ring atoms, but believes that social system to be the best in
> which the interests of the individual are made subordinate to
> the interests of society, while allowing freedom for the highest
> development of his own personality.[25]

It is only within socialism that individuals obtain and are thereby
assured the materials by which to fully develop themselves.
whereas capitalism continues to create "have-nots" who dwell
in misery within urban ghettos and have not the time nor energy
to develop their full range of capabilities.

Ransom is convinced that socialism is the solution to the problems faced by African American laborers and that the "battles of
socialism" must make use of all available hands — regardless of
color.[26] A civilization based upon unity of all peoples, and the full
expression of their talents, only comes through the implementation of this system. And African Americans must play their role
in the creation of this social transformation. However, Ransom
soon discovered that racism pervaded the socialist agenda. African
Americans found themselves excluded from "brotherhoods" and
"labor unions." Their sufferings at the hands of an unjust system
and its self-proclaimed reformers seemed perpetual. The continuing
oppression of black Americans regardless of reform efforts made it
imperative that Ransom address the issue of black suffering within
the context of his social gospel and socialist platform.

---

25. Ransom, "The Negro and Socialism," in Foner, 284.
26. Ibid., 289.

Why were black Americans facing such disproportionate suffering? Using the theory of chosen status provided by social gospelers like Josiah Strong, Ransom created a doctrine concerning the special role of African Americans in North American life. He asserted that African Americans provided a sense of spirituality that was missing from the American scheme, a sense of spirituality that was vital for the further development of American society. That is to say,

> [The Negro's] deep emotional nature will be the foe of tyranny and oppression and as a religious vehicle will convey the triumph of the King of Kings into the seats of pride and power, and over the dark and barren regions of the globe.[27]

White Christians had forgotten the mandate of the gospel, thereby giving African Americans responsibility for the destiny of the United States. African Americans held this task because they had maintained a true sense of Christ's teachings. Ransom also argues, in *The Negro: The Hope or the Despair of Christianity* (1935), that African Americans' contribution to American culture also rests in the vitality they instilled in a rather dry religion.[28] To this extent, blacks were responsible for a nascent theology of spirit which maintained some sense of continuation with African customs of dance and song. African Americans' contribution to culture combined with Ransom's sense of an immanent and active God sheds light on his response to the problem of evil.

Regarding this, Ransom was convinced that African Americans learned valuable lessons from their suffering, lessons necessary for their improvement and the fulfillment of their role in the development of North American society.[29] Related to this, Ransom provided black Americans with a creed: "We believe God to be not a cruel monster, but a loving Father, training and testing under severe discipline, the weakest and most unenlightened of his children." Furthermore,

---

27. Quoted in Morris, *Reverdy C. Ransom*, 50.

28. Reverdy Ransom, *The Negro: The Hope or the Despair of Christianity* (Boston: Ruth Hill Publisher, 1935), 22–25.

29. Ransom agreed with popular thought that African Americans experienced some "difficulty" in finding their place in North American society. Yet, he attributed this to a racist environment rather than inherent inferiority. Ransom continuously encouraged black Christians to make this critique (see Ransom, *Pilgrimage*, 299).

America is God's proving ground for the possibilities of the
Negro's capacity to win with faith and love what others have
failed to hold with wealth, privilege and power.[30]

In this way, the power and righteousness of God are proven
through the fruitful suffering of God's dark children. The divine
plan set out in historical garb was certain, but not without costs.
That is, "the pain and travail through which the Negro has passed
must produce results worthy of the things [they have] suffered."[31]
In a word, God had used severe means to accomplish divine goals.
The nature of Ransom's perspective on the problem of evil was also
shaped by his reliance on manifest destiny theory, liberal theology's
sense of human progress, and pseudo-Darwinian perspectives regarding people of color. One observes his manipulation of these
theories in the following lines from "Heredity and Environment
(1898)":

> God took the barbarians and fashioned them upon the anvil
> of Rome into what we now know as European civilization.
> God brought naked barbarians from Africa, put them upon
> the anvil of American Christianity and Democracy; under the
> white heat of denial and persecution, He is fashioning them
> with sledge-hammer blows into a new pattern from American
> civilization.[32]

Ultimately, it is through black Americans that the teleological
design is completed and global brotherhood (i.e., the Kingdom
of God) established. In addition to general statements concerning African Americans, Ransom makes a statement concerning the
special role of women in redemption:

> A few generations hence, when the womanhood of America,
> which constitutes its glory and its crown, shall be faithfully
> recorded by history, none shall outshine the achievements of
> the black women of America, who have cleansed their gar-
> ments out of the fire of degradation and humiliation to shine

---

30. Ransom, *The Negro*, 91.
31. Ibid., 91, 95.
32. Ibid., 97. Also see "The Spirit of John Brown," Second Annual Meeting of
the Niagara Movement, Harpers Ferry, West Virginia, August 17, 1906, 24–25;
"John Greenleaf Whittier, Plea for Political Equality." Centennial Oration, Faneuil Hall, Boston, December 17, 1907, 31–34. Both are located at the Schomburg
Center for Research in Black Culture, New York City.

forth in triumphant beauty as the choicest fruits that the American home and family life has produced.[33]

One notices that Ransom's analysis did not progress beyond nineteenth-century reaction to the "cult of true womanhood." Perhaps this results from the continued threat to black families and the desire to maintain certain perceptions concerning black family structure and middle-class status.

Maintaining the problem of evil argument forged in the nineteenth century, Ransom did not locate benefits within slavery itself; rather it was the "aftermath," so to speak, of oppression that was fruitful. That is to say, Ransom nuances his solution with a variation on the common theme of redemptive suffering. He asserts that black suffering is God's refining of African Americans' collective character in order to equip them for a special role in world progress. In a manner reminiscent of Henry M. Turner, Ransom acknowledges that oppression provides valuable lessons and tools which cannot be obtained otherwise. Although God does not directly inflict this suffering, God allows oppression to serve God's purpose and thereby controls human history and brings structure to seemingly chaotic occurrences.

---

33. Ransom, *The Negro*, 18.

Part One

Sermons and Speeches

Can a man reasonably be expected to love his neighbor when that neighbor is his landlord, exacting every thirty days, by the watch, an exorbitant rent, and refusing to fix the leak in the roof right over the bed? Can a man be expected not to covet when an overdue breakfast disappears down another man's stomach? Can you expect a man not to lie when a well-told lie is the only thing that has ever saved him from punishment or brought him a reward? Can you induce a man to abstain from illicit carnal pleasures when all his surroundings solicit him, and his status is so low that nobody considers it possible to disgrace him? No, these are some of the things that arise in the path of the church to hinder it in appealing to men to become Christians. Preaching as spiritual truth about an immaterial soul to be punished by a supposition remorse for finely drawn...irregularities in some future time, when duration shall have ceased and in some locus without dimensions, is not very likely either to alarm or charm the bullet-headed tough who "touches" the Sunday-school superintendent, and gets away with the swag.

— REVERDY C. RANSOM
"Trying to Become Too Much Too Soon"

Know all Men by these Presents,

That I, Daniel Alexander Payne

ONE OF THE BISHOPS OF THE

African Methodist Episcopal Church

IN AMERICA,

Under the protection of Almighty God, and with a single eye to His glory, by the imposition of my hands and prayer, have this day set apart

Deacon Reverdy Cassius Ransom

for the office of ELDER *in the said African Methodist Episcopal Church, a man whom the Annual Conference judges to be well quali-fied for that work; and do hereby recommend him to all whom it may concern, as a proper person to administer the ordinances of the*

Lord's Supper, Baptism, Marriage and the Burial of the Dead,

and to feed the flock of Christ, so long as his spirit and practice are such as become the Gospel of Christ, and he continueth to hold fast the form of sound words, according to the established doctrine of the Gospel.

In Witness Whereof, *I have hereunto set my hand and the Denominational Seal, this* 14 *day of* October *in the year of our Lord One Thousand Eight Hundred and* eighty eight

Daniel A. Payne

Bishop.

Done in Cannonsburgh Pa.

A. M. E. BOOK ROOMS, 681 PINE ST., PHILAD'A, PA.

Out of the Midnight Sky: A Thanksgiving Address

*Ransom argues, in the final years of the nineteenth cen-
tury, that history moves in such a way as to put humanity,
at times, between eras. This is currently the case as the
World's Columbian Exposition, the first Columbiad, marked
the emergence of a new era for the United States. This gathering of the nations in celebration of Columbus marked the
merging of ideas and technology, the movement toward a
glorious future — progress. However, the true mark of this
progress is spiritual renewal, a movement toward the will of
God fulfilled. And much of this is measured by the progress
of African Americans.*

•

In this year of grace heaven has bestowed her bounties with a lav-
ish hand. With music and song; with hallelujahs and doxologies;
with thanksgiving and praise, we meet to join with the nation and
unite in swelling the ascending tribute of gratitude which, from
stately cathedrals and exalted spires, from little chapels by the ru-
ral lanes, and from happy reunions round the firesides is going
up to God the giver of all Good. The skies have smiled upon the
fields, and the fields have answered back with abundant harvests of
golden grain. Scenes of beauty and notes of joy have followed the
pathway of the declining year, for the flowers have bloomed for
us, and the birds have not ceased their singing. Propitious winds
have come in from the sea, bearing moisture-laden clouds, whose
gentle rains have fallen like benedictions on the earth and given
refreshment unto man and beast.

God's great storehouse, the mines of the earth, has, at the touch
of toil and skill, yielded up the treasures of old geologic times, thus
feeding the wheels of commerce and manufacture, giving comfort
and reward both to capital and to toil. Neither blight nor famine
nor mildew has fallen on the land.

No national calamity has visited this land that can be justly
laid at the gate of heaven; if there has been destitution and suffering, if capital has been idle and labor unemployed, it is because
we have either squandered the munificent gifts of heaven, or have

---

Address delivered November 30, 1893, in Mt. Zion Congregational Church, Cleveland, Ohio (Cleveland: Praternal Printing and Publishing, n.d.), housed in the
Reverdy C. Ransom Collection, Payne Theological Seminary, Wilberforce, Ohio.

mismanaged the operation of the laws of trade, and laid violent hands upon the fruits of honest toil. As the influence of the Prince of Peace is brought to bear upon the nations, clouds of war do not so frequently arise out of the settlement of national and international questions. The pen is becoming mightier than the sword. Old despotism is being displaced by governments more humane. The suffrage is being extended and enlarged, and the people, the rightful kings and lords of earth, are asserting their right to rule.

America's First Columbiad

There are times in the history of mankind when the path of development and progress must be changed, in order that the feet of man may walk in broader ways, when gloom of ages must depart because a brighter light has arisen on mankind, when old faiths must be buried because they are dead, and a living faith is knocking at the door. All new eras, epochs, and ages have had their development and birth; there is a point which marks well the transition. Humanity stands for a moment "betwixt the conflux of two eternities," while the purest streams of the ages that have been empty themselves into the mighty current of some sublime event. It was so when the sounds of the hammer, which nailed the Man of the Thorn-crowned head to the cross of Calvary, mingled with the sounds of the hammer with which Martin Luther nailed his theses to the door of [the] Wittenberg church.

When during the past six months at Chicago, America celebrated her first Columbiad, with the splendors and magnificence of the World's Fair, it was the birth of a new era, [the] incoming of a higher civilization for America and mankind. Though the world could give the one that taught it how to love "nowhere to lay his head," to the emancipators of the human mind naught but a cup of hemlock or a dungeon, and to him who gave this hemisphere to the globe a weight of chains, the future held for them all a crown. The achievement and fame of Columbus could well afford to wait four hundred years to receive the splendid tribute and recognition which the whole world has joined with America in paying them this year. In no other year of all the four hundred which have passed could such well-won honors have been paid to his undying fame. To the World's Columbian Exposition came the nations of the earth. The beauty and perfection of art was there, speaking to the world "in forms of love and awe."

The best that the mind has thought in all the domain of literature was there thrown open to the world, every invention that ingenuity and skill could devise to minister to the welfare and comfort of mankind was there, proclaiming the mastery of man over his world, the gems and precious minerals of earth, the spices, fruits, and flowers of every clime were there, proclaiming the goodness and the beauty of the Lord; the representatives of all the nations of the earth were there, comparing notes, each showing to the other, what since the beginning of human history they had been able to do for civilization and progress. The presence of architecture was not hid, for she canopied the whole scene with sublime and harmonious forms of beauty. Thus within this year have the nations met; sharing each with the other their mightiest achievements and joining hands they have entered upon the pathway of a new era and the birth of a higher civilization.

The Parliament of Religions

In these closing years of the nineteenth century "progress" is a word upon every tongue. Men of every rank and calling conjure with this word. Literature, science and art, commerce, invention and manufacture, religion and statecraft have each written upon the forefront of their varying phases of development and operation this word "progress." But in common thought, progress is interpreted to mean the invention and multiplication of machines, the discoveries of science, the inductions of philosophy, the creations of genius, constitutional amendments, and the enactment of laws. These may be the signs of progress, but neither one of them, nor the whole of them, is "progress." A nation may possess them all, and yet be on the road to anarchy, to dissolution and decay. It was so with the nations that have been, which now are wrapped in the silence of centuries as with a shroud. The right development and true progress of humanity cannot be measured by inventions and discoveries. The ascending scale of human progress is best measured by Moses amid thunders of Sinai; by Jesus in Gethsemane; Paul before Agrippa; by Luther at the Diet of Worms; by Richard Allen's manly stand for manhood Christianity; by Abraham Lincoln laying the Proclamation of Emancipation before the Lord before he laid it before the people of the United States. Aye, this is progress — that man's heart may grow softer and his mind more clear while he daily strives to enter into eternal life. While the evening of the nineteenth century gathers round us, men stand amazed at the mighty strides of advancement which, within the measure at its years, humanity has made. But when the pen of history shall record the stupendous development of the century, and its marvelous achievement, when its unerring verdict shall be given, it will record the Parliament of Religions as the crowning glory of them all. At no time in the history of the world, "Since when at the tower of Babel, on the plains of Shinar, the God of heaven prorogued the first Parliament of Religions," has such an assemblage been possible. From Babel men went forth into the four quarters of the globe. Their strongest bond of union had been broken. They were no longer "of one speech"; God confused their language that they might not communicate to each other their schemes of wickedness. They went forth and formed nations, each separate and distinct, each to work out for itself its idea of God, its relation to the universe and to the divine. In God's harmonious world only man was inharmonious. The nations were separated not only by the confines of their territory but by religion, "language, institutions, and laws." Climate, food, and institutions were at work, forming race varieties, multiplying the barriers that kept men asunder. Here lies the world's greatest epoch, in the centuries that reach forth from Babel. But the arms of the Son of Man that were stretched forth on the cross of Calvary are stretched forth still, binding together every nation and kindred, and people in faith, brotherhood, and in love. Here lies the spring and secret of the world's triumph; the wounded hand of Christ has taken hold of the hand of sinful man, lifting him up from the gloom of ages to the light and liberty of the kingdom of God.

On the shores of Lake Michigan, in the Art Palace in the city of Chicago, but a few weeks ago, the representatives of the various forms of religious belief which are held and practiced by the major portion of the human race, met to tell their conceptions of God, His relation to the universe, and their relation to Him. From Egypt, Persia, India, China, Japan, Greece, Turkey, Russia, America, and the islands of the sea, the followers of Zoroaster, Buddha, Confucius, Mohammed, and of the multitudinous sects of Christianity met to give a reason for their faith. When the ablest exponents of the various religious faiths had declared their belief, it was discovered that in all nations "God had not left Himself without a witness."

They each recognized the existence of the one true God; agreeing with Aristotle that "God is one, only receiving various names from the various manifestations we perceive," and with Seneca, "that it is of little consequence by what name you call the first

Nature, the divine Reason that presides over the universe, and fills [all] parts of it. He is still the same God." Between the religions many points of agreement were found, and their respect for each other was increased a thousandfold. Like incense wafted from mountains of myrrh, like a divine symphony, without jar or break, men from the Orient proclaimed the doctrine of the brotherhood of man, and the men from the Occident proclaimed it back to them again. It is proper to remark that there was a reassembling here of the great branches of the human race, as well as a parliament of religions, and that our own bishop, B. W. Arnett, represented here the Negroes of the world, in doing which he has added the brightest jewel to his well-won crown of fame.

The Parliament of Religions has wrought mightily in preparing the hearts of men for the coming of the kingdom of the Son of God. When the light of the future ages shall reveal the causes that have shared for real the destiny of mankind, the Parliament of Religions at Chicago will be named the mightiest.

Out of the Midnight Sky

When emancipation and suffrage were bestowed upon the Negro, he thought that the night of adversity had passed, and that the daybreak of prosperity had dawned. But it was not the break of day for the race, but only a momentary coruscation of light, piercing through centuries of night, like the rising of the midnight sun in the Arctic latitudes, to look for a moment upon "the granite cliffs, ruddy-tinged, and listen to the peaceable gurgle of the slow-heaving polar ocean." The events of the year, touching the interests of the Negro in this country, have only served to add more gloomy chapters to the sad and melancholy history of the race upon these shores.

The Church, the School, the Home

The Negro has profound appreciation of the three great forces that belong to a high civilization — the church, the school, the home. He is endeavoring to qualify himself for citizenship and usefulness by taking advantage of all the aid which they afford.

In every community, where numbers are sufficient, he builds and supports a church. This he does voluntarily. The highest standard of Christianity and morals is both held and taught. If, as is so freely asserted, the "Negro" religion is a superstition and his morality a "sham," he would not make such sacrifices, and from his scant earnings contribute such large sums to maintain the Christianity of the New Testament and the ethics of the Bible. Upon the pages of that book wherein is written the names of them that love the Lord, his name is written large and full. The Negro has learned from courtesies of bitter experience that the chief disadvantage under which he labors when brought into contact with the more enlightened races of mankind is his ignorance. No people ever made greater efforts to free themselves from illiteracy than the American Negro is making today. He is thronging those light centers of civilization, the schools and colleges of the land. He is seeking to satisfy his insatiable thirst for knowledge by drinking deeply from every fountain in the domain of thought. The home circle of the Negro which, for centuries, was outraged by public sentiment, violated and destroyed by law, is becoming a circle of virtue and intelligence, and a source of national security and strength. The Negro is not of a migratory turn; he is not easily divorced from the scenes of his earlier years. With freedom now to act for himself, his home, wherever established, has the strength of permanence. While the fruit of his toil is adding to the comforts of his home, the elevated womanhood of the race is casting about it the mantle of refinement and chastity.

Negro Outrages

This year has witnessed no abatement of the barbarities which many American communities have long been wont to visit upon Negroes accused of crime. They are, indeed, in frequency and virulence increased.

Every time the sun has rose and set for twelve months past, his rays have fallen athwart the grave of some defenseless member of our race, who, by some mob, was either lynched or burned, for the alleged commission of an unproved crime. The revolver, the knife, the torch, the rope, and the Winchester rifle have stalked abroad through the southern section of our land, destroying, without legally established evidence of guilt, more members of our race than mark the number of the days contained in the circle of the passing year. The smell of burning flesh from Negroes consumed at the stake has been a pleasant odor in the nostrils of tens of thousands of American citizens. The awful agony and pain of victims who were being burned at the stake, in the shadow of schools and churches, have been greeted by women and children with the applause as of cannibals or fiends. That among the members of our race there should be criminals capable of committing revolting crimes is a matter of regret. These crimes should cease. The race forever stamps with the seal of its condemnation these criminals and their crimes. Criminals, black or white, should be duly punished by the law. But for these lynchings and burnings there can be no excuse, for the law is on the side of the lynchers; the courts, juries, [and] militia are in their hands, so that it is impossible for one guilty person to escape. But the unlawful slaying of the accused is only a part, and it may be the smallest part, of the injury done. When a human's life is taken by the mob, not only is the wretched prisoner slain, but the majesty and authority of the law is slain, public sentiment is slain, and society is slain also. Nay, it is more, anarchy seizing the scepter from the hand of constitutional authority. The sanctity of the home and the honor of womanhood should have both protection and respect. But the peace and security of a black man's home, and honor of a black man's wife and child, should be as sacred and as free from outrage and violence as though he were not black. This epidemic of mob violence, of outrage, and of crime is making deep inroads upon the nation's constitutional authority and moral strength. For the mob creates a thousand murderers to avenge one crime. From the outraged spot of ground which marks the grave of every mob-slain man there spring up, like the famous dragon's teeth, a legion of criminals in his stead. The slayers and the slain are recorded side by side upon the pages of the book of heaven.

The Press

The attitude of the press toward this reign of crime and barbarism is most discouraging. The southern lyncher, backed by public sentiment, has no need to seek cover for his crimes. The northern press chronicles daily these deeds of lawless men with scarcely a word of protest or condemnation. Southern writers, among them a Methodist bishop, have entered the great reviews and magazines with articles in defense of the burnings and lynchings. They are not only seeking to apologize for the crimes of their people, but also to impress the world that the Negro is so dangerous and inhuman; that he is without pale of law; that the southern lyncher is the true savior of southern society. Amid all unconstitutional acts, peril and fire and sword, the Afro-American press has been wise in counsel, patriotic in tone, strong in defense, and fearless in pleading the cause of the race before the world. Among the influences that mould sentiment and form opinion, the press is the most powerful; its attitude towards the interests of the race must be ever kept in view. Yea, as never before, our attitude toward society, government, and morals must be declared with all the ability of pen and voice at one command.

Is There Hope for the Future?

The Negro has tried every remedy for race elevation that has been proposed to him. The acquisition of learning and property, loyalty to country, patience in the midst of affliction, and abiding confidence in God, all these he has tried and is trying. Yet because in the language of many writers he still finds himself "a marked man," while his best efforts are discredited, many have grown faint and hopeless. But they are hopeless before all hope has fled. It is true that the field of opportunity is largely closed against us. But the man or the race who falters or retreats because the door of opportunity and endeavor is slammed in his face is unworthy of the goal he seeks. Armed with undaunted courage, education, virtue, and Christianity, let our watchword be "Forward! Onward to the heights of vantage!" When advancement is impossible, let us halt, resting on our arms with our faces to the foe.

"Paradise still lies under the shadow of swords," and only they are admitted who have won their right to enter there. The history of the undaunted, but hunted and persecuted, Jew has in it the tyranny of the pharaoh and the weeping willows of Babylon, yet he has lived to be present at the birth and death of empires for more than three thousand years. Many times conquered, dispersed, and scattered abroad, yet a conqueror still. Many who see no future for the Negro here talk of expatriation. All such idle schemes should have an end. To talk of expatriation is a confession of weakness and defeat. If the free and enfranchised descendants of a race that endured two hundred and fifty years of slavery in this land cannot survive after thirty years because opportunities are limited [and] liberties curtailed, neither would they become strong and powerful if environed by African jungles and savages, while every foot of surrounding territory was owned and held by the powerful nations of the earth. More powerful than governments and armies is that newborn ruler of modern times, Public Sentiment. Let the Negro continue to act the brave, the manly part.

> Like as a star that marketh not hate, that taketh not rest,
> Be each one fulfilling his God-given best.

And the sentiment, which is unfriendly or indifferent, out of which the present unhappy conditions spring, will give way.

The night of the Negro's suffering and trial has been long and dismal. It has been filled with the baying of the bloodhound upon the track of the fleeing fugitive, with sounds of the lash, with fetters and with toil, with the rope, the torch, "the law's delay," and the denial of "inalienable rights"! Out of centuries of night the sun is rising, but these monsters of the gloom will not greet his coming, for by the undaunted courage of an advancing race, they will be forever slain. If the Negro has done much for America, America has also done much for him. If this is not the hour of defeat, no more is it the hour when his shout of triumph should be raised.

This land of the Negro's suffering must yet bear witness to his triumph. Here, under the same stars where he was despised and fettered, he must yet be honored and free. The God of heaven still holds the scepter that sways the destiny of nations. When the generations yet unborn shall gather around their hearthstones to tell to their children at what cost America bequeathed the priceless heritage of "brotherhood, fraternity, and equality" to all mankind, how the Negro wrought to achieve this consummation will be the inspiration of their theme.

Lions by the Way

As mentioned elsewhere, Ransom believes that each nation has a unique and divinely ordained task to perform for the betterment of the world. For each group, the contribution made is influenced by the conditions under which the group lives. Hence, the work of African Americans has been hampered by the oppressive circumstances of life in the United States. Yet, this can change if the head and heart are worked upon. This type of work, he continues, must take place with young people. Ransom argues that children must be trained

---

From *The Disadvantages and Opportunities of the Colored Youth* (Cleveland: Thomas & Mattill, Printers, 1894), housed in the Reverdy C. Ransom Collection, Payne Theological Seminary, Wilberforce, Ohio, and in the Schomburg Center for Research in Black Culture, New York.

to take leadership within the world and in this way advance the cause of the race by avoiding useless vices such as gambling and strong drink.

•

The lion did tear in pieces enough for his whelps, and strangled for his lionesses, and filled his holes with prey, and his dens with ravin. Nahum 2:12.

In speaking to you, under the general topic for two weeks past, "The Disadvantages and Opportunities of the Colored Youth," my purpose has been to give inspiration and courage. We talked to you first from the topic under this head, "Race Soil." Last Sunday night we spoke to you from the topic, "Shall We Be Able to Go Up and Possess the Land?" Tonight we come before you to talk of "Lions by the Way." Permit me to say that in all I have said or may say, I have had no purpose and take no pleasure in showing up, or attempting to show the defects, the weakness or shortcomings of my race.

It is true we have been often flattered when the truth would have been more profitable, and I think it is not improper that once in a while we should step aside and take a look at ourselves and endeavor to learn the truth concerning us; but while all that is true, I would have my auditors understand that our enemies are always trying to get something against us. It has not been my purpose or desire to stand in this sacred place and furnish ammunition for the enemy. I have spoken because I believe it will be profitable for us to turn our eyes more directly upon ourselves and some of the phases of the unhealthy conditions by which we are environed. I want to speak the truth and nothing but the truth, in speaking from this topic. As I have done before, I shall have to use plain Anglo-Saxon, though I desire to say nothing that would make a blush come to the cheeks of the most chaste maidens, nothing that would be out of keeping with this time or sacred house. One thing further: my belief about the pulpit is this, that it ought not to be dumb, but vocal and articulate.

Any topic that relates to the welfare of mankind is not out of place here. This has been my endeavor and shall be until the end. I said to my church when I first came to this city that I would speak plain words in this pulpit, and it would be my purpose to know nothing but Jesus Christ and Him crucified. Last Sunday night our topic was "Shall We Go Up and Possess the Land?" We meant by that the fields of endeavor that are held from us. And now we come to tell you that there are some lions by the way. By this we mean the vices that are preying upon and destroying our people, in common with thousands and tens of thousands of others. Let me introduce this further, by saying to our young man and women, that I know what temptation is. Let me say to our boys and girls, let me say to our young men and women, that one thing we cannot afford to do is to imitate the vices and follies of the white boys and girls of this country.

The reason we cannot do it is this: the white boys and girls of this country have standing at their backs centuries of glorious achievements, and if they stop to play a little by the way, or if they stray from the way and give themselves to vices and follies, they have a foothold in the earth that you don't possess. They can afford, better than you, secret follies; they have power, you have not, your father has not. As you walk out Euclid Avenue and look at the mansions there, or downtown and look at the great banks and manufacturing establishments, remember these belong to white men and will descend to white men's sons.

The colored boys of this country, in attempting to get what others possess, have no time to stop by the road to get drunk; we are far enough behind without that. We have no time to stop on our way to the highest point of vantage, to take a game of cards with some fellow. On the way to business, we have no time to be lured by the siren's song onto the rocks of destruction, while attempting to get a foothold among men. These are reasons and others can be given why we cannot afford to stop and imitate the vices and follies of those by whom we are surrounded. In these talks I have so much to say that I regret I have to say almost everything so poorly. I know there are a great many of us who desire to be like other people. Some people tell us that we should strive to be like other people. Now what people would you desire to be like, if you had your choice? Like the Greeks? Socrates and Plato and Greece have passed away. You don't want to be like Greece — she fell.

Do you want to be like the Romans? Caesar, Cicero, and Rome have passed away. Something was wrong with that nation, she could not stand. Do you want to be like the Jews, scattered far and near? Many know not of the lions in the path of our progress. I place this one first. The lion, you know, is called the king, the strongest of beasts. One of the great roaring and devouring lions in our path is the lion of intemperance. You know he is devouring our boys and girls. My friends, if time permitted me tonight, I could tell you much as to its terrible ravages, and the inroads it is making among our people. Not only in Cleveland but all over this country, the lion of intemperance is making his way. I never saw but one building I wanted to curse and that was the Y.M.C.A. building in the city of Springfield, Ohio. Some of our people were so foolish as to subscribe five and ten dollars a year to support an institution our boys could not enter. I told them they ought to change its name and call it the White Y.M.C.A.

There was a door across the street unlike the Y.M.C.A. door. The door of the Y.M.C.A. swung in, but the door across the street pushed both ways; everybody could go in there, it was a saloon.

The fact of the matter is, my friends, if you want to take a header down, the doors are all open, and if you want to climb upward, many doors are barred as the Y.M.C.A.'s doors were. Intemperance is a demon, it is one of the devouring lions in the way, destroying the progress of our people. Say what you will, the lion of intemperance is making us his prey. I implore you to shun it. I remember a temperance lecture my mother once gave me: "My son, beware of the intoxicating cup. It has brought kings down from their thrones; it has brought statesmen down from their seats of power; it has blighted the prospects of the most brilliant men; it has come into the pulpit and dragged down the servant of the living God. Beware!" It has done that and more; of such an end beware. Young men, keep out of those places of drink; we cannot afford to enter them.

We of all people in this country can least afford to spend our money for drink. Taken from a financial standpoint, a man spends twenty or thirty cents a day for drinks and in eight or ten years he spends enough to buy a house and lot. From a financial standpoint we cannot afford to drink. I think that a man cannot afford to buy a piano for a saloon keeper's daughters. You bought his wife a carriage, but your wife and daughter have not one of these things. I am sorry to say that too many of our people are doing this very thing. It matters not what other people are doing in this respect, we cannot afford to do it. Anyone that has been in Chicago on State Street can appreciate what I am talking about. On the corners you can see anywhere from two hundred to three hundred colored boys, kingly looking fellows throwing themselves away in these saloons and dens. God save the flower of our youth from the lion's den! I remember the time when you could not get a colored woman to guzzle beer. And I cannot for the life of me understand why mothers send their children after it. This is the destructive part of the business. No matter what excuse you frame for a woman that sends her child to a saloon, I say there is something the matter with the mother-heart in that woman.

These are the destructive things and this is one of the lions that is doing much to destroy us and keep us poor.

In a little town in Kentucky, upon a hill where our people lived and had homes, there was an Irish family who kept a grocery. The man worked and his wife kept the grocery. She had a little keg of whiskey under the counter. She knew all the men by name and would pat them on the back and tell them they could have anything they wanted on credit.

With the groceries they bought a little whiskey, and then she got them to put their names to a piece of paper. It was not long before the Irishman owned the house across the street and after a while nearly all the houses on the hill, and they started on a few bars of soap and a keg of whiskey. Scenes similar to this are going on in scores of localities in this country, but we do not want to be engulfed by the lion of drink. Another lion which is preying upon our pathway is the vice of gambling. In destructive power I place it next to intemperance, for it is just as fascinating when it gets a hold on a man. I know gamblers that never touch a drink of whiskey. There are scores of our boys and girls going down to destruction, through the door of the gambling hell. There are some people who profess to think there is no harm in a game of cards.

I can't for the life of me see how any man or woman can apologize for a deck of cards. I do not care whether there is any harm in it or not, when a man is with a deck of cards he is in bad company.

When you get so you can play and play well, you desire to let somebody know how well you can play, you do not intend to be a gambler. Your friend has a quarter that says that he can beat you. That's the way it starts. You have a quarter that says he cannot. There are men at present in this city, dragging down their little children and wives in gambling hells of this town. The ravages of this vice are terrible. It has even affected some of our women. So infatuated are they that they will go out and wash all day and take the money to buy lottery tickets. These are some of the devouring lions by the way that are helping to destroy us, and I say to every young man, don't play a game of cards. I know the temptations of young men, and I know some of you have mothers off in distant cities praying for you. A young man goes to work in some hotel; after he waits his meals, he has no home to go to, and is at a loss what to do. Don't spend your money on gambling machines, keep it in your pocket; don't give it to those men downtown, for I think when a man spends his money he ought to get value for value. There is another thing of which I wish to speak; that is politics. A great many people think you can make men and women by legislation. You can't put a law on the statute books which will create men and women; they are not made that way. Our dependence on legislation and political parties has been one of the barriers in our way.

But my friends, salvation still comes through the church and that way only, and no political party can bring it otherwise. We are very important on election day. If you stay out on election day, so many men will be glad to see you, and when they want you to drink it is to serve certain ends. So we finally wake up to the fact that our salvation does not depend on any party. What have political parties done to help us? They have done more to destroy us.

I was shown into a saloon on election day, where I saw ten or fifteen colored men (among them an old brother of my church). They filled them full of whiskey and loaded them into a wagon and voted them like sheep. I do not say that you would do as those men did, but I do say that we can't afford to be governed by these bad principles.

Again, we are assailed by the lion of the white man's lust. I wonder that white women are not afraid to meet a Negro, after reading in the papers every day about "that burly Negro brute." I have no hesitation in saying that the outrages that are alleged to be committed by colored men upon white women bear no comparison to those which the whites commit with impunity upon colored women.

We had recently an instance in this state of a Negro assaulting a white woman. If he committed the crime, he deserved to die, and die a horrible death, but he did not deserve to die at the hands of the mob. The lions that are coming into the way, devouring the lifeblood and flower of our people, have their lair largely in the chivalric southland, but some of them are abroad in the North. In the first place there is no law for a colored woman south of Mason and Dixon's line. If a white man seduces her under avowal of love or promise of marriage she cannot sue him, for it would be a penitentiary offense for him to make her his wife. Therefore she has no law. In many of our states the law gives license to the white man's lust to feed at will upon the defenseless women of our race. A bishop of the A.M.E. Church is authority for the statement that there is a school district in Georgia where no colored woman can teach unless she consents to be the kept woman of the county superintendent. Both North and South it is notorious that indecent proposals are sometimes made to our mothers, wives, and sisters when they go to the stores to make purchases. You put the white woman in the colored woman's place and give colored men all the money and if they did as white men do I don't expect their girls would be found to possess [more] moral strength than ours. If when our young ladies go out in the streets, especially in the South, there is a crowd of southern gentlemen on the corner; they make any kind of remark about them they choose and to resent it would mean to precipitate "a race war."

Our womanhood is being degraded and desecrated, and this is one of the devouring lions. When you touch a man's home you are getting around the heartstrings of his life. In the North they don't do it in this way. Here when a woman goes out she is followed. But the northern villain will not persist if she pursues the even tenor of her way. But there is another side to this; we are saying these words not to injure, but to help. Some of you want me to preach of the land of Beulah; you object when the living present is preached. And while we are up yonder among the clouds, the devouring lions down here are despoiling us of womanhood and virtue. The fault is not altogether with our white brother, for there are women who belong to our race who surreptitiously associate improperly with the opposite side and want to be the first women among our people. I had an illustration of this a few years ago, when I had the honor to respond to a toast at the Lincoln banquet in Columbus, Ohio. In conversation with one of the gentlemen present, a state official, he asked me where I was located. When I told him he said, "I have a fine little colored girl in that city." He would not have told me that if the wine had not been flowing so freely. He called her name, and I was surprised to find she was high up in society and a leading member of my church. Women of this class do more than any other to call in question the integrity of the race. Recently a lamentation has gone up from white mothers of the South, because their sons marry so slowly. They prefer their colored concubines to the honorable estate of matrimony. The lion has her whelps in the person of degraded colored men and boys in hotels and elsewhere taking out strangers to seduce and destroy colored girls. Now, my friends, in the light of these statements it would be unjust for me to close without saying that I believe our colored women are among the grandest women under heaven. They have been loyal as mothers and sweethearts, in the darkest night and dreariest days, with every incentive to turn them from their course. As mothers they have been loyal to their children, ever loyal; as wives they have been faithful. Some of our friends say that the colored people are very religious, but their morals are bad. Read the papers and see whether the colored people have all the bad morals or not. We don't have to go down to Kentucky and run for Congress to advertise our morals. Not only have our women been loyal as mothers, but they have been loyal as sweethearts. In the midst of temptations, such as no other women in the land have ever faced, thank God, they have not lost their moral integrity. I preach faith in God. But tonight I preach, let us have faith in each other, faith in ourselves; we cannot be too loyal to each other. Loyal in business. A storekeeper, when asked to give a colored girl a clerkship in his store, said: "I can't put her in here. If I were to put a colored girl in this store I would lose lots of trade among your people. Do you know the reason? Some of your people when they came in and saw her behind the counter would not buy because they would be unwilling for her to know how much they paid for their dresses." That is the reason he would not take her. Frank James, the brother of the notorious Jesse James, is clerk in a store where our people spend thousands of dollars but could not get the most menial position. From these lessons we are admonished that our safety lies in loyalty to each other. Then let us not turn away from God; we must not lay God down. Why, don't you know some of our people are getting so progressive they actually spit on their mothers' graves. My brethren, we must hold on to God — our hope. Our mothers and fathers did not know much, but they knew God and they knew Jesus Christ in the dark days that have passed and gone. Through the long hours of the night have they gone and communed with Him, in their cabins, and the wind as it whispered through the chinks in the wall, spoke to them of the dawning of a brighter day. God has overthrown one race and nation after another; if we turn from Him He will overthrow us likewise. But if we hold on to God, He will lift us up. Let us smother pride. Do not turn from God back into darkness from which we are coming. God will lead us out of darkness into light and give us the strength of Samson to slay and overcome the lions that are by the way.

Deborah and Jael

Ransom assesses the role of women using two biblical fig-
ures: Deborah and Jael (see Judges 4–5). After this, he briefly
discusses the current and historical plight of African Ameri-
cans in the United States, in keeping with what he has noted
elsewhere in pieces published here. He argues that the great-
ness of black women was harmed by the harsh conditions
of life in the United States. Hence, in agreement with simi-
lar arguments made by Anna J. Cooper and others, Ransom
contends that black women's condition is not a result of in-
herent shortcomings; rather, it is a result of societal abuse and
neglect. Ransom continues that all of humanity has suffered
as a result of black women not being positioned to nurture
their community in healthy ways. Black men, because of their
own condition, have not inspired the best in black women.
However, this is changing. Black men are playing their role as
protectors of black women, and as a result black women are
doing their best to develop their children and their commu-
nity. Their nobleness is shining through. This club is playing
a role in this process by providing them with lessons in life —
domestic skills and the like.

•

We have with us tonight as guests of the church, who have come
to worship with us, the I.B.W. Woman's Club. We are pleased to
greet them and call attention, as a basis for our remarks tonight,
to the fifth chapter of Judges and twenty-fourth verse, which reads
as follows: "Blessed above all women shall Jael the wife of Heber
the Kenite be; blessed shall she be above women in the tent."

We have in this very beautiful chapter and in the one that pre-
cedes it presented to us two of the most remarkable women in
biblical history. Deborah was at one time the ruler of Israel. She
judged Israel at a time when, because the nation was threatened
by a neighboring kingdom her mighty men of valor and her men
of war had become awed into submission and had lost courage,
their enemies came up to fight against them; but Deborah sent for
Barak the son of Abinoam and told him to call the men of war to

---

A sermon to the I.B.W. [Ida B. Wells] Woman's Club, at Bethel A.M.E. Church, Chicago, June 6, 1897 (Chicago: Crystal Print, n.d.), housed in the Reverdy C. Ransom
Collection, Payne Theological Seminary, Wilberforce, Ohio.

arms and go out to battle to meet the enemies of their nation. But Barak, captain of the hosts of Israel, had not the courage to go to war leading the armies alone, and he said to Deborah, "I cannot go, except you go with me."

So, it was the patriotism and courage of a woman [that] inspired the men of Israel to go out to meet their Kanaanitish foes and fight until victory perched upon their standards. Side by side with Deborah, we place another woman, Jael, the wife of Heber the Kenite who, when the armies of Sisera were being routed and he had fled from his chariot, invited [Sisera] to come into her tent; and while he hid himself and had fallen asleep she took the tent pin and the hammer and drove it through his temple, pinning him to the ground, thus slaying the chief enemy and persecutor of her race.

We set these women before you tonight as the saviors of their race and of their nation and the deliverers of their country. And now we turn to sound through the gospel which we preach, the note of deliverance, for the gospel of the Son of God means deliverance — from everything that degrades, from everything that injures, from everything that tarnishes, from everything that destroys. Christianity can do nothing higher and better than to make man truly man. That is in part its mission in the world. Its highest and chief mission is the production of manhood, and of womanhood.

Whenever we lose sight of this truth, we have lost sight of the vital principle of Christianity. All of these services and sermons and means of grace are used by the church of God that men and women may be made better by being lifted up into a purer atmosphere and made to stand upon a higher and loftier plane; so that, as we have said, the mission of Christianity in the world is the production of manhood and womanhood. Not only so, but Christianity produces the higher type of man. When the gospel of the Son of God has wrought its processes on the heart and brain, it gives as the finished product the highest type of man that can be produced on the earth. Take the other forms of religious or of ethical beliefs and we find that the highest man that they produce does not measure up to the standard of the Christian man.

The very best Chinaman that you can find is a product of the very best that Confucianism can do in the production of manhood; but the highest type of man that Confucianism produces does not measure up to the highest type of man that Christianity produces. If you search in India, the highest type of man that you find in India is an example of the very best that the religion of Buddha can do in the production of manhood; but we do not believe that the Buddhist measures up to the Christian man. If you go to the Turkish Empire and find the best man in Turkey, you have an example of the very best that Mohammedanism can do in the production of manhood; but the men of these nations and of these religious beliefs do not measure up to the products of Christianity in Europe and this hemisphere. Turning to our land and our own institutions, we find that America produces the largest man of any other nation or civilization under heaven; the largest in heart and brain. America produces the most prosperous man on the face of the earth. These institutions of ours have given to the individual the largest degree of prosperity enjoyed by the masses of the people anyplace on the face of the earth. America produces the brainiest man on the face of the earth; because the foundation principles of our government rest upon manhood and not upon race, not upon creed, not upon blood; but the manhood of our race has suffered in this land — has been dwarfed in this land.

In the midst of their free institutions and under our flag, the Afro-American has suffered, the Afro-American has been dwarfed, the Afro-American has been defiled and despised; but if our manhood has suffered, through the horrors of slavery, our womanhood suffered more. It was degradation of womanhood to the lowest plane.

I believe our sisters will forgive me if, for a moment, I turn your eyes to that which is but recent history. Our womanhood was degraded by the slave hut. No woman under heaven could develop and grow into large proportions under those conditions. The miserable hovel or hut which she was compelled to call her home and the conditions under which she was compelled to live meant stamping out the higher and nobler instincts in her nature and the degradation of womanhood. The springs of maternal affection were almost sapped by the abominable and damnable system. Wifely devotion was made almost impossible. The purer instincts of our womanhood were deadened by the brutal system of slavery from which we have just come. Not only this but our womanhood was deprived of that which is necessary to womanhood everywhere. She was not permitted to inspire her men to deeds of noble action; and a manhood which lacks the inspiration of womanhood will never produce very many heroes, will never write its name very high in the annals of human history.

You may take any nation that has ever played a part in history and you will find that woman has been the inspiration of the poet's song, that woman has been the inspiration that gave the artist skill to handle the chisel and to mix his colors, that woman has been the inspiration of the warriors, of the philosopher, and of the king. But our manhood had not the inspiration of its women, could not have it; they could not inspire or cheer us to worthy and to noble service. While they were not permitted to do this, our manhood was not permitted to protect and defend them. Our womanhood has been unprotected and defenseless throughout all the centuries here and only within very recent years has it been protected. So that we could not expect a manhood on the one hand to be inspired to lofty and to worthy action, nor a womanhood which has not protected and defended by its men, to have that strength which was so necessary. But during the past thirty years our womanhood has had some delightful experiences — which have been as new as they have been delightful. For the first time she has had a home which she could call her own; or the first time she has had the delightful experience of seeing her children with their books marching away to school awakening in her breast new and pleasurable emotion.

At last her husband has become her protector and her king. No woman — no womanhood — can respect a man or manhood which is under the power of some other man; no race [of] women are going to respect their men when their men are subservient, held under authority and under the power of another class of men in the community; and it has been impossible for our womanhood — it is a hard thing to say, but it has been impossible for our womanhood to look up to our manhood with any inspiration, because they could not do so. They could not look up with confidence and be inspired by the life of a manhood that was kicked and cursed and driven by another class of men; they could not look up with confidence and pride to men who were not their own masters, but were mastered by other men; they could not look up with pride and confidence to a manhood which could not stand in the relation to them of protector, while some other man at his own caprice or volition could come and separate between him and her.

That has been the unhappy history and condition which our women have had to pass through all these dark and weary years. The wonder is that our womanhood has not been sunken and debased beyond all measure of comprehension. And after a few years our womanhood can look up to our manhood as one who has no master but God, who stands in the relation to her of protector. Today her husband is her "lord" and "king." She has no other — [nor] should have.

Women are natural hero-worshipers, more so than men; and there must be something akin to the hero in a man to take a woman's heart by storm, and to hold her affection and devotion throughout the years. But the kind of heroes that we have presented have not been very inspiring, and the women among us who have had some cultivation and intelligence have found in the ranks of our men in the years that have passed so few who were their equals. If our men desire to keep our women strong and pure and good and hold their admiration, they must show to our women on the one hand, that they have independence and strength, and on the other, they must stand on an equal plane with other men everywhere.

When our colored women, as they walk the streets of our cities, see the hosts of colored men whose personal appearance is such that as they look upon them, they can feel no swellings of pride, this fact has a tendency to render them a prey to temptation. I am glad that the time is coming, and has come, when the preacher is not the only man in the community who wears Sunday clothes through the week; because when there is only one man, or only two or three men who thus appear on other days except Sunday, it is dangerous. When our women walk the streets of the city day by day, morning, afternoon, and night, and see white men with clean clothes on, their shoes well polished, with every appearance of gentility, and then when they meet our men clumping along, looking all sorts of ways, it does not give to them that pride in our manhood which is one of the necessary elements to add to their strength. But now, as we have said, the time has come when our men are becoming to our women their kings, their princes and their protectors; and that is having the tendency to add unto their strength. Our women have had within the last thirty years the inspiring spectacle of placing their aspirations and their hopes upon the development and the training of their children, and they have been permitted to see their children, for whom they have made so many sacrifices, reach the goal, pass through the courses in our schools, in our colleges, in our universities and take respectable places in life.

A man said to me in the past week that one of the most inspiring spectacles that he had ever beheld was when, some years [ago], the man who stands before you tonight stood before two or three thousand people, after years of sacrifice, to speak his oration upon the day of his graduation. At the conclusion of that speech, while many were shouting and applauding, a woman arose from the audience, pushed her way through the crowd, made her way up to the platform, pushed by the dignitaries that were seated there, came and fell with her arms about him, and with her hot tears falling upon his cheek almost smothered him with kisses there. It was my mother; and he said, when he took that woman by the hand, he was almost shocked. He said, "That hand was as rough and as hard as the hand of some laboring man." But that hand had grown hard through the sacrifices inspired by love and maternal affection that her boy might reach the goal of his ambition, and that she might give him to the world to make an honorable place in life.

What was the inspiration of that mother (she was almost a god to me) has been the inspiration of thousands of others all over this country within the last thirty years. And these are some of the experiences that are new which our women are learning. Our women have seen, or are beginning to see, the beginnings of social life and culture. We find that we are not cultured yet, that social life among us is very crude; we have only the rudiments of it. Time was when all colored people indiscriminately mixed and mingled together, and if you refused to mix and mingle they would stone you as the Jews stoned Stephen. But there is coming a time — the day is almost at hand — when the better elements among us are beginning to class themselves together, and they are saying to those who are not fit for respectable association, "If you want to stand on this plane, you must qualify yourself by virtue, by intelligence and culture so to stand." It has long been the custom to class all colored people together without regard to intelligence, morals, or manners, but as we have said, we are beginning to find the rudiments of social life and that which may be with some propriety called society is beginning to make its appearance among us. If the lines are drawn with wisdom and intelligence, it will be for the advancement of our race and a blessed thing. If you were to ask me where is the society of Chicago, I would have to tell you that I do not know. It is none of my business either. I was not sent here for that purpose, neither for that purpose did I come; having a mission to all mankind, I love good and bad. But while that is true upon the one hand, it ought also to be true on the other hand that the lines would be so drawn that men who disgrace their manhood could not sit in the parlor of the respectable, that the man who, perhaps had the day before been in a place of questionable resort, or in the gambling "hells" of this city, could appear in the open gaze of the world with the best of our women leaning on his arm;

that our men could have, as they do have in some cities, "one girl downtown and another girl uptown."

But we are making a beginning, and the better elements among us, through the inspiration and growth of a better sentiment among our women, are beginning to appear and stamp with the seal of their disapproval that which tends to blight and mar the better life of our people. Our womanhood is getting a background which is permitting nobler qualities to be brought out. The best qualities of our womanhood could not be brought out against that dark and terrible background against which it had to stand during all the centuries of its life in this country. But now our women are getting a background, the background of a home which they can call their own — with their husband, their protector, standing there and their children round about them. With that background their nobler qualities are beginning to shine out and cause them to compare favorably with other elements of the womanhood of this country. Not only is this true but they are getting a background which is permitting their virtues to shine out and men are beginning to discover that the character and the virtue and the strength of our womanhood are not things that can be invaded at will. Our womanhood is beginning to lift its eyes beyond the horizon of its doorsteps. Just yesterday, so to speak, have they begun to do this, for they have been so busy in the last few years, within the home; but now we are beginning to produce a class of women who lift up their eyes and are looking beyond their doorstep, and they are beginning to study and think upon the great questions that affect them and the country at large and that affect all the larger interests of our whole life.

This is only the beginning. The signs have only just appeared within the past few years; but in almost every avenue, in almost every line of endeavor, our womanhood is showing its capabilities to take its place side by side with our manhood in the field of action in the greatest and largest questions of our day and time.

The organization which has come to worship with us tonight has a few representatives of this new departure upon the part of our women into the larger fields. And I want to say to the ladies that I honor you for doing honor to an honorable and a worthy woman. We have had so few women who have had an opportunity to distinguish themselves upon the larger fields of action. And when one has gone into the rich fields of endeavor and distinguished herself there, we should give her all honor that her deeds and achievements may be an inspiration to younger girls that shall come after her. Honor to whom honor is due. I speak no words of fulsome praise. The organization which meets here tonight has honored itself and honored Chicago and honored the womanhood of the race by taking the name it bears "The I.B.W. Woman's Club," a name which is known in almost every portion of the Western Hemisphere where the English language is spoken. A girl who started out in one of our southern cities as an orphan girl, left without mother or father at an early age, without protector or defender, by the strength of her own character she was mother and father, protector and friend to the brothers and sisters who had been left with her orphaned thus; going out as a girl to be an instructor and teacher of her people, and whenever her womanhood was trampled upon, standing up with all courage in defense not only of her womanhood but her citizen rights. When the men of Tennessee, standing face to face with the blood of their brethren who had been murdered in cold blood crying from the ground were silent, this girl had the courage to speak out, the courage to speak courageous words when the men and the manhood of the race ought to have rushed to the defense. For this she was compelled to be an exile or forfeit her life and started upon a mission to most of the larger centers of this country which heard such invective, such eloquence, such denunciation, such appeals to righteousness and truth under the Constitution and the laws as this country had never heard before. She met the opposition of leading men of the race, in the church and in politics; they thought it was a mistake. And yet she pushed her crusade in this country and across the waters until she filled the world with the cry of the Negro's wrongs. She so rang the story of the outrages in this country into the ears and into the hearts of the American people that now the great metropolitan dailies in this country and the public sentiment of England have been aroused; I say this tonight because I want to weave, while preaching to this club, a crown of evergreen and place it on the brow of that little woman who has wrought so gloriously in this cause for our race, and after this thirty years is an illustration of the kind of women that we can produce. She did not do it for fame; she did not do it for money. I have tramped the streets with her through the wind and the storm and rain, in mud and mire, that she might go to assemblies of men of influence and power and there plead to them the story of our wrongs and seek redress. And what I have known her to do she has done all over this country, so that tonight while receiving these guests with their honored name, we do double honor, by giving honor to whom honor is due. A character like that, God builds for war; He has got to make them in a certain way so they can fight; and He fixed her up with that kind of courage. He did not send her into this world to weave bouquets and to make apologies for wrong; but to speak straight out and talk right on, so that we have some of the first fruits of our womanhood here tonight. And while she has wrought in this field, in almost all of the larger fields her womanhood is beginning to secure a foothold.

We have perhaps foremost among the women that are engaged in the work of training our girls, that matchless woman Fannie Jackson Coppin, who in her school in Philadelphia has accomplished a wonderful work — an illustration of the growing strength of our womanhood; and we have in art Edmonia Lewis, who has won for herself a respectable place; and we have one of the first in that line, Hallie Quinn Brown, our elocutionist who, now in London, has gained some notoriety; and we have in song as one of the first fruits in that line, Selika — all honor to Selika the pioneer!

Now the hosts have come and are following in her footsteps. But these women among others have begun to make the way possible. In the field of literature and journalism there is rising up a host. One in our city is taking a respectable place — that is Mrs. Fannie B. Williams.

So Chicago and Philadelphia and the little countrysides are coming to the front with a type of womanhood that our race can produce. Now, another phase — and I shall detain you but a few moments more. These clubs are formed of the very best hearts and very best brains of our race to study the great questions of domestic economy, questions that relate to the home; and I tell you, my friends, that if ever there was a class of women that needed to study these questions, it is our women. They are not only studying questions domestic, but questions intellectual and questions social and questions political; and the organization which is here tonight, "the I.B.W. Woman's Club," is only one of a great number that are springing up in different parts of the country. Our womanhood is becoming aroused and awakened; and I only pray God that our manhood may be worthy of it.

And now, men, the thing that we must do is to protect this womanhood. Why is all this trouble in the country from time to time about white men putting to death with impunity colored men? Why, they say, "Our womanhood has been molested and the man that defiles our womanhood we will crush; we will kill." There is one thing that the Negroes of this country want to learn and that is to respect its womanhood, not to accost them too familiarly upon the street, but with all dignity and honor; and when their women are molested they should learn to defend them. Why, my brethren, in many cities of this Union colored men this very day, I am sure, every day, walk in the streets with their women, their wives, their sweethearts upon their arms and permit blackguards and ruffians to throw insults at them as they walk in their company. Is it not true? And as they walk the streets of this city — this northern city — our Chicago — it often happens that men presume because they see a colored woman on the streetcars, on the streets, and elsewhere that they may approach them with a familiarity that is not decent. Our men must come to the place when they will not permit it, and our women should conduct themselves with such dignity and propriety as not to invite insult.

I am a minister of the gospel and a man of peace, but the day that any man insults one of mine, I shall resent it with emphasis. And this is one of the lessons, if our womanhood is to be elevated, that men must learn, that womanhood has protectors and defenders. Another duty that we owe to our women is to support them as far as possible; take them not into the struggle for winning bread, but give them that opportunity, as far as it is in your power, for the development of those higher graces and qualities which are peculiar to the sex by supporting them properly in the home.

These are some of the lessons that our manhood must learn if we are to come up. How long, O Lord, how long! I speak tonight, men, not simply as a minister, but I speak as brother to brother, I speak as friend to friend; the work that we have to do means more than the service of religion, more than the work of the political reformer and of the legislator. It means that our manhood shall take a stand for the protection and support of our womanhood. The time has come now, in the condition in which we stand in this country, that any Negro that defiles or debauches, or degrades one of our little ones of the gentler sex is worse than a wild beast of prey; while I could not utter anything from this pulpit that would cause any man to perform an unworthy action that would lead to wrong, I believe that the men that lie in wait like a wild beast of the forest to destroy the virtue and uprightness of our women should be treated like a wild beast.

We have got some lessons to learn. Mark my words tonight, brothers! Our womanhood can never shine in all beauty and dignity and glory which is in store for it until it has our protection, until our women become our queens at whose feet we lay the richest trophies and highest honors we can win in the field of endeavor.

We wish to the I.B.W. Club, Godspeed, that no dissension may mar it that it may be worthy of the name it bears, that in good works it may be led up into still larger fields....

Thanksgiving Address, 1904

Recounting both the triumphs and tragedies of the year, Ransom proclaims in this sermon the nation's "duty and destiny." As suggested elsewhere in his writings, Ransom argues that the challenge for the individual and the nation is to fulfill their humanizing duty as opposed to simply asserting rights. Fulfilling this destiny entails having the necessary "tools" and "skills," and exercising them in healthy ways. In this way, Ransom seeks to rethink the United States's sense of manifest destiny — or a warped sense of divine privilege that allows for the abuse of others — and replace it with a commitment to the welfare of all humanity, both at home and abroad.

•

We need no proclamation from his excellency, the president of the United States, to remind us of our duty to give due observance to the proper celebration of Thanksgiving Day. The people of New England have observed, annually, a day of thanksgiving for generations, until it has become to them as a holy Sabbath unto the Lord. Thanksgiving Day is one of the institutions of New England. As her sturdy sons went forth to conquer this continent, fighting as they did, with the rocks of the mountains, warring with the elements of heaven, fording streams, bridging rivers, clearing forests, opening the untold mineral wealth of the bowels of the earth, making golden harvests of cereal and vegetable, fruit and flower spring from the virgin soil; while cities rose like magic from the wilderness and the prairie, among the mountains and by the sea, they established wherever they went the custom of observing this day, until now it is no longer local, but national.

Address delivered at Bethel A.M.E. Church, New Bedford, Massachusetts, originally published by L. I. Jenkins, printer, n.d., contained in Ransom, *Duty and Destiny: A Thanksgiving Address,* housed in the Schomburg Center for Research in Black Culture, New York. Reprinted by permission of the AMEC Publishing House (Sunday School Union).

This has been a year of such unprecedented calamities, and such climatic horror, as to make the blood run cold, while ashen lips could only speak with bated breath. Fatalities by accidents upon railroads, incineration in the awful holocausts of the Iroquois Theatre at Chicago and the ship *General Slocum* at New York, are chief of many appalling disasters.

The peace of Europe and the diplomatic amity of the nations of the world have been threatened by the titanic contest of arms between Japan and Russia on the other side of the world, where the ground has run red with the blood of thousands, even the blood of tens of thousands of the slain.

But nature has lifted high her cornucopia and poured out bountiful harvests, so that our barns and storehouses have been filled. We have enough and to spare. The dove of peace has spread her wings over the nation; we are at peace with all the nations of the world.

This day is a time of reviving memories: memories of bygone days; memories of the sights and scenes of youth and childhood; memories of the old home and hearthstone and of the circle that surrounded it there, from which, alas! how many forms have vanished, how many lips are silent forevermore!

We have made our Thanksgiving, not a fast day, but a feast day. It is the time of family reunions, when feet that have wandered far retrace their steps and turn back home again. It becomes a kind of domestic sacrament, when children and children's children are gathered around the sumptuously laden family board. The heart of age grows young again, and hope rejoices in fruition, while parents welcome back from the busy world children whose lives are a crown of glory to their gray hairs.

And now, while today we count our blessings and reverently give thanks to Almighty God for His mercies and all His benefits, both in individual and national life, may we not consider, for a brief space, some of the elemental forces, influences that lie deep in the problem of our life....

Duty and Destiny

How strangely, indeed, are we begirt, in the midst of this mighty current of humanity of which we form so small a part. How did I become what I am? How was I fashioned thus, in thought, character, and in circumstance? Did I become what I am because of what I was? Does what I shall become depend unalterably upon what I am? What of these paths that lead, one to poverty, another to wealth; one to fame, another to oblivion; one to political subjugation, another to political control?

Is individual or national destiny a part of a fixed order in the scheme of things? Or, is destiny something to be attained, achieved; something under the influence and guidance of capacity, courage, and character. I doubt not that each individual, as well as nation, has felt within him at least a dim foreshadowing of his destiny. A race conceives that destiny has decreed it to be superior and therefore it has a right to hold and treat all others as inferior; a nation feels that destiny has given it the scepter of empire and therefore it has the right to subjugate and govern, without their consent, certain other peoples; the individual feels that destiny has decreed him the enjoyment of certain rights in human society, and therefore to achieve his destiny he is justified in fighting for his rights.

Jesus Christ, in dealing with the great question of human destiny, speaks not once of human rights. He does not teach men how to obtain their rights, but how to fulfill their duties. He teaches that the loftiest exercise of our faculties and powers lies in the fulfillment of our duty toward God and man. [Giuseppi] Mazzini, the great Italian patriot, wisely based his teaching and philosophy upon this doctrine — that rights could only be attained by the fulfillment of duties. I should refuse to be a slave, because it is my duty to be free; I should refuse to be kept in ignorance because it is my duty to be enlightened; I should refuse to be under tyranny of another man, because it is my duty to be also a man. It becomes thus, then, a greater thing to fulfill a duty than it is to assert a right.

The Man of Destiny

We have heard much of the man of destiny in ancient times, and even in modern times he is thought to have occasionally appeared. Was it the star of destiny that led the invincible legions of Julius Caesar back to Rome? Or was it not rather that Brutus, the envious Casca, and Cassius, "with the lean and hungry look, who thought too much," were eclipsed in oratory, literature, statesmanship, and war by Julius Caesar, who thus became "the foremost man of all the world"? Napoleon flashes up, meteor-like, from the streets of Paris, until he has all the armies of Europe in his train, unable to curb or break his power, because he outmarched, outmaneuvered, and outfought them, upon contested ground. Fortunate indeed is he, and we doubt not that such there are, who feels that destiny has chosen him for a certain calling, marked him for a certain work, appointed him to some high task, or led him to the doing of a great deed. But even when destiny seems to be clearly set before us, I hold that it is always conditional. One, to fulfill the destiny he conceives to be appointed to him, must first be properly equipped, both from within and without; he must employ all means, power, and influences conducive to that end, and he must walk courageously in the path that leads to it.

The American Youth

The possibilities that lie before the youth of America are dazzling to the imagination — limitless. There are no objects of ambition to which he may not aspire, no prize in life for which he may not compete, no path of human endeavor he may not tread, no height of usefulness and honor he may not hope to scale. For here, each one is supposed not only to be entitled to, but to be actually given "a man's chance." Neither rank nor title, wealth nor blood are supposed to stand as a barrier to the youth of most lowly origin or humble birth. It is our boast that in America, "each holds his destiny in his own hands." This is, indeed, the very breath of life with which this republic was born. It was the spirit of the Pilgrim Fathers when they took their destiny in their hands and set sail for these shores; it was the power that inspired the patriots of the revolution, when they refused taxation without representation and launched this nation upon the untried waters of self-government. When opportunity is hedged about by caste, race, or class barriers and distinction, personal responsibility for what an individual may become is not large; but when the pathway of opportunity is made so free that all may walk it with unfettered feet, responsibility for individual destiny becomes a sacred trust. Would a young man never be unemployed? Let him be thorough in his work and faithful to the interests he serves. Would he be prosperous? Let him practice rigid economy and honesty. Would he be honored by society? Let him fulfill his moral, social, and civic duties.

A Nation with a Mission

From the time the foundations of the government were laid, America has regarded herself as a nation with a mission. Each epoch in her history has been ascribed to "manifest destiny." America regards herself as a nation raised up by God, to establish and pre-serve certain great principles. It is hers to keep watch and ward over personal freedom, individual liberty, and free self-government established upon no other foundation than manhood citizenship.

Other nations may have their ruling families, but here each family is a ruling family. Others may limit the number of those permitted to participate in the administration of the government; here there is but one qualification and but one test which applies to all. We give to each individual the opportunity to make out of himself all, and the very best, he is capable of becoming.

While we make no war upon monarchy or absolutism, we say to the crowned heads of all the earth that we must be left free to work out here upon these shores the great task to which we have dedi-cated ourselves. Until within the past few years we have worked out the problem in comparative isolation from the rest of the world; we have left to the governments of Europe the questions of the expansion of empire, the subjugation of strange peoples, the ex-ploitation of savage races, and the establishment and government of colonies.

Within the past few years the nation has entered upon the path of a new development. We have acquired territory outside our bor-ders and are now governing strange peoples across thousands of miles of sea on the other side of the world. In this new departure some of the wisest and most patriotic men see the beginning of the republic's end. But however loudly they may shout their notes of warning, the great mass of the nation is borne forward by the cur-rent of events. The step, once taken, cannot be retraced. In a new sense we have become a world power. But our destiny to continue to be a free self-governing people will not be changed if we do our duty by ourselves and by the people with whom we are brought in contact.

While other nations subjugate alien peoples, we must liberate them. While others exploit the material resources of foreign lands, we must develop them. While others force the yoke of their pe-culiar civilization and government upon unwilling peoples, it is this nation's mission to take them by the hand and assist them in the establishment of a form of government and the development of a civilization suited to their peculiar temperament and climatic conditions.

While within our own borders, with all the commingling of races, the mantle of citizenship must be large enough to enfold them all. When money comes to be more influential than manhood, when color comes to be more potential than the constitution, then indeed is the ax laid to the roots of our tree of liberty.

Social Awakening

Of all the movements of modern times, the social is destined to wield the greatest influence. The social awakening of the peoples within the last century has brought into organized society a new force. The distant thunder of the tread of marching millions now at last is heard. The American eagle from his mountain height of freedom was the first to see them coming from afar, but now have they drawn so near to courts of justice and thrones of power that even the Russian bear trembles with alarm at their approach.

The groanings of the social spirit in travail to be born are now often viewed with apprehension. What shall be brought forth, the wisdom of statesmanship cares not now to know. Intrenched wealth says it may be a usurper of its accumulations, while conservatism avers that the time of its delivery is not at hand. But the hour is struck. The hands upon the dial-plate of progress cannot be reversed. The process of the readjustment of the relations of men to society has begun, and while many blunders will be made, the work will go on until men have learned to live together upon a new basis, both of interest and of service.

Gone is the time when the many shall toil for the benefit and pleasure of the few. Gone is the time when the few shall be surfeited with goods, with houses and lands, while the many perish or are but poorly housed and fed. The mass of humanity has grown to look up — look with aspiration and desire — to all the vast domain of social and industrial advantage from which they have been so long debarred. They will continue to look up, until they rise up, and march in their might as God's children coming into their own.

While these look up, those who are above intrenched in seats of power must look down, not in derision or scorn, not in malice or alarm, but with willingness to surrender to their disinherited brothers the estates they have so long withheld.

Segregation or Solidarity

The great questions which we and the other enlightened nations of the earth are now seeking to solve and settle are being fought, with either segregation or solidarity for their war cry.

For thirty centuries, in the great drama of human civilization, segregation has held the center stage. The line of cleavage between man and man, class and class, race and race, nation and nation has ramified into every phase of human relationship. From of old it has been found that the sun of destiny only shone to light the path of certain privileged classes or races. Men could conceive that certain classes or that a particular race or nation had a destiny worth fighting for; nay, so priceless as to be worthy to be preserved if one must die for it.

That the Jews had a destiny, let even the mountains round about Jerusalem proclaim it. That the Greeks had a destiny, let the marble of Phidias breathe it and the muse of Homer give it voice; that Rome had a destiny, let the Tiber hear the proclamation from her seven hills and hear the message on into the sea; that the white race has a destiny, let the hoarse voice of his cannon thunder it as, robed in blood, he goes forth upon his mission of the subjugation of the world.

At last a new conception is dawning upon mankind and human speech is becoming vaguely articulate, but nonetheless articulate, in uttering a new word — solidarity. The destiny of the individual, the race, the nation is becoming less and less and will have decreasing influence as a rallying cry, only as it includes the common destiny of man. An individual life, a race or national life, which only sees its duty and views its destiny from the angle of these narrow limitations will become more and more a thing to be despised. The necessity for cooperation among men, their mutual interests, and the common good are bounded by no race or clime. The destiny of our race is bound up with the destiny of humanity, even as the destiny of our nation is bound up with the destiny of the world.

You may call me a dreamer when I tell you that my vision beholds the fetters of race and class broken from the limbs of humanity forevermore. I see humanity with arms so long that brother joins hands with brother across the broad expanse of sea, until, in a circle that girdles the globe, man to his brother is joined in a loving handclasp around the world.

I see the men of a new civilization rejoicing in the fulfillment of our golden dreams, when from the centuries of its wanderings humanity comes back to its common unity, knowing but one family altar, that the altar of humanity; but one brotherhood, that the brotherhood of man; but one fatherhood, that the fatherhood of God.

The Spirit of John Brown

As has already been established through other documents, Ransom gave special attention to those who fought for the full rights of African Americans, using them as examples of the attitudes and activities proper for the true securing of democratic practice in the United States. In this speech, his attention is turned to John Brown. In so doing, Ransom links Brown with great biblical figures who fought to secure the will of God in human affairs, even when this meant fighting against established powers. Unfortunately, Ransom continues, the efforts of John Brown and similar figures have not completely removed the tragic manner in which African Americans are dealt with in the United States. Hence, the struggle continues.

•

Great epochs in the world's history are hinged upon some spot of land or sea, which becomes historic and sacred forevermore. There are Mt. Sinai and Mt. Calvary, the Jordan, the Euphrates, the Nile and Rubicon, Thermopylae, Runnymede, Waterloo, Gettysburg, Appomattox, Port Arthur and Manila Bay; *while John Brown has made Harpers Ferry as classic as Bunker Hill.*

The leonine soul of this old hero-saint and martyr proves how important and defenseless are tyranny, injustice, and wrong, even when upheld by the sanction of the law, supported by the power of money, and defended by the sword.

If modern history furnishes a solitary example of the appearance of a man who possessed the spirit of the prophets of ancient Israel, it is John Brown. The sublime courage with which he met the Goliath of slavery in mortal combat was not surpassed by David, who went forth to meet the Philistine who had defied the armies of the living God. He was commissioned by the same authority and bore the same credentials as did Moses, who left his flocks in the Midian desert to go and stand before Pharaoh and demand in the name of "I Am That I Am" that he should free his slaves.

Address delivered at the Second Annual Meeting of the Niagara Movement, Harpers Ferry, West Virginia, August 17, 1906, housed in the Reverdy C. Ransom Collection, Payne Theological Seminary, Wilberforce, Ohio; in *The Spirit of Freedom and Justice: Orations and Speeches* (Nashville: A.M.E. Sunday School Union, 1926), housed in the Schomburg Center for Research in Black Culture, New York. Reprinted by permission of the AMEC Publishing House (Sunday School Union).

John Brown left his flocks and fields at Mt. Elba, New York, and fought at Osawatomie to make the soil of Kansas free; at Harpers Ferry, where his brave followers fought and delivered a blow against slavery in the most vital part, and fired the gun whose opening shot echoed the sound of the death knell of slavery.

Melchizedek of Modern World

This old Puritan, whose steel gray eyes gleamed with the spirit and courage that possessed Cromwell at the battle of Dunbar, took literally "the sword of the Lord and of Gideon," as both battle cry and watchword. Men like John Brown appear only *once or twice in a thousand years*. Like Mt. Blanc, the king of the mountains, he towers high above the loftiest figure of his time. The place he occupied in the affairs of men is unique. He is the Melchizedek of the modern world [see Genesis 14]. He had no predecessors and can have no successors. Any picture of him which does not have its proper setting amid the background of his time makes him appear quixotic, rather than the heroic figure that he was.

A Man of Action

Like Moses, Joshua, Cromwell, and Touissaint-L'Overture, he defies classification. He belonged to no party, was a disciple of no school; he was swayed neither by precedent nor convention. He was a man of achievement, of action. Garrison could write and Beecher could preach, while the silver-toned voice of Phillips pleaded; this man performed the *doing of it*. He could not choose his course; the hand of the Almighty was upon him. He felt the breath of God upon his soul and was strangely moved. He was imbued with the spirit of the Declaration of Independence and clearly saw that slavery was incompatible with a free republic. He could not reconcile the creed of the slaveholder with the word of God. While dealing with the border ruffians of Kansas he had seen the slave power seek to justify itself and extend its sway, by the murder of peaceful citizens; he had seen the prairies illuminated at night by the flames of their burning homes, their crops destroyed and their cattle and valuables stolen.

An "Act of God" Needed

The government was cognizant of this and also acquiescent. Statesmen and politicians were making concessions and compromises to
quiet the demands of the South in behalf of its cherished institution. The nation found itself bound to a body of death whose
foul decay was spreading its influence to the highest sources of its
life. No time, then, for Missouri compromises and Kansas and Ne-
braska acts; what was needed then was an *act of almighty God.*
Slavery leaning upon the arm of the law was defiant, it could
only be attacked by appealing to "the higher law." John Brown
appealed.

Traitor to Country to Be True to Slave

God sent him to Harpers Ferry to become a traitor to the government in order that he might be true to the slave. This nation
was established by men who took up arms to fight against a tax
on tea, and the universal verdict of mankind approves their action. When John Brown fought at Harpers Ferry he commanded
his immortal band with the sword of Frederick the Great, which
had been presented to George Washington, and posterity has given
him a fame no less secure than that of these two great captains who
unsheathed in no worthier cause.

It has been fifty years since Osawatomie, and fifty years, less
three, since an old man, whose austere manner and flowing beard
gave him prophetic mien, *introduced Harpers Ferry to history.*
Since then the armies of the North and South have marched across
the country in a robe of fire and blood, to fall upon the field of
battle locked in the embrace of a death of lead and iron.

Brown a Puritan

The true value and merit of a man lie embalmed and treasured up
in the life he lived, and the character of the service he rendered to
mankind. The whole life of John Brown was serious and purpose-
ful. He was a [descendant] of one of the company who landed from
the *Mayflower* at Plymouth Rock, and from ancestors who fought
in the Revolutionary War. He had all of the moral uprightness and
strict religious character of the Puritan, as well as his love of liberty
and hatred of oppression and tyranny.

From a child he loved to dwell beneath the open sky. The many voices of the woods and fields and mountains spoke to him a familiar language. He understood the habits of plants and animals, of birds and trees and flowers, and dwelt with them upon terms [of] familiarity and friendship. His heredity and environment were just such a school as was needed to shape his character and prepare him for his God-appointed task. For he believed himself sent upon a *mission under the authority of heaven.* When he wrought like a mighty man of valor, whether in Kansas or at Harpers Ferry, he believed with all the modesty of his truly great and heroic soul that he was only doing his duty. He proved the sincerity of his motives, the unselfishness of his purpose, and his entire devotion by sacrificing upon the altar of human freedom his money, goods, wife, and children. When God's clock struck the hour, he cried, "Ill-timed, premature"; education and respectability shouted, "Monomaniac, madman, fool!" Posterity hails him a hero, and crowns him martyr.

Armed Slave to Free Himself

The distinctive act which has given the name of John Brown to immortality was his attempt to organize *and arm the slaves to rise and strike for their freedom.* This deed aroused the nation and *startled the world.* His was not an attempt to assist them to break their chains in order to flee to Canada, but to forcibly assert and maintain their freedom in the Southland where they had been held as slaves.

The Negro will never enjoy the fruits of freedom in this country until he first demonstrates his manhood and maintains his rights here *in the South,* where they are the most violently protested and most completely denied.

What is to be the final status of the Negro in this country cannot be settled in New England or settled in the North. There will be no rest or peace, or harmony upon this question until it is settled, and settled justly, *on southern soil,* where the great majority of the Negro Americans make their home.

Rights Must Be Won in South

In the days of John Brown a handful of slaves found freedom in flight to Canada and the North. But this did not change the condition of the enslaved millions, or the attitude of their cruel oppressors, while it did cause the Supreme Court of the United States to make every white man of the North a detective and an agent of the South, in the detection, capture, and surrender of fugitive slaves.

Today Negroes are coming North in increasing numbers. But this does not change or modify a revised constitution in any southern state, abolish one Jim Crow car, or stop a single lynching. In the days of slavery the Negro had a few devoted friends in the North and also in the South, but those in the South dare not speak or act; while some in the North were outspoken, they were backed by no public opinion which would support radical action. So today, the Negro has sympathetic friends and helpers, but public opinion nowhere sustains agitation or action against the conditions that prevail.

Nothing New in Country's Attitude

The present manner of dealing with the Negro question is nothing but the old method in a new disguise. The former attitude of the North was to confine the institution of slavery within the boundaries it occupied and to permit the inhabitants of new territory to settle the question among themselves. Today the South is unmolested in its disfranchising constitutions, by which two score seats are occupied in Congress in violation of the Constitution. The Jim Crow car is also kept within these borders.

President Never Mentioned Suffrage

While no president has been so voluminous a writer of messages to Congress, or traveled so extensively in every section of the country, speaking freely and at length on a wide range of subjects, the present occupant of the White House has been *absolutely silent* on the question of the enforcement of the Fifteenth Amendment; while his secretary of war has admitted the violation of the Constitution, he has recently in a notable address openly condoned it, if not tacitly, indeed, *endorsed* it. On the admission of Oklahoma and the Indian Territory, as in the case of Kansas fifty years ago, the Negro question reappears, and it is never to be unconstitutional to separate the races in public schools, which opens the door for legislation that will discriminate against the colored citizen.

In the early sixties scores of northern regiments and 185,000 Negro soldiers went into valorous action, singing as they marched, fought, and fell, "John Brown's body lies moldering in the tomb, and his soul goes marching on." The dreams of this dreamer at last found fulfillment as his soul went marching on in the Proclamation of Emancipation, in the Thirteenth Amendment to the Constitution, abolishing slavery, the Fourteenth Amendment, bestowing citizenship, and the Fifteenth Amendment, giving the elective franchise to the Negro to protect and defend his citizenship and rights under the Constitution and laws.

It is, indeed, paradoxical that a nation which has erected monuments of marble and bronze to John Brown, Frederick Douglass, William Lloyd Garrison, Charles Sumner, and other abolitionists; a nation which proclaims a holiday that all classes, including schoolchildren, may decorate with flowers the graves of the men who fought to preserve the Union and to free slaves; a nation which enacted into organic law the freedom and political status of a race that have been bought with blood, now sits supinely down, silent and inactive, while work of the liberators is ignored, while those who fought to destroy the government, *regain in the halls of Congress the victories they lost on the field of battle,* while the Constitution is flouted and the Fifteenth Amendment brazenly trampled underfoot.

The Charter of Rights Annulled

It is thus that the charter of the Negroes' rights is being annulled. The North is busy with its moneymaking and money getting. Northern manufacturers think more of the southern market for their goods than of the rights of the loyal Negro citizen. Every few months a captured battle flag is returned to some southern state, to be followed by a proclamation that the gulf between the North and the South has disappeared and that the wounds of the war have been healed. *Southern men* are neither *cajoled nor flattered* by these overtures. Their determination to refuse to recognize the political equality of the Negro remains unaltered, while their purpose to fix his social status and reduce him as far as possible to a condition of industrial serfdom is firm.

Political Action Needed

The Negro regards the Democratic Party as his traditional and hereditary foe. Tradition, gratitude, sentiment, bind him to the Republican Party with an idolatrous allegiance which is as blind as it is unpatriotic and unreasoning. *Today there is very little difference between the two parties, so far as their attitude toward the*

Negro is concerned. While the Republicans do not, perhaps, *initiate* legislation unfriendly to the Negro, neither do they, on the other hand, openly attack, defeat, or *veto* such legislation. It has been demonstrated repeatedly that a *Republican* cabinet and a Republican Congress will make the Negro's civil and political rights a matter of barter and trade, to secure Democratic votes in the interest of tariff schedules, interstate policy relating to commerce, or some scheme of our expanded republic relating to its possessions and dark-skinned subjects in the islands across the Pacific Ocean.

Taft Calls Us Political Children

Secretary [of War] Taft, speaking for the president, chides us by saying that the Negroes are political children, that they have shown their incapacity to maintain their political rights. It is true that the Negro had a *childlike faith in the Republican Party,* believing that it would administer the sacred trust which the fortunes of war and the constitution had imposed upon it, and that it would not use him like a gambler's stake in the game of politics.

Scales Falling from Our Eyes

Thank God, at last the scales are falling from the Negro's eyes. He is being disillusioned by the acts of a *Republican Congress,* the speeches of members of a *Republican cabinet,* and the silence of a *Republican president.* He has reached his political majority. It is his patriotic duty to emancipate himself from his political fetish and cast his influence and his vote where they will make for the preservation of his liberty and the welfare of his country. He should not hesitate to *repudiate his former friends,* who have betrayed him, nor refuse to *fraternize with former enemies,* who are willing to give him aid. While he remains a political issue he must insist upon making his power felt and his rights respected.

Negroes Divided among Themselves

There never has been a time when the American people have not sought to fix the status of the Negro in this country, in every phase of its life, within limitations and boundaries more or less definitely defined. But our fathers have told us that in the darkest days of slavery, when this nation fancied that they were contented with their lot, which they bore with so much patience and submission, they secretly cherished the hope of someday reaching the goal which was set before their white fellow countrymen.

There is not now, and never has been, any division among the Negroes as to the place they hope to occupy within this nation. But there is a division among them as to methods and the choice of ways leading to the coveted goal. It was one of the defensive weapons of slavery to keep the Negroes divided among themselves, lest they unite to the injury and destruction of that institution.

The race has not wholly survived this heritage, nor have the whites ceased in their efforts for division among us by pitting one Negro against another, and the condition in which we are placed tends to make this practice more or less effective. The 10,000,000 Negroes in this land, despite their seeming acquiescence in the inequalities and restrictions placed upon them, are determined, [if] it takes a thousand years, to enter, as an equal, every avenue of American life.

Today two classes of Negroes, confronted by a united opposition, are standing at the parting of the ways. The one counsels patient submission to our present humiliations and degradations; it deprecates political activity, ignores or condones the usurpation and denial of our political and constitutional rights, and preaches the doctrine of industrial development and the acquisition of property, while it has no word of protest or condemnation for those who visit upon us all manner of fiendish and inhuman indignities.

This form of teaching is alike acceptable to the North and to the South. It tends to keep the Negro in his preconceived place and eliminates him, both as a factor and a cause of irritation, [from] politics and all that vitally relates to civic and social affairs.

Position of the Agitators

The other class believes that it should not submit to being humiliated, degraded, and remanded to an inferior place. It neither seeks nor desires that a special place be made for it within this nation, separate and apart from other people. It believes in money and property, but it does *not believe in bartering its manhood for the sake of gain.* It believes in the gospel of work and in industrial efficiency, but it does *not believe in artisans being treated as industrial serfs,* and in laborers occupying the position of a peasant class. It does not believe that those who toil and accumulate will be free to enjoy the fruits of their industry and frugality, if they permit themselves to be shorn of political power.

Founded as this nation is, it does not believe that submission to injustice, the surrender of rights for the sake of an opportunity to labor and save, is the road to the goal of the manhood and equality which we seek. It believes the Negro should assert his full title to American manhood and maintain every right guaranteed him by the Constitution of the United States, and having these, all other things will be added.

The White South Frank

However we may regard them, we must respect the frankness and honesty of the southern people. They do not disguise their attitude. They boldly declare that they seek not to deceive the Negro, the nation, or the world. However high the Negro's character and education, however large his accumulation of money and property, however industrious and efficient as a laborer, they do not intend to permit him to enjoy with them political equality or any other kind of equality. They are not deceived by the Negroes who are seeking to *delude them by submission to* present conditions, in the hope of outflanking them by a circuitous march. The Negroes who are aggressively fighting for their rights have the press against them and the weight of public opinion. They are branded as disturbers of the harmony between the races, but they have the same spirit that animated the founders of this nation. *In them the soul of John Brown goes marching on.* Unless the Declaration of Independence is a lie, and the throne of Almighty God breaks down, they will at last take their place in our national household as an equal among their brethren.

Need Unusual Voice and Issue to Arouse the Nation

Like the ghost of Hamlet's father, the spirit of John Brown beckons us to arise and seek the recovery of our rights, which our enemy, "with witchcraft of his wit, with traitorous gifts" has sought forever to destroy. John Brown was thought by many, even among his friends, to be insane. But an exhibition of such insanity was required to arouse the nation against the crime of slavery and to bring [about] the Civil War. *No weak and ordinary voice can call the nation back to a sense of justice.* A commonplace movement or event cannot influence or change the present attitude and current of the public mind.

Rights of Citizens the Battle Cry

The rifle shot at Harpers Ferry received defiant answer from the cannon fired upon Fort Sumter. This nation needs again to be aroused. The friends of truth and justice must be rallied. But men cannot be rallied without a rallying cry; and even with this upon their lips, there must be a lofty standard to which they may resort. Cannot the hearts of men warm as earnestly to the cry of the rights of an American citizen as they did to that of the freedom of the slave? Will the nation that could not tolerate the enslavement of human beings sanction the disfranchisement of its citizens?

Abraham Lincoln set before this nation in its darkest hour preservation of the Union as the standard for all loyal men. Can the men of the present take higher ground than to make secure the life and liberty of the black men who helped sustain it when it was tottering to its fall?

The gage of battle has been thrown down. The lines are clearly drawn; the supremacy of the Constitution has been challenged. In fighting for his rights the Negro defends the nation. His weapons are more powerful than pikes and Sharp's rifles which John Brown sought to place in his hands at Harpers Ferry. He has the Constitution, the courts, the ballot, the power to organize, to protest, and to resist.

The battle before us must be fought, not on the principle of the *inferiority of one race and the superiority of the other,* but upon the ground of our common manhood and equality.

Socrates drained the cup of hemlock to its dregs, Jesus Christ suffered crucifixion on a cross, Savonarola was burned in the streets of Florence, and John Brown was hung from a gallows. But the cause for which they willingly became martyrs, the principles they advocated, and the truths they taught have become the richest and most glorious heritage of mankind

Before the strife and hatred of race and class have vanished, many will be called upon to wear [the] martyr's crown. A new birth of freedom within a nation is always accompanied with great suffering and pain. How much greater, then, the travail through which humanity must pass to bring forth its last and highest birth, for which all preceding ages have worked and waited until now.

We see it in the tyrant's face, in the oppressor's cruel wrongs;

we read it in the statute books of every unjust law; we hear it in the strife of human conflict; we feel it in the universal aspiration of the soul; it comes to earth by many signs from heaven. The spirit of human brotherhood is unbarring the gates of life to admit a civilization in which it can reign incarnate, while out of the many threads of human life upon this planet we are weaving the royal garments it shall wear.

Thanksgiving Sermon: The American Tower of Babel; or, The Confusion of Tongues

Within this sermon, Ransom discusses the lingering "Negro question" by making reference to the biblical tower of Babel (Genesis 11) and the confusion resulting from human arrogance. After rehearsing some of the major events resulting from the nation's dislike of African Americans (including the Civil War), Ransom notes that the confusion due to different languages that marks the tower of Babel story resurfaces with respect to the various opinions concerning African Americans' role in industry, education, politics, and social equality. In addition, he makes mention of the pseudosciences used to justify the inferior position of African Americans. Yet, this is countered by scientific proclamations that there are no biological grounds for the inferior position of African Americans. Unfortunately, according to Ransom, in the early twentieth century common opinion is beginning to favor the language of African American inferiority, as mass violence against blacks demonstrates. This move is oddly justified through a double standard with respect to morality. African Americans, according to Ransom, must point out this dilemma and through example highlight the common humanity of all.

•

Sermon delivered at Bethel A.M.E. Church, New York, November 25, 1909, in *The Spirit of Freedom and Justice: Orations and Speeches* (Nashville: A.M.E. Sunday School Union, 1926), housed in the Schomburg Center for Research in Black Culture, New York. Reprinted by permission of the AMEC Publishing House (Sunday School Union).

Text: Genesis 11:9, "Therefore is the name of it called Babel; because the Lord did there confound the language of all the Earth."

The fruits of the field and the vine, the products of forest, quarry, and mine, the rains of heaven, freedom from pestilence and disease, lie in a realm in which the power of man does not enter. They are the gifts of God.

It is a long-established custom in this country, when the harvests have been garnered and all the bounties gathered from the lap of nature have been safely laid by, to call a solemn assembly to return thanks to the Giver of all these benefits.

It is also a time of reunion, when children who have gone forth from the family rooftree, some to be wife and mother, others to make their way in the great world, return and, around the family fireside and the well-provided family board, rehearse old memories and revive the affections of the years gone by.

We are assembled here this morning to join with our fellow countrymen in thanks to God Almighty, for these and innumerable blessings that have come to us.

During the year our nation has enjoyed peace and prosperity. Speaking broadly, labor has been generally employed and capital has received its just reward. We have had peace with all the world; no pestilence or great catastrophe of nature of appalling proportions has visited our shores. It is our prayer that this nation may more and more seek to stand so firmly upon the foundations of justice and righteousness that it will merit a continuance of the blessings of God.

Turning from this phase of those considerations which give its chief emphasis to this day, I, in common with the large majority of clergymen in this country, have chosen to take up for discussion a phase or phenomenon of our national life; to discuss a question which is national in its aspects and vital in its relation to peace and the future well-being of this nation.

I have chosen for my theme "The American Tower of Babel; or, Confusion of Tongues over the Negro."

The Negro and the Negro question have passed through many phases, dating back nearly three hundred years ago when he first set foot upon this soil. The Negro question first came up for discussion at the time the foundations of the government were laid. For in the Constitutional Convention there were friends of freedom, some of whom were slaveholders. As a compromise measure over the adoption of that instrument, it was agreed that the slave trade should be prohibited after the year 1808. The question next appears in the discussion over the boundary lines of slavery, that is, as to whether slavery should be confined to the territory south of the Mason and Dixon line and as to whether within such territory, new states might be formed as slaveholding states, and finally as to whether new territory north of the Mason and Dixon line might be admitted into the Union as a slaveholding state.

Along with the discussion of these questions come[s] the Fugitive Slave Law, involving the right of the master to take his slave even from the boundaries of the free state and carry him into slavery. Another and by all odds the most momentous and burning discussion of this question arose over the subject of emancipation. Over this the tides of battle ebbed and flowed for more than a generation. The best statesmanship of the nation, ministers of religion of the highest standing, reformers, poets, writers, and thinkers of every school brought their contribution to this discussion. It caused great religious bodies to divide asunder; it separated families; it severed the ties of friendship, and finally brought on one of the greatest wars of modern times, until more than a million men stood in the field of battle in the awful carnage of war, until in the red streams of the blood of the slain the question of freedom triumphed. Abraham Lincoln's immortal Proclamation of Emancipation has been signed and sealed by none more enduring and omnipotent than the superscription and seal of Almighty God.

While there was much division, yet speaking in general terms, the nation was of one speech in the adoption of the Thirteenth, Fourteenth, and Fifteenth Amendments to the Constitution. It was felt that these great amendments had fixed forever the place of the Negro in this nation, that the awful cost of treasure and blood was not too great a price to pay for equal freedom and liberty to all men under our flag.

The South, devastated, impoverished, defeated, was for a time helpless yet sullen and in a sense defiant and unrepentant. The North was busy with its work of reconstructing the nation after the awful ravages of four years of bloody war. There was a brief lull after the conflict and then confusion began to arise, first over the question of the Negro's civil rights. Charles Sumner's Civil Rights Bill was an attempt to settle this matter finally, but the enemies of the Negro were again active, and this bulwark for his protection was ruthlessly set aside by the Supreme Court of the United

States declaring it unconstitutional. This was the entering wedge, to be followed by all the tides of indecencies, injustices, humiliations, degradations, insults, and outrage that have come in under that form of legislation known as the Jim Crow laws. There are no Jim Crow laws in northern states, yet so powerful does this react that the Negro meets, at almost every place of public entertainment and in all those phases of conduct which in the line of business and duty must bring men together, the spirit of the same proscription which animates the Jim Crow laws of the South.

From this point and around this point the confusion of tongues has been increased and multiplied for the last thirty years; it has concerned itself in the discussion of his place socially. In the South the Negro's place socially is always interpreted to mean social equality. I have never believed that the South was sincere in its pretended fear of social equality, and so far as the Negro is concerned we are quite sure that it is a question which gives him no concern. He only asks to be permitted, like other men, to walk unhindered in the path of men.

The confusion has gathered volume and increasing virulence around the question of the Negro's sphere industrially and as to the kind of education he should receive. Some of his opponents justify their attitude by appealing to Heaven, on the ground that God himself has decreed that the Negro's place is one of inferiority and that only in the capacity of a menial should he be permitted to make his contribution to our industrial life. The trade unions have largely adopted this view by debarring Negro artisans from membership and excluding them from employment wherever possible, so that it has come to be that the millions of Negro toilers in this land have less protection and receive less incentive to produce, up to the limits of their capacity, at just reward, than any class of toilers in this country or enlightened nations of Europe.

The question of Negro education is one which for twenty years has divided even the friends of his advancement. So persistently and so skillfully has the view that a special brand of education should be prescribed for the Negro been propagated that willing ears in the North, as well as in the South, have accepted it as just. This view holds that he is to be trained to constitute a great black peasantry in this land; while there are others who hold the view that the Negro, being a citizen and a man, should be educated just as the children of the Irish, the German, the Italian, and the Jew are educated, to qualify him to take his place in any phase of the nation's life, side by side with his fellow countrymen, and make the best contribution of which he is capable, according to his capacity and his powers.

While these are the great vital questions around which the voices of men are divided, there is still another and persistent note which seriously vibrates, on the question of deportation or immigration of the Negro to Africa, or to some other country outside the boundaries of the United States. Not having the courage to meet and face this question on the ground of justice and right, white men have adopted this view; not having the courage to stand up and fight, to suffer and endure, Negroes of prominence have acquiesced, but up to now they have received no sign from Heaven that Jehovah is crying aloud to the American people to let the Negro go, as He did in the case of Israel in Egypt in the day of Pharaoh.

The Negro was able to maintain himself for more than two hundred and fifty years in slavery here. For more than forty years of freedom he has increased, multiplied, prospered, in the face of obstacles and opposition discouraging and at times almost insuperable. The agitation of this question has not ceased and may not for a long time, but in the midst of it all, the Negro will continue to root and entrench himself so firmly in the nation that he cannot be uprooted without overturning the nation to its very foundation. He is here to stay.

The confusion of tongues over the Negro question in this country is illustrated by the attitude of the most intelligent and progressive Negroes. We have on the one hand Dr. Booker T. Washington and his adherents; on the other hand Dr. W. E. B. Du Bois and his adherents; while outside of these there is a great unclassified host. Now the adherents of Dr. Washington speak one language and the adherents of Dr. Du Bois speak another; neither can understand the other. Therefore, like the confused tower builders of the plains of Shinar, they go into different camps and take their separate ways, while the unclassified host to which I have referred stands hesitant and halting between the two conflicting bodies of opinions.

Mr. Washington says, "Eschew politics," and Mr. Du Bois says, "Vote." Mr. Washington places largest emphasis upon vocational training which shall be chiefly industrial, while Mr. Du Bois insists upon no special brand but the largest opportunity for that which is highest and most liberal.

The attitude of these two champions may be best illustrated by referring to the National Negro Business League, of which Dr. Washington is president; and to the Niagara Movement, of which Dr. Du Bois is president; or by considering the contents of Dr. Washington's chief book, *Up from Slavery*, and of Dr. Du Bois's chief book, *The Souls of Black Folk*.

If we turn to the government itself, the Constitution of the United States speaks one tongue and the Unites States Supreme Court another. In each instance, thus far whenever the vital interests of the Negro have come up before this body, it has seemed to be unable to understand or to rightly interpret the express mandates of the Constitution. Or we may turn to former president Roosevelt and the present occupant of the White House, Mr. Taft. President Roosevelt, whatever may be our attitude as to his conduct with reference to the Brownsville affair, stood unequivocally for a square deal, for the open door of opportunity, and for an equal chance for all men, while on the other hand, the present occupant of the White House has gone out of his way to make public proclamation of his intention to appoint no Negroes as federal officers in communications where such appointments were displeasing to the white people of that community. His attitude in the matter of the taking of the census, now about to be under way, would seem to indicate that for the first time since our enfranchisement we are to be practically eliminated from this important service.

If we turn to the domain of science we find the same confusion here. We would expect that here there would be nothing but unbiased search for truth and for pure deductions of logic, the collection of data and the classification of facts without regard to where they lead, but not so. Science on the one hand is lending its high authority to the doctrine of Negro inferiority, by seeking to prove that because of the shape of the skull, the convolutions, weight, and size of the brain, the Negro is naturally inferior and that therefore treating him as an inferior is treating him according to nature and setting him in his proper place. But on the other hand science declares that the shape of the skull, the convolutions and the weight of the brain have nothing to do with intellectual capacity — that the Negro's brain is no smaller than that of the Swiss, Italian, and others, and that his cranial capacity is no less, that there is absolutely no difference between the brain of the Negro and that of any other man.

If we turn to the halls of legislation, the confusion increases. Georgia, Mississippi, and South Carolina advocate one set of laws; New York, Massachusetts, and Ohio another. Senator Tillman speaks one tongue and Senator Foraker quite another.

In literature confusion reigns. In the editorial rooms of the great newspapers and magazines there is no agreement of opinion.

If we turn to the realm of religion the confusion increases. When the pulpit is not hesitant or incoherent, it is absolutely dumb. What has religion to say to lynchers, to the disfranchisers, the despoilers of womanhood when it is black, and to the degradation of manhood by humiliation and ostracisms? There is no speech or language which is common to the different denominations, or even to various pulpits of the same denomination.

At the tower of Babel those who spoke the same language traveled in the same path as they took their way. So today those who hold the same views on the Negro question camp together.

But admittedly, the number of those who differ over the Negro question is growing less and less. There is forming in this country a large body of opinion unfriendly to the Negro; the various groups are more and more coming to a better understanding.

The lynching of Negroes or their burning at the stake no longer fills the country with horror; now great crowds of women participate in this human holocaust. There are no protests in Congress against disenfranchisement. The Supreme Court of the United States, as in the case of Berea College, may declare that the state has a right to prohibit white and colored youth from being educated in the same school, and, as Justice Harlan declares, that according to this opinion, they have the right to prohibit them from going to the public market at the same hour, or from walking upon the same side of the street.

The North, if we are to take the recreant Senator Cullom as authority, is coming over to the view that we are to acquiesce in the complete nullification of the Fifteenth Amendment, in order that the financial interest of the South and the tenure of power to the Republican Party may find a basis of union, and be it remembered that Senator Cullom resembles Abraham Lincoln in features, that he comes from the home of Lincoln, and was the friend of Lincoln.

Nothing could be more disastrous to the Negro at this time than the harmonizing of the divergent and conflicting views in regard to his status, if thereby his manhood is compromised or his citizenship circumscribed.

Amid the Babel of tongues over the Negro question in this country, the latest comes from an article in a recent number of *Leslie's Weekly,* in which the writer claims to quote from a man who was a government official under former president Roosevelt and who claims to have been in Mr. Roosevelt's confidence.

He says that the real object of Mr. Roosevelt's trip to Africa is not to hunt lions or to gather specimens for the Smithsonian Institute, but to find what he believes to be the true and only solution to the Negro problem. He quotes Mr. Roosevelt as saying that he has been convinced ever since he lunched with Dr. Booker Washington at the White House that no amount of education or other qualification could lift the Negro high enough in this country to cause him to be recognized as an equal, and that after thinking long and deeply over this question, the president had gone to Africa in an effort to work out a solution there. He said the president took a large quantity of trinkets with him to be distributed among the native tribes in the heart of Africa, in order to get on friendly terms with them, and that the president hopes to be able to get permission to take over a large section of the northern Sudan, east of the German sphere of influence, as this is one of the largest and most desirable portions of Africa not yet seized upon as a sphere of influence by the nations of Europe. When Mr. Roosevelt bursts from the heart of Africa next April he will declare his solution to the world. His plan will be, as an entering wedge, to persuade this country to repeal the Fifteenth Amendment; then he will propose that the states issue bonds, which are to be guaranteed by the national government, and that these bonds are to be used to pay the Negroes for the property they own in this country and to pay the cost of deportation to Africa, giving them 160 acres of land and all the necessary tools of industry. He claims that with the Fifteenth Amendment repealed, the property of Negro as may be taken, just as the land of the Indians was taken, and as the Indians were pushed back, so the property of the Negroes may be thus taken and the Negroes deported to Africa. The Negro in Africa, with the flag of this country over him, would furnish a check to further aggression of Germany and other European nations and also give the United States greater power as a factor in the partition of Africa, aside from settling for all time our race problem.

The thing which perhaps, more than any other, is undermining the foundations of individual and national character is America's double standard of morals. It has one moral standard for the white people and another moral standard for the colored people. This is aptly illustrated in the case of Senator Stone of Missouri, who not long ago assaulted a colored waiter on a dining car. In court Senator Stone pleaded in justification of his act that "he did not strike a man, he only slapped a nigger."

When a Negro is accused of a crime, the presumption is always in favor of guilt, thus reversing the very fundamental principle of our legal structure, that a man is presumed to be innocent until he is proven guilty. Severe sentences for misdemeanors visited upon Negroes in the South are far more excessive than those which would be imposed upon a white man who had actually been proven guilty of a crime.

Or take the question of the division of the school funds in the southern states, with perhaps two or three exceptions. They will apportion anywhere from 60 percent to 90 percent per capita more for the education of the white children than for the black.

But the application of the double standard of morals for the two races accomplishes its most destructive and degrading work in the relations of white men to colored women and of colored men to white women. If a colored man is accused or even suspected of a crime against a white woman, the vengeance with which he is put to death, without the process of law, reaches the height of madness and ferocity. If a colored man and a white woman are suspected or known to have relations which are entirely mutual, the very best that the Negro may hope is to be permitted to leave the community on pain of death.

In the South, if a colored girl is seduced by a white man, she has no redress at law; even if they were willing, they could not legitimatize their offspring, because it is a penitentiary offense for the two races to marry. She could not sue him for support, because this would be both against the law and public sentiment.

The white people of the South acquiesce in the immoral relations between young white men and colored girls, on the ground that it is a protection of the young white women of the South.

It is in this relation that the whole fabric of southern chivalry falls to the ground, their boasted reverence for womanhood, for virtue; yet they regard with absolute indifference and contempt all womanhood, except in the person of their fair sister, and make it a boast that the virtue of their black sister is their legitimate and proper prey.

Our confusion will grow more confusing until we as a nation comprehend the fact that the ethics of Jesus, as set down in the New Testament, is not an iridescent dream; that foundation stones of this nation have their last resting place upon the ethics of Jesus Christ, that of brotherhood based upon the fatherhood of God. Out of this, through all the struggles of our national life, we have been seeking to realize liberty, fraternity, and equality.

America is based not only upon the ethics of Jesus, but upon democracy, as set forth in the spirit of the Declaration of Independence. This means all men should be permitted here to achieve the highest possibilities of which they are capable.

The American Negro does not ask his white brother to take him on faith but on sight, and to recognize his worth as it is proven — his manhood, his industry, his skill, his patriotism, his ability, as they are demonstrated day by day right before his eyes.

The Negro himself can perhaps do more than any other to silence confusion by proving for himself and for the blacks throughout the worlds that he is capable of attaining to the very highest and best within this civilization. For the Negro here is the only Negro on the face of the earth in vital daily contact with the white man within the same government on terms of equality. If he fails through ignorance, incapacity, laziness, shiftlessness, courage, in a sense the black race throughout the world has failed.

We are to prove that the indifference of color which divides us is only superficial and entirely nonessential. We are here to prove our common humanity and manhood. From the shores of this country the Negro and the white man should go forth, hand in hand, to teach Russia, Japan, England, India, Europe, and Africa how men of different races may live together upon terms of equality, of fraternity, and of peace.

I see, as from the tower of Babel, the scattered groups returning from the confusion that has so long kept them separated and divided. They have learned that despite all differences of speech, they have at all times had one word in common — that word is MAN. Now we learned to articulate in unison another word — that word is BROTHER. Now standing face-to-face they say — "MAN AND BROTHER." The recognition is instant. Barriers are broken down, the confusion is silenced, and in brotherly cooperation they set themselves the task of building their civilization a tower of strength, because all men who toil and strive, who hope and aspire, are animated by a common purpose that is peace, happiness, and the common good of all.

Charles Sumner: A Plea for the Civil and Political Rights of Negro Americans

In keeping with centennial celebrations for other figures, Boston sought to recognize the leadership of Charles Sumner, and Ransom was selected to give a speech about him. After presenting biographical information on Sumner, Ransom discusses Sumner's work on behalf of African Americans, work that must be continued by able hands until full democracy — justice — is achieved. During his speech, Ransom remarks that the Fifteenth Amendment to the Constitution giving African Americans the right to vote is of fundamental importance in the securing of full rights. Ransom states that Sumner foresaw the battles that would need to be waged in order to continue moving toward African American progress, and he worked to assure the continued enfranchisement of African Americans.

•

Not until the latter half of the nineteenth century did the American people seriously set their faces toward the realization of the Declaration of Independence. The centenary of the men who had most to do with the new birth of freedom within the nation has fallen upon the opening years of the twentieth century. As becomes our best traditions, the citizens of Boston have, on each occasion, gone to Faneuil Hall to extol their deathless deeds and pay reverent tribute to their imperishable names. Our first centenary celebration in recent years was that of William Lloyd Garrison, which, in order, was followed by that of John Greenleaf Whittier and John Brown. Tonight we celebrate Charles Sumner's, within the walls of historic old Park Street Church, while before the close of this year the centenary of Wendell Phillips will occur. The patriotic impulse that has prompted us to hold these public assemblages in their honor is strong testimony to the fact that however much obscured for a time, the spirit of liberty and justice is not dead. These men were not timeservers, seeking personal or partisan advantage, political preferment, or popular acclaim. In the words of Garrison — they

Boston centennial oration, January 6, 1911, Park Street Church, Boston, sponsored by the New England Suffrage League, the Massachusetts branch of the National Independent Political League, and the Citizens Auxiliary Committee, housed in the Reverdy C. Ransom Collection, Payne Theological Seminary, Wilberforce, Ohio. Reprinted by permission of Mrs. Ruth L. Ransom and her son, Louis A. Ransom, Jr.

were in earnest — they did not equivocate, they did not excuse — they did not retreat a single inch. In their day as in ours, on the question of the Negro's rights, there was as much stubborn prejudice and frozen apathy in the northern states as in the South. With a nobler resolve than the Spartan warrior, who pledged himself to return from battle with his shield or on it, they stood for right against wrong, for liberty against oppression, for justice against tyranny.

The soul of Charles Sumner was cast in a classic mold of Apollo-like perfection. His eloquence was lofty, the form of his periods was chaste and beautiful, but the power of his logic was as terrible as justice. There are men, black as well as white, who occupy positions of commanding influence and posts of the highest honor, *who have so compromised or repudiated the principles for which Sumner gave the best fruits of his life that any word they might utter in an hour like this would be a profanation of his memory.* And unless we, who have assembled here tonight to honor his memory, meet the problems of our day in the same resolute spirit he met the problems that confronted him, this meeting will have been held in vain, our applause a hollow mockery, our words a sounding brass and a tinkling cymbal.

Mr. Sumner was elected a United States senator from Massachusetts as a member of the Free-Soil Party. When he entered the Senate as an avowed and uncompromising opponent of slavery, he soon took and held a place as the northern champion of freedom, quite as conspicuous as that which had been previously occupied by Calhoun as the southern advocate of slavery. When Sumner embarked on his career as a commanding figure in national politics, he found the slaveholding oligarchy and its influence arrogant, aggressive, sensitive, brutal, entrenched everywhere. Its baneful influence controlled the press, the pulpit sought to defend it by divine sanction, the Supreme Court upheld its judicial decisions; it dominated Congress, which it awed by threats of nullification and secession if its assumptions were questioned or assailed.

The second great effort of Sumner after he entered upon his senatorial duties was his speech entitled "The Crime against Kansas." He based his arguments upon the Constitution, upon broken faith in relation to the Missouri Compromise, and pleaded to keep the soil of all the territories of the United States forever free from the invasion of human slavery. While free from bitterness, it was the boldest and most powerful arraignment of the assumptions of the slave power which, up to that time, had ever been delivered in the Senate; its logic was unanswerable. The speech inflamed to madness the advocates of the extension of the domain of slavery. The spirit of slavery was shown in the characteristic reply which it made to his arguments, by the unprovoked assault which was made upon him by Congressman Preston Brooks of South Carolina, who beat him into insensibility with a bludgeon while he sat at his desk in the Senate occupied with his duties. This speech and the consequences to which it led were more powerful in arousing and influencing public opinion than the heroism of that stern old patriot, John Brown, who at Osawatomie fought for the freedom of the soil of Kansas.

Sumner's speech "The Barbarism of Slavery," delivered more than four years later, after he had returned from his travels in Europe, whither he had gone to recuperate from the effects of the murderous assault made upon him by Brooks, left slavery completely unmasked. It was shown to be wholly evil in its tendencies and degrading in its influence. All arguments in its defense were answered; its apologists, North and South, were either overwhelmed with confusion or provoked to that madness which led to treason, while friends of freedom took heart and within in a few months thereafter girded on their armor to fight for liberty and union.

Providence seems to have willed it that the Negro should be present and participate in the events which have marked every turning point in the history of this nation. Though in chains, he was among the early settlers of this country. While denied the exercise of those rights which the Declaration of Independence pronounced to be "inalienable," he fought with distinction in the armies commanded by Washington; he was with Commodore Perry on Lake Erie, with General Jackson at New Orleans; he was with the armies of General Grant until he received the sword of Lee at Appomattox, and in the ranks of the armies that destroyed the power of Spain in this hemisphere, and for weal or woe, started this republic on the road to empire. When the life of this nation trembled in the balance, it was the valor and patriotism of 180,000 Negro soldiers that caused the scales to turn in favor of the Union and freedom. *The blood of 30,000 Negroes who gave their lives in defending the flag against secession and slavery has sealed forever the rights of this race to enjoy a white man's chance, wherever floats the flag of the nation they helped to save.*

Mr. Sumner lived to see the downfall of the Confederacy and the Union restored on the basis of freedom. With him and the men who stood with him, there was no room for evasion or compromise. They believed that the fruits of freedom should be made secure to the freedmen and their descendants, that it would be worse than criminal to withhold from them the ballot as a weapon of defense against reenslavement by their former masters.

The ratification of the Fifteenth Amendment was regarded as an act of justice by the president, by Congress, and by the public opinion of the North. In one of the longest speeches ever delivered by President Grant, he said, in response to a delegation which called upon him[:]

"I can assure those present that there has been no event since the close of the war in which I have felt so deep an interest as that of ratification of the Fifteenth Amendment by three-fourths of the states of the Union. I have felt the greatest anxiety ever since I have been in this house to know that was to be secured. It looked to me as the realization of the Declaration of Independence."

Mr. Sumner's position on the political rights of the Negro is perhaps better expressed in a letter written by him to a colored national convention at New Orleans. Among other things, he said:

"In maintaining your rights it will be necessary for you to invoke the Declaration of Independence, so that its principles and promises shall become a living reality, never to be questioned in any way, but recognized always as a guide to conduct, and a governing rule in the interpretation of the national Constitution, being in the nature of a bill of rights, preceding the Constitution.

"There can be but one liberty and one equality, the same in Boston and in New Orleans, the same everywhere throughout the country. The colored people are not ungenerous, therefore, will incline to any measure of goodwill and reconciliation; but I trust no excess of benevolence will make them consent to any postponement of those rights which are now denied. The disabilities of the colored people, loyal and long-suffering, should be removed before the disabilities of the former rebels, or at least, the two removals should go hand in hand. It only remains that I should say, Stand firm!"

The Negro should have been unyielding in the past, and there should be no compromise today of that liberty and those rights which a sense of justice caused to spring from the heart of this nation when it was still bleeding from the wounds which had drenched it in blood and scourged it with fire in the awful carnage of the Civil War. The Garrisons, Phillipses, and Sumners stood for us when we could not stand for ourselves. Aye, "stand firm" is the strength of our position now as it was in the past. Since the fetters of our bondage have been broken and *our political rights written into the national Constitution, if we do not stand firm to preserve inviolate this priceless heritage which has been bequeathed to us, we have small ground for compliant if others are not concerned to stand for us.*

All of the rights that we or other citizens possess are bound up in our right to vote. Where this is denied or abridged, the bulwark of our protection is destroyed, leaving the way open for the invasion of any or all other rights combined. The enemies of the Fifteenth Amendment well understand this. Any voice which counsels either compromise or surrender is singing to us a siren's song which would lure us and our posterity upon the rocks of political destruction.

We have more to inspire us to stand for our rights today than in the sixties and seventies, when Frederick Douglass was the recognized leader of our cause. Then we were illiterate and penniless; our feet were just crossing the threshold of the path that leads to prosperity. Today we own in the southern states not less than 30,000 square miles of land, an area equal in extent to that of Vermont, New Hampshire, Massachusetts, Connecticut, and Rhode Island combined. We pay taxes on over $550,000,000 worth of property, we have dotted the landscape with homes, schools, and churches, engaged in business, have a million children in the public schools, and are eager to maintain the best standards of American work, wages, and living. Added to all this, after having taken a drink so long and deep at the fountains of political liberty, as to have tasted the sweetness of its life-giving waters, we will not now consent to drink from the bitter pools of the Marah* of political serfdom.

The denial of the right to vote, either by intimidation, violence, or legal subterfuge, has caused that bastard birth of American political liberty — our nationwide Jim Crowism — to brazenly usurp the legitimate place of the civil rights of ten millions of Negro citizens. As Preston Brooks, armed with his murderous bludgeon, and Charles Sumner, armed with right and justice, represented the spirit of slavery and of freedom, so Jim Crowism, armed with a million suppressed ballots, would assail both the Declaration of Independence and the Constitution, to reduce the Negro to a condition of slavery. It was not only Sumner that Brooks was attempting to strike down, but freedom, truth, [and] justice. Jim Crowism, by insult, degradation, humiliation, and dehumanizing assaults, strikes

---

*Or *ma'-ra*, meaning bitter; see, e.g., Exod. 15:23. –Ed.

not only the Negro, its intended victim, but human equality, life, liberty, and the pursuit of happiness, and our Constitution and Christianity; yea, "it hits the very image of God in the eye." While the act of Brooks was applauded in the South, *it found apologists in the North;* so today the attempt to proscribe the Negro to a condition of degrading inferiority is justified in the South and accepted, without resistance, in the very birthplace of liberty.

We are well aware of the present attitude of public opinion in regard to the place the Negro should occupy within the nation and the treatment that should be accorded him. Our country is so sensitive to the discussion of the Negro question in the light of equality and justice that more passion and unreason may be aroused over it than upon any single question that touches our religious, social, or political life. For this reason, religion keeps in the background, the press ignores it as much as possible, the Supreme Court avoids squarely facing the issue, while our statesmanship, when not wholly silent, deals with it either in platitudes or in the heat of passion. We have actually arrived at the place where it requires courage and may entail sacrifice — political, moral, or financial — for a man, black or white, to plead for justice for the Negro. The white man who does is regarded as one who neither knows nor understands the Negro, a fanatic who would foist upon the white people social equality with the blacks, while making them in some sections politically dominant. The Negro who stands up for his manhood, as well as his constitutional rights, is regarded as one who alienates his white friends, "a breeder of strife," "dangerous," "bad," "a disturber of harmony between the races," and as "one of the worst enemies of his own race."

To all demagogues, faithless politicians, cowardly moral and social reformers, tyrannical oppressors, and to those Negroes who are either seeking ease and peace at the price of liberty, or who are yet slaves at heart, we have no apology to offer for the position we assume; but all who honestly differ, we meet on the grounds of Christianity, the Declaration of Independence, the federal Constitution, and our common humanity and manhood. There is not an argument advanced today against the agitation for the rights of the Negro that was not used, in some form, fifty years ago against those who opposed human slavery. As of old, our prophets have no vision, our statesmen no message, and our money changers are busy in the marketplace, while they cry in unison — "Peace, peace, let us have peace!"

We do not prophesy, but point to the fact that we are storing up materials for the greatest explosion that ever menaced our democracy or Christianity. We are storing them up by the prevailing attitude of the South, the courts, the Congress, the president, and by the growing self-respect, intelligence, and wealth of the Negroes. In some critical situation a very small event may light the fuse which shall precipitate the catastrophe. That the Negro will not be annihilated, our church spires pointing heavenward are the pledge; he will not be deported or colonized, because he will not, neither would our modern Pharaohs let him go; he will not be reduced to a condition of serfdom because his spirit has been illuminated by the quenchless flame of liberty. We agree with those who counsel patience and moderation, when they include justice also. Those whose repose is disturbed by apprehensions as to the consequences of our insistent demands for our rights, we urge to *remonstrate with the aggressors and not with the aggrieved.* Let no man chide us for resisting the thief who would despoil us of our goods, but rather let the culprit be apprehended and restore that which he has unlawfully taken away.

While a statue of General Robert E. Lee occupies an honored place in the Capitol at Washington, and Justice Edward Douglass White, an ex-rebel, is appointed by a Republican president, chief justice of the highest court of the nation he fought to destroy, may we not boldly demand that the Negro be given every right by the nation whose flag he has always defended, whose honor he has never tarnished, whose loftiest ideals he cherishes, and for the preservation of whose life he willingly yielded up his own upon the field of battle?

Mr. Sumner clearly foresaw the perils that awaited the newly enfranchised citizens; for this reason he labored with all the power at his command to have his Civil Rights Bill enacted into law. His attitude on this question is well set forth in a letter to a Negro convention in Columbia, South Carolina, in the fall of 1872, in which he says:

"In the first place, you must at all times insist upon your rights, and here I mean not only those already accorded, all of which are contained in equality before the law. It is not enough to provide separate accommodations for colored citizens, even if in all respects as good as those for other persons. *Equality is not found in an equivalent, but only in equality.* In other words, there must be no discrimination on account of color. The discrimination is an insult and a hindrance and a bar which not only destroys comfort and prevents equality, but *weakens all other rights.* The right to

vote will have new security when your equal right in public conveyances, hotels, and common schools is at last established; but
here *you must insist for yourselves, by speech, by petition and
by vote.* Help yourselves, and others will help you. Nor has the
Republican Party done its work until this is established."

If there is anywhere ignorance, confusion, misapprehension, or
doubt as to what constitutes our American race problem, let it now
be dispelled. It is the denial to the Negro of those rights for which
Sumner worked and pleaded, almost with his dying breath. *Let
these be conceded and our race problem will quickly be solved.*
It is the denial of these rights that is warping the decisions of the
courts, nullifying the Constitution, making Christianity a sham,
logic a lie, retarding the development and civilization of the South,
and increasing the friction between the races. Until the full and
equal enjoyment of the rights common to white men is conceded to
Negroes, however much men may legislate, nullify, oppress, compromise, or surrender, there will be no peace. We do not contend
that, after less than fifty years of freedom, the Negro is able to
measure arms with the white man on a footing of equality in every
department of endeavor. That would be against the laws of human
development and progress. What we ask is a man's chance — that
no door be closed against us that we are qualified to enter, that we
have freedom of opportunity to rise to the level of our highest and
best capacity. No one but a conscienceless hypocrite would contend
that discrimination against the Negro, whether under the guise of
law or otherwise, is ever carried out in the spirit of justice and
fair play. On the question of the Negroes' civil rights, the South
with the approval of the North, has sought to salve the national
conscience by pretending to provide separate but equal accommodations for the Negro on public conveyances. Be it said to their
shame, many Negroes have not only acquiesced, but some have
even advocated this arrangement. If the separation of the races
were based on the ground of character, conduct, intelligence, or
bodily cleanliness, it might find some ground for justification. But
to Jim Crow an entire race on the ground of color alone is as
abhorrent as it is degrading. Again, for the sake of emphasis, we
quote Mr. Sumner: *"Equality is not found in an equivalent, but
only in equality. The discrimination is an insult and a hindrance
and a bar which not only destroys comforts and prevents equality,
but weakens all other rights."*

It is not true that the Negro and white man can be as one in the
things that relate to industry and business relations and yet in all

other things be as separate as the fingers on the hand. Yet, in the
North as well as in the South this sentiment has been applauded to
the echo. Yea, it has been capitalized and is coming to be accepted
as the proper solution of our race question. But let us not make
up the verdict before we have heard all of the evidence. St. Paul,
the great apostle to the Gentiles, says: "But now are they many
members, but one body. The eye cannot say to the hand, I have
no need of thee; or the head to the feet, I have no need of thee.
God tempered the body together, giving more abundant honor to
that part which lacked; that there should be no schism in the body;
but that the members should have the same care one for another.
And whether one member suffereth, all the members suffer with
it; or one member is honored, all the members rejoice with it."
There can be no harmony or equality between the races, except
of master and servant or superior and inferior — when they are
one only in the things that relate to the purely physical side of life,
but separate in all of those broader and more complex relations of
intercourse where human life at its best really begins. If in the light
of the evidence the decision is against us, we appeal to the Superior
Court of justice on the ground that "there should be no schism in
the body," even in the body politic.

With respect to the Negro's political rights, the Fifteenth
Amendment is openly set at defiance by the former slaveholding states. No one pretends to believe that the revised constitutions
of the southern states were framed with any other end in view
than the suppression of the Negro vote, or that their provisions
are fairly administered. There is no longer concealment or evasion;
the Negro is to be eliminated as a political factor regardless of
his wealth or intelligence. But here again, as in the case of the
denial of civil rights, it is sought to palliate the injustice. We are
told by white men of great influence, and by the only Negroes that
the South will tolerate or the North hear with patience, that the
Negro should eschew politics and devote himself to agriculture,
the trades, business, and the saving of money and the acquisition
of property, thus gradually, in time, a few will be admitted to the
franchise. *No clearheaded man, white or black, should be deceived
by this cunningly devised strategy, by which a whole race is to be
delivered into political bondage.* Without being able to participate
in electing men by whom he is to be governed, how is the business
Negro to protect his business? How is he to secure the same educational advantages for his children? Georgia with her suppressed
Negro vote has not a single school for Negroes. What security has

he that he will be permitted to enjoy the blessings of prosperity? What do sheriffs, constables, policemen, mayors, courts, school boards, aldermen, etc., care for the rights of a voteless citizen? Whatever be their care, a public official or a political party which does not stand in fear of retribution at the polls, and cannot be called upon to give an account of its stewardship, will have small consideration for those who can neither give nor cancel their lease of political power. Once the Irish were ignorant, poor, and despised, both in Boston and in New England. But the Irishman had a ballot which he used as a weapon of defense. Who dares despise the Irish now and whisper it above his breath, while Boston has an Irish mayor?

But we are told that such protests as we voice tonight are "whining." If this be whining, we shall not only continue to whine, but to cry aloud against injustice. Again, we are told that we are not constructive. Admittedly, we are working to tear down the last vestige of injustice and tyranny. The men who threw the tea into Boston harbor, the men who fought at Bunker Hill, the men, who like Sumner, assailed the institution of human slavery were all destructionists.

Under the tactics by which the Fifteenth Amendment is nullified and degraded by the humiliating insults of Jim Crowism, the Negro can build nothing but a hideous caricature of American citizenship. So long as it rests upon submission, compromise, suppression, and discrimination, the foundations of our citizenship are built upon the sands. We must destroy before we can build a citizenship that will rest upon every affirmation of the Declaration of Independence and every guarantee of the Constitution. It is said that we are weak and defenseless. But we are no weaker than our courage and determination; neither are we defenseless. We can uphold the flag, support and defend the Constitution, and in all these pivotal states of the North we may divide our vote, or cast it where it will make for our political protection and the restoration of our rights.

This was Mr. Sumner's advice contained in a letter addressed to the colored people more than thirty-five years ago, in which he said: "I am sure that it cannot be best for the colored people to band together in a hostile camp, provoking antagonism and keeping alive the separation of the races. Much better will it be when two political parties compete for your vote, each anxious for your support. Only then will that citizenship by which you are entitled to the equal rights of all have its full fruits. Only then will there be harmony, which is essential to true civilization." By his slavish devotion to the Republican Party the Negro has rendered himself politically impotent, so that now a Republican president makes the insulting announcement that he will not appoint Negroes to office in any community where the white people object. True, we have been repelled and opposed by the Democratic Party. But we are not shut up to a choice between the two dominant parties. If the Republican Party holds us while the Democratic Party robs us of our rights, we need choose neither. Let us not be for parties, but for men. There are men in both of the old parties willing to concede to us the rights which are now denied. Or better still, we can unite with the Socialist Party, as did the Negroes of Oklahoma in the last election, when it stands for equality for all men, regardless of race, class, creed, or color.

The Negro has not advanced in character, education, or wealth, because he has, perforce or otherwise, let politics alone; he has advanced in spite of it. *Is anyone so bereft of reason as to believe that the South has driven the Negro from political power, so that he might devote himself to industry and the acquisition of wealth?* Yet, this is the argument which the so-called best friends of the Negro, and those Negroes who are most tolerated and subsidized, are continually presenting as "a solution." Whatever may be the outward semblance, no question is ever settled until it is settled right. The greatest of all questions among men is the question of government — the condition under which men may live together in society. In the eighteenth century, beginning in Europe, the great struggle was over the battle for democracy, until it found its noblest birth in our great American democracy. In the nineteenth century the tide of battle raged between freedom and slavery. With fire and sword and the awful music of the cannon's roar, the victory of freedom was proclaimed. The twentieth century opens with the lines forming for the battle for equality and brotherhood. This happy consummation is not more impossible or remote than was the realization of democracy or freedom. The present attitude of compromise and submission must be brushed aside, our inequalities must be leveled, race and class hatred must take wings and fly away, every stronghold of tyranny and oppression must be captured and destroyed. The sun of the twentieth century is rising to banish the age-long darkness that has so long obscured the recognition of brotherhood between man and his brother; it will not set until it has gilded with gold the steeples of a new civilization in which equality and fraternity have triumphed over prejudice and pride.

Wendell Phillips: Centennial Oration

The condition of African Americans has been a cornerstone question for the United States, and the progress of the African American is a sure measure of the nation's development toward democracy. Those who have worked to help African Americans include Wendell Phillips, the abolitionist who denounced the Constitution as a slaveholding document. Yet, he worked to bring the Constitution in line with the democratic ideals of the Declaration of Independence. And, Ransom argues, those concerned with justice must follow the example established by leaders such as Phillips.

•

The tree of liberty will only bear fruit after its kind. It will not flourish when the foul birds of tyranny and oppression nest amid its boughs. It will not yield vitality or strength to any wild branch of slavery or serfdom that may be entangled on its limbs. There are many, both at home and abroad, who are slow to learn that, while ready to acknowledge our debt to England and to Europe, we are a new nation, in a new world, with a new form of government whose type of democracy is distinctively American.

When John Hancock laid down his pen and George Washington sheathed his sword, the fathers of the Constitution completed the task of launching this republic to take its unique place among the nations of the earth. The compromises growing out of the slavery question that were inserted in the Constitution were the chief blemish of their otherwise almost perfect work. This vital flaw prevented the realization of their high ideals and the fulfillment of their hopes. It at once arrayed against each other two hostile forces; it undertook the impossible task of uniting two irreconcilable principles — freedom and slavery.

The Negro question is the pivot around which this nation has revolved at every crucial hour of its history, from the foundation of the government until now.

While the Indian may rise against us in judgment, the Negro is now and ever has been the sure and final test of the strength and

Address delivered November 29, 1911, Plymouth Church, Brooklyn, New York (n.p., n.d.), housed in the Reverdy C. Ransom Collection, Payne Theological Seminary, Wilberforce, Ohio. Reprinted by permission of Mrs. Ruth Ransom and her son, Louis A. Ransom, Jr.

progress of American democracy and Christianity. Would you behold the skyline of our Christianity and democracy today? I point you to the present attitude of this nation toward the Negro.

From the adoption of our federal Constitution until the abolition of slavery, there were those who saw and felt the enormity of the crime of ownership in human flesh. Of this increasing company, worthy to be called America's immortals, William Lloyd Garrison was the chief, while Wendell Phillips was preeminent among those who stood in the foremost ranks.

One hundred years ago today, Wendell Phillips was born. His unselfish devotion to the cause of humanity has made not only black men, but liberty-loving man and women everywhere, his debtors. His career is unique in the annals of American achievement. He has been called the "Knight Errant of Humanity." His noble figure moved among us with all the kingly grace of a knight of the days of chivalry. He met the burning question of his time with dauntless courage and a faith that never wavered. His sword once drawn was never sheathed until the foe was vanquished. He counted not the odds against him, his confidence in the righteousness of his cause.

Wendell Phillips was not a child of the backwoods. He was born in Boston. He did not spring from the common people. Providence worked through six generations of the best Puritan stock of New England, to evolve in him an American gentleman of the highest type. His was not a struggle against poverty. The child of wealth, he was environed by an atmosphere of refinement in the most cultured city in America. A graduate of Harvard, he was admitted to the bar as a member of the legal profession with every prospect of a brilliant career. While a young man, as yet comparatively unknown, he stood in Faneuil Hall and heard James T. Austin, the attorney general of Massachusetts, justify the men who murdered Lovejoy at Alton, Illinois. Hot with indignation, he mounted the platform and delivered, impromptu, a reply in scathing terms and with such crushing effect that at a single stride he stepped from obscurity to fame. From that hour he broke the barriers of his social position, became deaf to the blandishments of wealth and honor, and with a self-abasement akin to that of the Son of God, he made himself of no reputation to become friend and advocate of the lowly and despised.

The surroundings amid which these commemorative exercises here tonight are set are significant, while lending added inspiration to the hour. We are within the walls of Plymouth Church, whose pulpit Henry Ward Beecher made famous throughout the English-speaking world. At a time when the American pulpit was, for the most part, either dumb upon the evils of [slavery], or threw about the iniquitous institution the sanctions of religion, Henry Ward Beecher stood here, a mighty Jove, hurling the hot thunderbolts of his wrath against it. He was one of the best friends the cause of freedom ever had. He has demonstrated the power and influence of the unmuzzled pulpit. He was much more concerned with the acts of the supporters of slavery than he was about the Acts of the Apostles. He had the courage to do that for lack of which the church and the unchurched masses are perishing today; he stood on the banks of the Hudson instead of the banks of the Jordan and applied the gospel to the moral, political, and social problems of his time. That which concerns us now is not that St. Paul, a member of a despised race, had his Roman citizenship insulted, but that ten millions of black American citizens may be robbed of their most sacred rights under the protection of our flag. Which today is of more vital importance, that St. Paul received thirty-nine lashes upon his back, or that thirty-nine American citizens have been lynched with fiendish ferocity in this year of grace?

After he had been mobbed out of two halls in New York City, Mr. Beecher, with characteristic courage, opened Plymouth Church to Mr. Phillips, to whom he refers as "the unagitated agitator — so calm, so fearless, so incisive — every word a bullet."

One of the chief distinctions Wendell Phillips earned and so well deserved was to be called an "agitator."

"Agitation," said he, "is an old word with a new meaning." Sir Robert Peel defined it to be "the marshaling of the conscience of a nation to mold its laws." Its means are reason and argument, not appeal to arms. Eternal vigilance is the price of liberty; power is ever stealing from the many to the few. Only by continual oversight can the Democrat in office be prevented from hardening into a despot; only by unintermitted agitation can a people be kept sufficiently awake to principle not to let liberty be smothered in material prosperity. Republics exist only on the terms of being constantly agitated. Never, to our latest posterity, can we do without prophets like Garrison, to stir up the monotony of wealth and reawake the people to the great ideas that are constantly fading out of our minds — to trouble the waters that there may be health in their flow.

This favored epithet of injustice and oppression is today brought forth from its proslavery archives to be hurled at the noble men and women who are standing for justice to the Negro, in an effort to nullify and discredit their influence. "Agitators!" "Impracticables!" "Breeders of strife between the races!"

We should not count it strange that many who have enlisted in the unpopular cause of our poor and despised race have had their ardor chilled by the cold indifference and unresponsiveness of their friends, while many continue with us as advocates of our cause, would compromise our blood-bought and inalienable rights for political gain and social peace, to placate opposition and silence the voice of ridicule and censure from the weathervane press of America.

I voice the sentiments of millions of our race when I take the liberty to use the rostrum of Plymouth Church as a megaphone tonight, to say to the American people that the Negro wants neither the money nor the sympathy of those who do not believe in his equality of manhood and who do not accord him the same political rights, the same educational advantages, and the same freedom in every pathway of opportunity. He is neither ungrateful nor unresponsive, but having been so often plundered and betrayed, he prefers to stand and mark time rather than follow the leadership of men, organizations, or parties, the genuineness of whose credentials he has not thoroughly examined and the unrightness of whose motives has not been clearly disclosed. The traitors within the ranks of our race are known. They have neither our confidence nor our hearts. What standing they have is due to the powerful support which is given then by misguided men of great wealth, by politicians who, for personal or partisan advantage, would use them to profit by the vanishing remnants of the Negro's political power, and by a newspaper press whose approving voice is the mouthpiece of a decadent public opinion which would let the Negro question "work itself out" under the baneful influence of the many degrading forms of Jim Crowism.

At a time of recredence [recrudescence] of sentiment against the Negro, the friends of freedom have eagerly seized upon the celebration of the one hundredth anniversary of the birth of William Lloyd Garrison, John Greenleaf Whittier, Elijah P. Lovejoy, John Brown, Charles Summer, and Harriet Beecher Stowe, as a means of awakening the public conscience and creating a public opinion in favor of justice to the Negro. So tonight in this celebration of the centenary of the birth of Wendell Phillips, we are here not so much to tell what he did then as to point to what we, who would honor his memory, should do now. He stood for truth, the whole truth, and nothing but the truth, for equal rights and justice to all, without equivocation or compromise. While his spirit looks down upon us tonight from the star-crowned heights to which he has ascended to sit enthroned high by the side of Garrison and Summer, we are here to reconsecrate and dedicate ourselves anew, not only to the cause of justice and equality to the Negro, but to humanity, without regard to race or sex, to color or to creed. The carrying power of our voices may not reach, perchance, the ears of this mighty metropolis, much less the country at large, but if under the power of this new baptism we continue to cry aloud with no uncertain sound, the nation, the Supreme Court, the press, and even the pulpit will hear. The spirit in which we agitate is needed for rescue and perpetuity of our American democracy; it is needed to arouse the Negroes themselves; to arise and take an unyielding stand while a vestige of the rich dowry, which was handed them on the point of a million bayonets, remains. This is not the time to use rose water or the speech and manners of the drawing room. To paraphrase the words [with] which Daniel Connell justified his course in seeking to wring from England justice for Ireland: The hearts of Negroes are so cowed, and most white Americans are so arrogant, that it needs independence verging on insolence, and a defiance that will touch extreme limits, to breathe self-respect into my own race, teach aggressors manners, and sober them into respectful attention.

Wendell Phillips was a Disunionist for twenty years. At the beginning of his career as an agitator, he took his stand outside of the church; he wore the label of no political party; he refrained from voting and repudiated the Constitution as a slave-holding document. Thus he stood, a man without a country, free and untrammeled to wage relentless warfare against a slave power and all of the influences that upheld it. Garrison's slogan — "No Union with Slaveholders" — was on all occasions his "Delenda est Carthago." The course which Mr. Phillips persistently followed until success crowned his labors is best justified in his own words:

"I was a Disunionist sincerely, for twenty years. I did hate the Union, when union meant lies in the pulpit and mobs in the streets, when union meant making white men hypocrites and black men slaves. I did prefer purity to peace — I acknowledge it. I did prefer disunion to being the accomplice of tyrants. I, indeed, thought man more than constitutions, humanity and justice of more worth than law."

But when God's hour struck in answer to the signal from Fort Sumter, "Missouri Compromises," "Kansas-Nebraska Bills," and

"Fugitive Slave Laws" were swept aside as dust in the balances, and Wendell Phillips found himself at last within the Union. He was among the organizers of the first black regiments, the Thirty-fifth and Fifty-sixth Massachusetts, which, under the leadership of Colonel Shaw and the Hallowell brothers, marched down State Street in Boston to the music of "John Brown's Body" over the very spot where a Negro, Crispus Attucks, gave the first blood to consecrate America to freedom.

Wendell Phillips labored to make the Constitution conform to the Declaration of Independence. Lincoln's Proclamation of Emancipation, the victories of Sheridan and Sherman, Meade and Grant, put Jefferson Davis to flight and completely subdued the South's power of armed resistance. The South sued for peace, not because it had changed its attitude, not because of its baptism of fire, though four years of bloody war had converted it to Sumner's view of barbarism of slavery, but because God had made it helpless by pressing the bitter cup of its iniquities to its lips, until it had been drained to the dregs.

When the Thirteenth Amendment to the Constitution, abolishing slavery, was passed by Congress, Mr. Garrison and other influential members of the Anti-Slavery Society believed that it should dissolve, that its members should work through other channels to accomplish that which remained to be done for freedom. Mr. Phillips differed; Frederick Douglass, Robert Pervis, and a large majority of the society stood with him. He believed that the freedom of the blacks should be sealed, not alone by emancipation, but by citizenship and the ballot. Without civil rights and citizenship they were only half free. On the question of the Negroes' enfranchisement, he declared, "The black man without the ballot is the lamb given over to the wolf." He held the American Anti-Slavery Society together, as its president, until the Fourteenth and Fifteenth Amendments were passed by Congress and ratified by the requisite number of states. This act of Mr. Phillips reveals the full stature of the man; it shows the breadth of his comprehension of the whole question involved in freedom, and entitles him more than any other to our gratitude and veneration.

Harsh as it may sound in this hour of compromise and surrender, we hold that Wendell Phillips was right when he declared, "I want a right hand stern as death, and a sword, rough ground; like those with which Wellington went into [the] battle of Waterloo, held over every southern state, to secure that peace which promotes industry." If the South had conquered the North it would indeed have called the roll of its slaves on Bunker Hill and put its flag over the Capitol at Washington. The events of the past forty years have abundantly demonstrated that the spirit of the rebellion, though humbled, has never been conquered. The climax at Appomattox should have been followed by planting in the South the civilization of the North — respect for free labor, the North of equality, education, toleration — the North of books and brains. The South did not lay down its arms when Lee surrendered his sword to Grant. It only changed its weapons. Now it works by intrigue, fraud, nullification, dishumanizing laws, and by blackening the Negro's character before the world by painting him as a monster who menaces the safety of its womanhood and the preservation of good government and civilization. Its most effective emissaries are not the Tillmans, Hoke-Smiths, and Vardamans who may sit in Congress, but the soft-voiced women and men of engaging manners who sit in northern drawing rooms and insidiously make converts to the South's method of dealing with the Negro. Bright southern boys are on the reportorial staffs and in the editorial rooms of the great daily papers of the North, to season every news item relating to the Negro with the southern flavor, and to paint him in a manner generally that either discounts or discredits him. They have even invaded the theater, and under the guise of the drama seek to inflame the northern prejudice.

In the face of this systematic campaign, the North has stood by with its old antebellum attitude of concession and compromise, while the South, through these means and an obliging United States Supreme Court, has regained all it lost upon the field of battle. Under slavery the South counted three-fifths of the blacks in the enumeration for representation in Congress; now it counts them all, but by unconstitutional methods excludes them from the franchise. It has thus, under freedom, increased its proportion of representation in Congress over the North, by two-fifths of the number it held under slavery.

The question of the South's method of dealing with the Negro has come to be as sacred as was the question of slavery in the days of Mr. Phillips. To demand the enforcement of the Fifteenth Amendment today is to be branded as "an enemy of both races," "a fanatic," "a mischievous agitator." To all outside interference the South says, Leave the Negro to us, we understand him, and we know best how to deal with him, both for his own good and the peace and the welfare of the South. President Taft, who has boldly committed himself to the doctrine of race discrimination, pipes his grand diapason in harmony with this sentiment by declaring that the Negro "ought to come and is coming more and more under the guardianship of the South!" With far more justification, we reply on behalf of the Negro, Leave the southern white people to us. We have lived among them for two and a half centuries; we both know and understand them. We have nursed their children, built their homes, and for more than two hundred years, we have fed and clothed them. When they took up arms to destroy the Union in order to bind us in perpetual chains, we did not fire their cities with the torch, nor rise in violence against them, but protected their property, their helpless women and children. Leave them to us. We have imbibed, not the ideals of feudalism, but of democracy; we are Americans filled with the spirit of the twentieth century. Leave them to us, and we will make the free public school universal throughout the South and open alike to all, without regard to race, creed, or color. We will make free speech as safe in Mississippi as it is in Massachusetts; we will abolish lynching and usher in a reign of law, of courts and juries, instead of the shotgun, the faggot, and the mob. We will abolish peonage, elevate and protect labor, and make capital secure. Leave them to us; our chivalry shall know no color line, but all womanhood shall be protected and defended, and all citizens, regardless of race or color, shall be permitted to participate in the government under which they live. Leave them to us, and we will make them know their place and keep it, under the Constitution as amended. We will remove that last vestige of Jim Crowism under the forms of law, and make the places of public necessity, convenience, recreation, and amusement open alike to all without respect to race or color. We will make intelligence, character, and worth, instead of race and color, the sole test of recognition and preferment for all. Thus as North and South divided over the Negro, so would the Negro unite them in the only bond of union that can stand the test of time — fraternity, justice, righteousness.

There is a strong effort to make out a case against the Negro as "the sick man of America." His case has been diagnosed by doctors of every school of thought, who have treated him for all deadly diseases in the mental, moral, social, industrial, and political catalogue. Yet he continues to grow strong on the same meat and exercise that are daily bread of all normally healthy Americans. The trouble is not with the Negro but with the physicians who are paranoiacs on the Negro question.

There are those today who tell us that the enfranchisement

of the black man was a mistake, that it should have been left to time to gradually prepare him to exercise the ballot. So there were those calling themselves abolitionists, who advocated "gradual emancipation." But Wendell Phillips, with Garrison and his compeers, stood for "immediate and unconditional emancipation." After nearly fifty years of freedom, are the disfranchising states seeking to gradually prepare the Negro for the franchise, when they obstruct his path to the ballot box with every obstacle that legal ingenuity can devise? Does any honest person believe that the disfranchising states ever would, if left to themselves, or ever will, if left alone, permit the Negro to become gradually prepared for the ballot? Let us be honest and say that this lament about the untimeliness of the Fifteenth Amendment is a dishonest subterfuge and a lie. Let us be frank, as some are, and declare that "Constitution or no Constitution, character, education, and property to the contrary, this is a white man's government and white men are going to rule it."

As Wendell Phillips took his stand outside the Constitution while it sanctioned slavery, so today the only impregnable position we can take is to plant our feet upon the Constitution as amended and stand there without compromise, not altering a clause or changing a single word. The Fifteenth Amendment a mistake? If we erase the names of the men who supported its adoption, with them would be blotted out the major portion of names that have made our country's history worth recording for the last fifty years.

Wendell Phillips was the friend and advocate of liberty and justice for humanity throughout the world. He cheered the triumph of the labors of Mazzini and Garibaldi for the liberation of Italy; by sympathy and cooperation, he made himself the friend and fellow countryman of Curran and Grattan, O'Connell and Parnell in their labors for home rule for Ireland. He was one of the earliest advocates of woman's suffrage and took his stand with Mary A. Livermore and Lydia Maria Child. He espoused the cause of organized labor and affirmed, "as a fundamental principle, that labor, as the creator of wealth, is entitled to all it creates." But we will not trespass on the limitations placed upon us to dwell on his activitie' in these and other fields; nor yet upon his tender devotion to h' wife, whom he nursed through forty years of invalidism, playi the lover's part with such a wealth of affection as to make tł domestic life idyllic. It is ours to make his services on beha' freedom the burden of our theme.

Wendell Phillips was the relentless foe of the caste spirit of his day. As early as 1846 he appealed to the school committee of Boston to admit colored children to the public schools with the whites. He continued, with the cooperation of the enlightened colored people, to press the cause until the point was won. This victory he pronounced "the triumph of law and justice over the pride and caste of wealth." Now, after more than fifty years, comes forth the Honorable William Howard Taft, president of the United States, by grace of the Republican Party, to declare that the Negroes should be educated differently from the whites. He allows us a few colleges where our ministers, teachers, lawyers, and doctors may receive a liberal education, but gives us no place in the great universities, scientific and technical schools of this, our native land. Would the president dare offer such insulting suggestions or advice to his Irish, Jewish, or Italian fellow citizens? This from the head of a nation which professes to give, without distinction, equal opportunities to all.

Why does this learned judge so interpret the spirit of our American democracy? Is it not because he believes he voices the sentiments of the majority of the American people? Is this because the Negro has demonstrated his incapacity to take his place in all the avenues of the nation's life? No, it is because he, and those who think with him, would train their black fellow citizens to continue to hold an inferior or secondary place — to be America's black peasants.

Men tell us we should point the Negro to things of solid achievement rather than assail the barriers that obstruct his way. Have the Irish waited for banks and farms and industries during the four hundred years they have agitated for home rule? Did the colonists wait for these things before they rebelled against the tyranny of George III? Of what value are artisans and mechanics, money and lands, if a city council or state legislature may prescribe the locality, or spot of ground, whereon you may breathe God's air under your own vine and fig tree?

We are told to get money, to get land, and to qualify for practical service and then we will get our rights. Why not tell that to the Jews of Russia or to the Armenians under Turkish rule with whom this country so strongly sympathizes? Give us those rights for which a million men faced death through four years of bloody war, those rights which the most enlightened statesmen since the days of Lincoln, Grant, and Sumner have labored to secure — the rights common to other citizens — and then, like other citizens,

we will willingly work and wait with patience, for business and money, houses and lands to be added unto us.

The apologist for slavery, who sought to gild the iniquity with elegance, called it "industrial subordination." So now, disfranchisement and other forms of Jim Crowism are defended in the name, not of democracy, but of "the preservation of Anglo-Saxon civilization." None of the elements of our population, except in the color of their skin and the lust for blood, are more purely Anglo-Saxon in character, aspirations, and ideals than the American of African descent.

In the time of Wendell Phillips, the slaveholding oligarchy made the Democratic Party the bulwark of slavery; the Liberty Party, the Free-Soil Party, and the Whig Party each recognized slavery under various forms of compromise; he would have none of them. He refused to recognize slavery as either local or sectional; he believed that freedom should be universal.

As Mr. Phillips believed he could best serve the cause of freedom by refraining from all political affiliation, so we today can best secure our complete emancipation by aggressive political independence. Our most powerful weapon of defense is the ballot. How much do our opponents care for the force of our logic or the power of our arguments? We must have [a] voice in choosing the hands that hold the reins of power.

The Democratic Party has not placed upon the statute books of the nation a single law on behalf of justice to the Negro. Today it defends disfranchisement and upholds repression. The Republican Party, once the friend and champion of justice and equal rights, in its worship of the golden calf, has belied its professions and betrayed the trust of a confiding race. If the socialists have the courage to be true to their program and take up the great moral questions which the old parties have abandoned, then all men who love justice and hate oppression may turn to them.

Tie on a party name when it does not mean as much to a black man as it does to a white man, as much to a poor man as it does to a rich man, as much to a woman as it does to a man. The Negro should rally to the standards of justice by whomsoever carried, regardless of party name. He should seek to drive from office every man who, by vote or influence, has joined with the enemies of his race, and rather let his arm be paralyzed than cast a ballot for a man who will not unequivocally pledge himself to equal rights and privileges for all.

The Negro must keep books, record events, and remember

names. He must refuse the leadership of those men of his race who have surrendered the rights of their people for honors and emoluments of office or the bribe of gold. When charged with ingratitude because he refuses to follow those who have deserted the cause of freedom, let him remind them that the Arch Deceiver, the devil, was also once an angel of light.

Let no one be deceived by the prophets who prophesy lies, or by the wise men who image a vain thing. Just in proportion as the Negro has grown in character, wealth, intelligence, and industrial efficiency, so has he been disfranchised, Jim Crowed, and relegated to the place of a menial in the industrial world. Standing under the flag whose folds, on behalf of freedom, have been consecrated by the blood of our fathers, may not the men of this race plead for equal justice before the war amendments to the Constitution have been repudiated and the principles of Wendell Phillips have perished from our land?

We offer no newly discovered panacea for the ills that afflict us; we have no chimerical scheme for the solution of our race problem. The ground we stand upon is as old as justice. The Negroes are not going to be colonized into a separate state or territory; given a man's chance, they are satisfied to remain where they are. They are not going to Africa, except it be to follow the cross of Christ, or the flag of our country, on some errand of humanity or civilization.

We have resolved that this country shall [be] neither our prison nor our tomb. Our ears have heard a strange music through the years — the clanking of chains, the crack of the lash, and the breaking of fetters amid the cannon roar. We have heard the shout of triumph and the song of freedom rise above the voice of mourning where a nation wept over the graves of the slain. Since we came from the darkness of slavery, the white light of freedom has not blinded our eyes to the unscaled heights that lie before us. We are not pointing backward to monuments of achievement in the past, but forward to the heights we would attain. We are carrying a weight of ignorance and poverty, we confess; we ask not that others bear our burden; but do not obstruct our pathway, and we will throw off our burdens as we run. The white man held on to us in the days of slavery; we are holding on to him in the day of freedom, and we will not let him go until we are seated securely by his side in the full enjoyment of every right which he holds as his most sacred heritage.

Robert G. Ingersoll

In this address, Ransom pays tribute to another prominent figure in race relations in the United States. Using his poetic style, Ransom gives an account of Ingersoll's efforts on behalf of human freedom and democratic practice. A version of this speech is printed in another volume of the The Review *("Ingersoll, the Humanitarian"). Readers might also find the following article of interest. It is not included in this volume because it is available elsewhere: Reverdy C. Ransom, "Centennial Oration of Reverdy C. Ransom at Faneuil Hall, Boston, December 11, 1905, on William Lloyd Garrison," with handwritten corrections (Boston: Boston Suffrage League, 1911), housed in the Reverdy C. Ransom Collection, Payne Theological Seminary, Wilberforce, Ohio. This document is also available in Alice Moore Dunbar's* Masterpieces of Negro Eloquence: The Best Speeches Delivered by the Negro from the Days of Slavery to the Present Time *(New York: G. K. Hall, 1997). It is also found in Carter G. Woodson's* Negro Orators and Their Orations *(New York: Russell & Russell, 1925, reissued 1969).*

●

(In answer to many requests which have come to me through the years, I am printing this address which I delivered at the Memorial Service for the late Colonel Robert G. Ingersoll, held in the Studebaker Theatre, Chicago, in 1901.)

The perspective of the years is not yet sufficiently distant to permit us to justly estimate or correctly measure the work, the worth, and influence of Robert G. Ingersoll.

He stood for years the unyielding storm center of much religious, or rather irreligious, controversy. Even now the kindly mention of his name causes the muttering of theological thunder and the generation of polemical lightning.

Passion and prejudice are alike unreasoning and unjust; they pervert our judgment and becloud our vision. Until these are softened by time, and we view him standing out against the background of at least a century, we cannot clearly see the extent of his influence upon the life and thought of his age.

First published in the *A.M.E. Church Review* (April 1922): 252–54. Reprinted by permission of the *A.M.E. Church Review*.

> Too many a man is honored over-much,
> The worthiest souls are ever scarce and few;
> And ere we crown them (if at last we do)
> They first are outcasts whom we shrink to touch.

The tribe of Abu Ben-Adhem still occupies too small a space in the book of gold wherein the angel writes the names of those who love their fellowman. Ingersoll was a man! He based his manhood not upon a religious creed, not upon any political party, nor upon wealth — the mud-god and man-maker of our time — but upon the kinship and affinity he felt toward mankind of every condition and of every race.

When ministers of religion laboriously searched the Scriptures to find sacred sanctions in defense of American slavery, while statesmanship from the Supreme Court to the Capitol threw around it the strong arm and protection of the law, the sword of Colonel Ingersoll flashed upon the field of battle to strike slavery dead upon the ground running red with the blood of the slain. Now that the din of conflict here is stilled, now that he sleeps, to dream of battlefields no more, in the thought of every Afro-American who loves a lover of his kind, we would "mold a statue of enduring brass, out of the broken chains of slaves set free."

When there came to Peoria that prince, that king "crowned in the shambles and the prison pen, the noblest slave that ever God set free," Frederick Douglass,

> Whose form was like Apollo's and his brow
> Like what the sculptors carve for Zeus's own,
> With his dark visage and his frosty pow [head]
> As god-like as was ever cut in stone,

all doors were closed against him there save one. Colonel Ingersoll received him into his home, recognized him not as a mere human thing but [as] a man.

When citizenship followed emancipation, the voice of Colonel Ingersoll, with all his splendid eloquence, was used to cheer the newly made citizen on his way. He was not of that later brand of pygmy statesmen, nor of that late addition to our chivalry, who, clad in red shirts, ride like demons robed in blood, to slay defenseless men and helpless women, declaring that the Fourteenth and Fifteenth Amendments to the Constitution were a mistake. Ingersoll never dishonored the flag of his country, made sacred by the blood of our patriot dead, or spat upon the graves of his comrades in arms, by silently consenting to surrender in time of peace the results of the victories of war.

Today, individual states are so strong, the interpretation of the Constitution so narrow, and the government so weak that whole-sale murder and disfranchisement may occur without restraint when black men are the victims. Ingersoll declared that the Four-teenth and Fifteenth Amendments were but a just price for the nation to pay for the Negro's two hundred fifty years of slavery, and but a small reward for his services upon the field of battle in helping to save the Union.

Ingersoll believed in the reign of law. He was opposed to violence, injustice, or cruelty in any form. When thousands of American Christians left their places of worship to greet with cheers the tortures of a human being burned at the stake, he denounced it as an outrage upon the law and a crime against civ-ilization in terms which stand in fine contrast to the acquiescent or half-apologetic attitude of government officials, and the sacri-legious justification or silence of some of the dumb preachers of our land.

For, however much the pulpit may execrate him, it might also emulate him by being as vocal and articulate, if it cannot be as eloquent, upon all questions that relate to the welfare of mankind.

The literature, poetry, and art of Europe and America have made God and all of the angels white. The devil of course is black. In China, God is represented as a yellow man, and so with ever-changing variety among the nations of the earth. But the recognition of a universal God, the principles of whose religion will lead all men to meet as brothers in every relation of life, is the greatest need of the world.

Ingersoll was one of the first fruits of the evolution of humanity away from tribe and clan and race into a manhood bounded only by humanity. He saw no black peril in America or yellow peril on the other side of the world. He saw only man and believed that all should walk by the light of reason under the sway of the scepter of liberty and justice. He has made the world's heart softer and its brain more clear.

Bigotry, passion, and prejudice may seek for a time to dim the luster of his fame and to tarnish the crown in the splendid realm of oratory, where genius crowned him king. But with the widen-ing of years, when man shall be more sacred than a book, when fires upon our altars of sacrifice shall be kindled by devotion to our home, our country, and mankind, when prejudice and greed and tyranny shall lean less upon the arms of faith, those themes of abiding interest which the genius of Ingersoll has clothed with surpassing beauty will become the common property and heritage of mankind.

Ingersoll loved liberty. He was the ideal plumed knight pictured in one of his impassioned periods, who hurled his lance full in the face and through the shield of those who sought to enslave the soul, the mind, or body of his fellowman. He would have all men free, free in every realm. He would remove the fetters from the mind, give wings to thought that it might soar upon unhindered pinions through the wide realm of truth.

He would have the slave to know that he is also a man. That being so, the price of liberty cannot come too high, nor its safeguards be maintained with a courage and vigilance too sleepless and unyielding.

When slavery sat in the seats of power, holding a lash over Congress, dictating iniquitous decisions to the Supreme Court, while ministers of religion were seeking to justify and perpetuate it by finding sacred sanctions in the Bible, Ingersoll took his place in the ranks of that band of immortals of whom Lincoln was the chief, and stood for a country which should be free and united, with liberty for all.

Ingersoll did not delight in blood or in the suffering and sorrow of mankind. He had tenderness for tears, sympathy for sorrow, and the poor and the struggling never had a better friend. He buckled on his sword and went to war to preserve the integrity of his country and to make men free. The richest materials for an epic poem since the days of Homer are to be found in the history of the Negro on these shores. What strange fate has brought together here the descendants of the Pilgrim Fathers and the children of the slave! How the one has had freedom of opportunity to tread the path of progress and to feed the intellectual life upon the choicest viands in the treasure house of thought, while the flaming sword of the law kept back the other from the tree of knowledge, while the wind as it sighed through the cane and moaned round the cabin door toyed with his chains.

The children of each have fought side by side from Bunker Hill to San Juan. Each according to his opportunities has helped to rear this civilization which is the common heritage of all. Slavery is dead. Its fetters are broken, but they have left their marks and scars upon our religion and literature — the heart and brain of all. We do not want one sphere, one plane, for white men and another for the black. We do not want a little Ireland, a little Germany, or a little Africa in the United States; we want no secondary place, but full-orbed American manhood for all. For this Colonel Ingersoll pleaded with all his strength of voice and pen. He was strong amid the strong, and gentle, too.

We boast our light, but the mists and clouds are about us all. What lies beyond the pale kingdom of the dead does not most concern us now. The life of man upon this planet is daily confronted with problems which it has not solved. Each needs the help of all. And when such a helper of his kind, as he in whose memory we have met tonight, has ended his journey in the paths of men, we cannot with brush or chisel, tongue or pen, enough perpetuate, enough make known, his value to the present and to the coming time.

Like the Grecian matron who took the ashes of her husband and placed them under the hearthstone of her home, the family of Robert G. Ingersoll, with affection and grief too deep for words or tears, have enshrined within an urn a little handful of ashes, too small to make sport for the passing summer breeze, all that is mortal of that once splendid presence.

> The gods are dead, and all the godlike men,
> Are dying too! How fast they disappear!
> For death seems discontent to fill the grave
> With common bones, but downward to his den
> Drags, like a greedy monster, year by year,
> The men most missed — the good, the wise, the brave!

The National Republican Convention

According to Ransom, African Americans have been loyal to the Republican Party. However, he cautions that the Republican Party does not provide African Americans full participation in U.S. life because their disenfranchisement is the result of systemic racism which is not limited to any particular party. In fact, it is not limited to the United States; racial prejudice in Cuba, for example, Ransom argues is a

From *The Spirit of Freedom and Justice: Orations and Speeches* (Nashville: A.M.E. Sunday School Union, 1926), housed in the Schomburg Center for Research in Black Culture, New York. Reprinted by permission of the AMEC Publishing House (Sunday School Union).

consequence of U.S. race relations. The struggle of black Cubans is similar to the struggle of black Americans. Hence, Ransom opposes U.S. intervention aimed at establishing a "white man's government." Furthermore, African Americans, according to Ransom, should refuse to fight when it will mean the harming of blacks who struggle for freedom as African Americans do. The remainder of the essay entails a discussion of the two Republican candidates — Taft and Roosevelt — giving support to the latter, while making it known that African Americans will not vote Republican out of tradition but will look to their own interests.

•

At a meeting held at Bethel A.M.E. Church, Thirtieth and Dearborn Streets, Chicago, on the night of June 17, Rev. Reverdy C. Ransom of New York spoke in part as follows:

This is the eve of the Republican National Convention. We are about to witness the climax of one of the bitterest as well as one of the most spectacular contests ever waged within the ranks of the Republican Party. We are assembled here as American citizens, most of whom are or have been Republicans. Ever since the shadow of our fathers' fathers first fell across the borders of this nation, we have been a cause of division and strife, not because of anything we have done to create it, aside from our physical presence within the nation, but because of what others desired to do with us.

Let no man deceive himself. Anyone who thinks that the convention to assemble here tomorrow, whatever may be its platform, whoever may be its nominee, will bring to us the political millennium, is doomed to a rude and speedy disillusionment.

The Caesars, Anthonys, and Brutuses who have marshaled their cohorts here in battle array are taking little thought of us or the condition of our people save as they may attempt to bribe or flatter us for the moment in order to enhance their personal fortunes.

The feeling of indifference or hostility to the Negro as relates to his life, liberty, and freedom of opportunity is confined to no party or section. It is reflected in the attitudes of sheriffs, mayors, and governors, until it extends to the Chief Executive of the nation. It is disclosed in the decisions of courts, acts of Congress and state legislatures, in the employment of labor in business and trade. It has even invaded the sacred precincts of religion and polluted with its withering touch the things that are held to be most sacred and divine.

We as a race are much divided and bewildered. We have trusted too long in a sycophantic, compromising, and time-serving leadership while our liberties have been invaded and our rights annulled. If we run from pillar to post in response to the cries, "Lo, here," and "Lo, there," it is because in desperation we are seeking a safe asylum where our rights and full political inheritance will be made secure.

The recredence [recrudescence] of sentiment against the Negro is not alone peculiar to the United States. It appears with more or less virulence in all parts of the world where Anglo-Saxon influence has penetrated and wherever the white man has gone to proclaim his lordship of the black or dark-skinned peoples of the earth. At this very hour it is being vividly illustrated almost at our very door in Cuba. What but American race prejudice is responsible for the present conflict between the whites and blacks in Cuba? The overwhelming majority of the inhabitants of Cuba are Negroes. Under Spanish rule, however great may have been the faults or shortcomings of the government, it cannot be charged that it fostered race discrimination and animosities.

The chief glory in the struggle for the freedom of Cuba rests with the Cuban Negroes who fought from within and the American Negroes who from without won imperishable glory in the battles [of] El Caney and San Juan Hill. The patriots of Cuba are fighting at this very hour for the same principle that has caused us to assemble here tonight within these walls, namely, that they shall not be denied the right to participate freely in the government of the nation which has been saved by their blood and which must depend for perpetuity upon their patriotism and industry.

We are against any American intervention in Cuba whose object is to set up a white man's government on that island. If this government by its might crushes the present revolt of the blacks of Cuba against injustice, it may by its intervention proclaim peace, but it will be the peace of despotism and everlasting disgrace to a nation whose chief claim to greatness rests upon the fact that it stands for free self-government without distinction of blood, religion, or race.

We would rather see every Negro soldier in the United States army discharged or court-martialed and imprisoned for desertion than to see them follow the flag of this country bearing arms to crush the aspirations of brown men in the Philippines or black men in Cuba to a free and equal participation in all the affairs of their own government.

Whoever may be the nominee of the Republican Convention, we do not expect that he will be able by proclamation to the people or message to Congress to still the currents of injustice, or lay the ghost of slavery which stalks abroad through the many forms of Jim Crowism. The best we can do at the present time is to give our support to the man who will set his face most strongly against it."

Taft and Roosevelt

The Republican Party is divided between the adherents of President Taft and former president Roosevelt. At the very beginning of his incumbency of the presidency, Mr. Taft disclosed his attitude toward the Negro by making the gratuitous declaration that he would not appoint any Negro to office in any community where such appointment was objectionable to the white people. From that hour intelligent and patriotic Negroes began to turn from him.

Mr. Taft has never realized that the Negro of 1912 is not the Negro of 1872. That the Negro has nothing to hope from him is disclosed by such declarations of his as "The Negro should be held in tutelage to the white people of the South," and "The Negro youth of this country should be educated in a different manner from the whites." No man, however benevolent his intentions, can do justice to our people when he does not believe in our future in this country and is not willing to accord us equal rights, privileges, and opportunities.

Pitted against Mr. Taft is Col. Roosevelt, and so far as he is concerned the whole world knows how bitterly the Negroes of this country resented his action in discharging without honor a battalion of the famous regiment, the Twenty-fifth Infantry. We think he was wrong then, we believe he has been wrong ever since, and we believe he is wrong now, so far as that action is concerned. It is the one black spot in his record so far as the Negroes are concerned, but before this act and since this act, down to this very hour, he has stood for justice and a square deal to the Negro. If his whole career has been one of friendliness and justice to us as a people, we cannot consign him to everlasting punishment for one error of judgment, however unjust.

Be it remembered that William Howard Taft was the secretary of war when that battalion was discharged. Be it also remembered that while Secretary of War Taft did suspend the order of discharge, he also made it effective before any word came from the then president Roosevelt, who was absent from the country at the time. Be it also remembered that Mr. Taft is the inventor of the term "a conspiracy of silence." When no confessions or incriminating evidence could be obtained from the discharged soldiers themselves, it was Mr. Taft who said that they had entered into a "conspiracy of silence." It was Secretary of War Taft who asserted that the soldiers were guilty. In a letter to President Roosevelt reviewing some of the testimony and dated January 12, 1907, he says, "I venture to say that no one can read this evidence judicially without being convinced beyond a reasonable doubt that the men who committed this outrage were Negro soldiers from Fort Brownsville and therefore the Twenty-fifth Infantry stationed there."

While President Roosevelt did discharge one battalion of Negro soldiers for what he believed sufficient cause, he did not discharge the whole regiment nor did he discharge or threaten to discharge the other three Negro regiments of the regular army. There were one hundred and seventy-two men in the battalion discharged by President Roosevelt, who drew on the average from $20 to $22 a month, while Mr. Taft has directly or through the influence of his acts discharged over four hundred federal employees, drawing from $100 to $300 per month. The places of the men discharged by Theodore Roosevelt were filled by colored men, but when President Taft puts out a Negro he puts a white man in his place, and when he does not put a white man in his place he puts a Negro in his place who can pass for white.

Here is a situation that is most paradoxical. Mr. Taft's Negro support comes from the South, yet here is where he has made a clean sweep of Negro federal office holders. Mr. Taft's chief Negro appointees are northern Negroes or Negroes from the South to positions which bring them North or take them entirely out of the country. Yet, the overwhelming majority of northern Negroes are opposed to Mr. Taft's nomination. He cannot stem the rising tide of opposition to him by his death bed repentance in appointing a handful of Negroes to inconspicuous jobs which bear high-sounding names.

A great many people are trying to inflame popular opposition to Mr. Roosevelt by flaunting the "third term" bogey. They claim that to break the precedent of not giving one man more than two terms in the presidency is to menace or destroy our Republican form of government. I am a Methodist preacher. Our time limit in any one charge is five years. There are those in our denomination who declare that to remove the time limit would be to destroy our itinerant system. The M.E. Church has removed the time limit for pastors, but it has not destroyed the itinerancy. The people themselves take care of the itinerancy. They know when they have had enough of a minister and have a way of telling him when it is time for him to move on.

We have not yet had one full term of Mr. Taft, yet the majority of the Republican electors in the great states of the East, North, and West have declared at the polls that one term for him is quite sufficient. Nominate and elect Theodore Roosevelt president, and if he fails to make good four years hence, the Republican electors will act toward him then as they have acted toward Mr. Taft now. They will repudiate him. It is not so much a question of tenure of office as it is a question of service to the country.

The Negro should take up these new political doctrines proclaimed by Mr. Roosevelt. We have had the referendum with a vengeance for many years, but it has been the referendum of the mob upon our guilt or innocence and executed its will with the rope, the shotgun, and the torch. We want a referendum which will give us the power to initiate laws and elect men to office to protect the sacredness of human life.

The Negro has been a stand-patter for forty years. He has let Republicans ride into the presidency on his back and hold a majority in Congress by counting him on the basis of apportionment for representation. While the Fifteenth Amendment has been nullified and he has been degraded by Jim Crow laws, he has stood pat. Now he should arise and join the ranks of the insurgents and fight this thing to its overthrow. If white men may grow insurgent over the question of tariff schedules and the regulation and control of trusts, surely black men may grow insurgent over mob rule, Jim Crowism, and the nullification of the Fifteenth Amendment.

As to the question of appealing judicial decisions, we have always been sound on that subject. Neither is action in this matter anything new. The Dred Scott decision was appealed from. That appeal was carried from the Supreme Court to the high court of the field of battle, and was overruled finally when Lee surrendered his sword to Grant. We would recall the unjust judges who upheld Jim Crow laws, and we would recall the judicial decisions where judgment is rendered not in accordance with justice but according to the complexion of the litigants.

We have not spoken of the Democrats or Democratic Party here tonight. We know that we have little hope from that source. Some of our leaders have felt that by turning to the Democratic Party the Republicans could be chastened and made to give us a larger measure of justice, but so far as the Negroes are concerned, the Democratic Party is today as of old controlled by southern sentiment, which is in favor of injustice to the Negro and would today, if it had the power, repeal the Fifteenth Amendment, as it has already nullified it.

These white men who will contend for supremacy when the convention doors spring open tomorrow may not consider what we say here tonight. Let that be as it may, but let us serve notice on them here tonight that we will compel them to take note of what we do at the polls next November. The right to vote will not be denied us in these great states of the North and West which, with the present dissension within the ranks of the Republican Party, they have no chance to win without our united aid. With William Howard Taft as their standard-bearer, they can under no circumstance count on our support. Let them not be deceived by the reassurance of Negro officeholders who think more of their jobs than they do of their rights. The great rank and file of the Negro Republicans of the nation will unite to follow in unbroken rank, as they will no other man, Theodore Roosevelt.

Crispus Attucks, a Negro, the First to Die for American Independence: An Address

Ransom notes that progress toward peace often required the shedding of blood, and the blood of Crispus Attucks continues to call for the liberation of African Americans. The progress of African Americans is a just outcome of the blood and work they have put into the building of this country. The will of God for the United States entails the full democratic participation of African Americans. And the work and progress of African Americans will send a message to the world and will encourage other peoples of color. Attucks's

Address delivered at the Metropolitan Opera House, Philadelphia, March 6, 1930 (Philadelphia: Printed by A.M.E. Book Concern, n.d.), housed in the Reverdy C. Ransom Collection, Payne Theological Seminary, Wilberforce, Ohio. Reprinted by permission of the AMEC Publishing House (Sunday School Union).

sacrifice for democracy has sparked a movement that must end in the full incorporation of African Americans.

•

Every good gift has been bought with blood, not by League of Nations, World Court, or peace pacts. The warm lifeblood of heroes, patriots, saints, and martyrs is the price we have paid for Magna Charta, the Bill of Rights, the Declaration of Independence, and the Proclamation of Emancipation. Of the first human blood that stained the earth, God said, "The voice of thy brother's blood crieth unto me from the ground." With a voice resounding through this nation for one hundred and sixty years, the blood of Crispus Attucks, the first to be shed to consecrate America to freedom, has cried unto God for freedom and justice for his race.

Massachusetts has her Paul Revere, celebrated in song and story. Over in New Jersey stands a towering monument to Molly Pitcher, of Revolutionary fame. Washington Monument stands in chaste beauty outlined against the dome of our national Capitol, while here in Philadelphia the riven throat of [the] Liberty Bell hangs in the cupola of old Independence Hall, the sacred shrine of national glory and achievement. But, none of these takes precedence over the immortal deed and deathless fame of Crispus Attucks, the Negro who bared his breast to British bullets and died the first martyr to American independence when he fell, facing the foe on State Street in Boston, one hundred and sixty years ago. We are told in fable and legend that Romulus and Remus founded Rome. The Romulus and Remus that founded this mighty democratic republic are the black men and white men who fought side by side in all the great battles of the United States. Peter Salem, who shot Major Pitcairn at the battle of Bunker Hill; Salem Poor, who fought with such bravery at the battle of Charlestown — he was reported to Congress for his behavior as an excellent soldier. More than three thousand Negro soldiers fought under Washington and Lafayette. They were in the battle of Long Island; more than seven hundred black men were in the battle of Monmouth, fighting with distinguished courage. The graves of one hundred and seventy Negro patriots extend from Bunker Hill to Lexington and Concord. White women have no exclusive claim to be members of the Daughters of the American Revolution; hundreds of colored women descendants of black Revolutionary patriots have every right to a place in the honorable circle of the D.A.R.

America was created for the high destiny. This is the first nation ever born with the Bible in its hands. While there is no specific mention of Jesus Christ or the Bible, either in the Declaration of Independence or the Constitution of the United States, our democratic doctrines of liberty, equality, and brotherhood spring direct from the teachings of Jesus.

To those who declare that Negroes are an alien and inassimilable race, we reply, "Who by their valor and their blood established the independence of the United States?" There can be but two possible claimants for that great honor, namely, white men and Negroes. America is ours, and the Negro is a fool who does not stand erect, hold his head high, and claim everything in it. . . . Our fathers did not fight for restricted liberty or partial equality; arms of ebony and bronze wrought mightily to establish American independence. Our national foundation stones of liberty and equality rest upon their bones and are cemented by their blood.

For nearly a century we tried to sustain a free government upon a cornerstone of slavery. But not even a government can abide if founded upon a lie. The lie may be buttressed with wealth and power, it may be gilded with gold and buried under a mountain of flowers, but because it is a lie, it will cause division, insecurity, and unrest until it is removed. Abraham Lincoln clearly perceived this when he said, "A nation cannot exist half slave and half free." Again he declared, "A house divided against itself cannot stand."

Under the providence of God, America has had no decisive hour, no turning point in her history without the presence and aid of Americans of African descent. These two peoples, the black and the white, are inseparably united by every link in the chain of American history. Legal heirs of a great legacy, joint beneficiaries of the greatest political inheritance ever bestowed, Negroes fail to push their claim before the high court of public opinion for the restoration of their full and complete political, social, and economic heritage.

Frederick Douglass used to say that the picture of Perry's victory on Lake Erie, which hangs under the dome of the Capitol at Washington, is "a painted lie." For he represents the white man standing in an attitude of bold defiance under the guns of the enemy, while the Negroes are cowering in fear. But Commodore Perry reported that the Negroes who fought with him in that battle were so courageous that when they fell wounded to the deck of his ship, they begged to be thrown overboard lest they should be in the way and hinder the fighting.

In the War for American Independence, there was opposition to the enlistment of Negroes as soldiers. It was thought by some that Negroes should not be permitted to take part in struggle between white men. John Hancock was of this opinion. Others feared that if the Negroes were armed, they might turn against their masters, or go over to Great Britain. The Continental Congress at one time instructed Washington to discharge all Negroes. But in his strait at Valley Forge, Washington enlisted a battalion of Negroes. The Continental Congress by pressure of events was forced to reverse its position, and we find Negroes generally enlisted throughout the colonies.

If Negroes [fought] to establish this government, the part which they played in its preservation during the Civil War constitutes the most thrilling epic of devotion, courage, and loyalty recorded in the history of modern times. At first there were the same grounds against Negro enlistment of Negro soldiers as had once been urged in the struggle for independence. But the fortunes of war compelled the government to arm the Negroes. The glorious deeds of valor performed by the Fifty-fourth and Fifty-fifth Massachusetts regiments remain one of the immortal chapters of courage and fidelity rising out of the Civil War. Our nation was not established without the Negro's aid; nor could it be preserved from disunion save by the strength and loyalty of the bayonets borne by one hundred and seventy-eight thousand Negro soldiers who brought back the wandering stars of the Confederacy to our flag and mingled their blood to seal them there forever. A generation later, in our little war with Spain, their courage and bravery on the battlefields of Cuba brought new luster to the invincible feats of American arms. Here for the first time in our history we have some colored regiments commanded by Negro officers from corporal to colonel. The men showed a submission to discipline and the officers such capacity and soldierly bearing as to forever settle the question of the discipline and morale of Negro soldiers when officered by members of their race. In Mexico and the Philippines, in both cavalry and infantry, the Negro soldier splendidly upheld the military record their race had borne for more than one hundred years. His aptitude for arms, as well as his loyalty and courage, having been tested upon every battlefield of the Republic, the government has never called the Negro to arms until driven to do so by dire necessity out of repeated defeats. In not one single instance has it ever laid down its arms in victorious peace without the presence of the Negro soldiers as a deciding factor in her triumphs. And yet in every contest of arms in which our nation has engaged, the Negro has always had to fight for a chance to fight. After each victorious contest, our nation has always been reluctant and grudging to share with the Negro the fruits of victory in the paths of peace.

After America entered the world war, about two hundred thousand Negro soldiers were sent to France. There they were compelled to work and fight under abject and humiliating conditions, so far as most of their white officers were concerned. Yet under these conditions they added to the military glory of their country. The first members of an American military unit to receive from the French government the Croix de Guerre were two Negro soldiers. These soldiers, together with thousands of Africans who fought under the flag of France, have made the whole world their debtor by their sacrifice and noble daring in Champagne, the Argonne forest, and at Metz and [the] Marne.

In any future war in which this country may engage, if Negroes do not refuse to enlist and fight under our flag, except under exactly the same conditions of rank, assignment to duty, promotion, honor, and reward as are accorded to their white fellow citizens, they shall deserve all the insult, humiliation, and contempt that may be visited upon them.

Just now the great powers are holding a naval conference in London, the ostensible purpose of which is reduction of naval armaments. They solemnly assure us they are working in the interest of international peace. No doubt there are many sincere men sitting at that conference table. But knowing the ruthless and bloody character of these oppressive and grasping capitalistic nations, we are skeptical as to their real purpose and design. They want peace for their commerce and trade; they want financial stability; above all they want the ruling white nations to be at peace among themselves in the face of the dark-skinned world of Asia and Africa, which holds two-thirds of the population of the world. Africa has been partitioned among the nations to the satisfaction of everybody except Germany and the Africans themselves. England holds her Indian empire with trembling hands. China is regarded as [the] legitimate prey of all at any serious crisis in her affairs. True, Japan is there, but only welcome so long as she cooperates with the white nations in preserving the status quo among the myriad millions of dark-skinned peoples of the Orient. The menace of the dark-skinned world, developed and united, is ever in the background of every conference among the white nations to establish international peace among themselves.

Nowhere else on the face of the earth are the white and black people as inextricably united as they are in the United States. Claiming no other nation or country as distinctly their own, Americans of African descent are in a strategic position. They owe a duty not only to themselves and their white fellow citizens, but more to the entire world of dark-skinned humanity. They must demonstrate forever and to all, the ability and capacity of the black race, in competition with the white race, to win and hold complete political, social, and economic equality. They must engage in the business of putting the white man in his place, and insist it shall be that of an equal, nothing more.

There are more Negroes in the United States today than there were people comprising our entire population in the days [when] Daniel Webster and Henry Clay in statesmanship [and] William Ellery Channing and Lyman Beecher in the pulpit were at the zenith of their power. The Negroes of the United States own more land than comprise the combined area of the states of Massachusetts, Vermont, Rhode Island, and Connecticut. Their educated men and women are increasing at the rate of twenty thousand graduates annually from schools, colleges, and universities. With this mighty lever properly [wielded] upon the fulcrum of united purpose and a dauntless will, they can capture every stronghold of prejudice and opposition that would obstruct their progress and achievement. The white man yields nothing, even to his own poor laboring masses, through sympathy or love. He yields not to the persuasion of logic or the sanctity of his religious creeds. He only yields or compromises in the face of aggressive, determined, uncompromising power. We can most signally honor Crispus Attucks and the men of our race who have fought to establish and preserve this nation by emulating in the paths of peace the virtues they displayed in war.

We can only gain our rights by our fights. Aggressively contend for the things we desire, ceaseless agitation to arouse and stir the indifferent and sluggish of our race, keep the organs of public opinion vocal with our cries, solidify and defend every advanced position we may gain. Even then only ceaseless vigilance and perseverance can prevent the enemies of our progress from causing us to fail to retain the ground we have gained at the cost of so great peril, labor, and sacrifice.

For centuries the white people have made it clear just what kind of Negroes they want. They have decided it by acts of legislation, by decisions of the courts, by denial of economic opportunity, by social degradation, by disfranchisement and segregation, by inferior educational facilities, by mob violence, lynching and the burning of our bodies at the stake. But the descendants of Crispus Attucks, Peter Salem, and Frederick Douglass must decide for themselves just what kind of Negro Americans they intend to be.

We have covered much ground since Attucks fell a martyr to liberty one hundred and sixty years ago. We have come from general illiteracy to doctors of philosophy, from universal poverty to a financial strength where we may name some millionaires, from the slave pens to beautiful homes, from the auction block to the presidency of banks and insurance companies, and from the fields of corn and cotton to the Congress of the United States. All of this we have accomplished in less than a century while opposed and challenged on every side.

We have not yet begun our great offensive against the political, social, and economic strongholds that would either bar or limit our entrance within their gates. We are not yet on our march. So far we have done little more than skirmish. We are equipping, drilling, training, spying out the land. While we mark time, we are schooling ourselves in patience, fortitude, and self-control. We are reconnoitering every stronghold of the opposition. We are girding up our spirits, keeping our brains clear and our hearts warm, while we decoy our opposition into positions of false security. We are waiting for the schools and all the forces that make for righteousness and strength, to send up reinforcements and equip us with invincible weapons against every invention of our foes. A few decades hence, when the mighty leaders of our race shall order the complete destruction of every barrier of color and race, fifty million Negroes, born and reared on American soil, shall advance to the charge in ranks that cannot be broken. Then shall Americans, black and white, lead the way for all the peoples of the earth to equality and brotherhood in the paths of peace.

My fellow citizens, as we are met here tonight to review the past that revolves about the name and fame of Crispus Attucks, it should also be an hour of rededication to liberty. Then let the words that phrase our consecration be the burning words with which William Lloyd Garrison dedicated himself to freedom's cause:

Oppression! I have seen thee face to face,
And met thy cruel eye and cloudy brow;
But thy soul-withering glance I fear not now —
For dread to prouder feelings doth give place
Of deep abhorrence! Scorning the disgrace
Of slavish knees that at thy footstool bow,
I also kneel — but with far other vow
Do hail thee and thy herd of hirelings base;
I swear, while lifeblood warms my throbbing veins,
Still to oppose and thwart, with heart and hand,
Thy brutalizing sway 'till Afric's chains
Are burst, and Freedom rules the rescued land,
Trampling Oppression and iron rod;
Such is the vow I take — so help me God!

The Church That Shall Survive

*Bishop Ransom outlines the strengths and potentials of the
A.M.E. Church through an appeal to its ability to address the
full range of human needs. He argues that if the church is to
live up to its potential, its leadership must be called, committed, and visionary. If the church does not make itself relevant,
it will not survive because its importance is not based simply upon tradition and history; rather, it is based upon its
response to current crises.*

•

Text: Exodus 14:15, "And the Lord said unto Moses, Wherefore criest thou unto me? Speak unto the children of Israel,
that they go forward."

The quadrennial sermon to a General Conference is no ordinary
occasion. The speaker is called upon to address the elected delegates of our constituency, representing more than three-fourths
of a million souls, scattered throughout all parts of America, the
Islands, South America, West and South Africa. In approaching

Sermon before the thirteenth session of the A.M.E. General Conference, New York,
May 6, 1936. Reprinted in George A. Singleton's *The Romance of African Methodism: A Study of the African Methodist Episcopal Church* (New York: Exposition
Press, 1952), 146–56. Reprinted by permission of Mrs. Ruth L. Ransom and her
son, Louis A. Ransom, Jr.

the task, I was immediately confronted with the question, "What should be the scope and character of a sermon to meet the requirements of the occasion?" Our program says a "sermon" — not a lecture, not a formal address, but a "sermon." Now, a sermon should always deal not only with the subject of religion, but its emphasis should always be placed upon the revelation of God through Jesus Christ, His Son. The occasion asks not only for a sermon, but for a quadrennial sermon (that is, one which should look both backward and forward). It should look backward at least to the things through which we have come for the past four years, and these things have naturally derived from the things in [the] past which make the history of our church up to this hour. But more than this, it should look forward, facing the future as it relates to our opportunities, our duties, and our tasks. No institution, whether church or state, can stand still without beating a retreat or moldering to decay. It must go forward. I do not mean that activity is synonymous with progress. There is much activity which is engaged in threshing old straw or simply beating the air. We should be active by forever enlarging our vision to meet the changed moral, social, and spiritual conditions of the succeeding generations in which our lot is cast. We must always have in mind that widening our activities through engaging in work on behalf of schools, hospitals, Y.M.C.A., temperance, world peace, and in forms of work for help and mercy do not constitute a church. They may, and should, grow out of its life and spirit; but the church is now, as of old, a body of believers however large or small, who are united through saving faith to Jesus Christ as Redeemer, Lord, and Master of their souls.

If the A.M.E. Church as a body is to be simply nothing more than just one of the religious bodies, holding the same standards, choosing the same aims and objectives, and attempting to do the same things as are being done by others, many of whom have far better equipment and resources than have we, there is really nothing unique or distinctive about it; there is no rallying point that stirs our zeal, kindles our enthusiasm, or causes us to be willing to lie upon the altar of self-denial, of suffering, and of pain.

Richard Allen and his followers achieved a place in the high company of men like Martin Luther and John Wesley because they met a turning point in religious history with intelligence, courage, and faith. They were the first to strike a blow for independence, freedom, and equality in the church for Negroes in the United States. There was no thought of prestige, power, honor, or reward. They were engaged in the task of achieving for themselves that freedom which belongs to all persons who have been born of God through faith in Jesus Christ. Negro organization, Negro self-confidence, self-respect, self-support, management, and control date from that very day.

"The Church That Shall Survive" is the theme for today, and my text may be found in the fifteenth verse of the fourteenth chapter of the Book of Exodus, the words of which are "Speak unto the children of Israel, that they go forward." While I may not, in what I shall say, directly refer to the text at all, it constitutes the main thread around which all I say today shall be woven.

The A.M.E. Church was born ten years after the Liberty Bell on Independence Hall in Philadelphia split its throat in ringing out tidings of American independence, which was the same year [1787] that our federal Constitution was signed. At that time, the spirit of freedom and independence filled the air.

Richard Allen's ears doubtless heard [the] Liberty Bell ring out its defiant challenge. His eyes doubtless saw Washington, Jefferson, Franklin, and Adams passing through the streets of Philadelphia while engaged in the work of building a new nation. Richard Allen was a resident of Philadelphia when the spirit of the times gave prompting, inspiration, and courage for the momentous step he took. The stage for his appearance as an historic figure was perfectly set. The A.M.E. Church was born in due time. God set the stage and chose the actors to play the leading roles in producing its opening scenes.

It created nothing new in the religious doctrine or church policy but took over bodily what it found in the Methodist Episcopal Church from which it withdrew. What was new about it, and the thing that made it distinctive and unique, is the fact that it is the first organized movement by Negroes in the United States of America for freedom, independence, and equality. How Negroes of every rank throughout the nation rallied to its standard through the power it made to manhood, how its different departments were organized, its schools and colleges established, are now a matter of history.

No race since Israel came out of Egypt has traveled so far or gone as fast within such a brief period of time. Slavery with its degrading influence lies behind us; ignorance and degrading poverty are being overcome by leaps and bounds; self-confidence and self-respect are being achieved under our own leadership, management, and control.

As we stand here today, we can judge the vitality, the spirit, and morale of our church by the manner in which its leadership and following have met and faced the depression during the past four years. We have splendidly stood the test. We are alive and functioning. But this by no means assures our future as we face the dawn of a new age where the social end of our civilization itself is confronted by the most revolutionary changes in history.

Where past and present meet the future begins. We have arrived here today largely through the impact of the inertia of the past that has come from our fathers, rather than any power or foresight we have achieved ourselves. He who clings to the past, without at the same time going forth in the light of the present to meet the future, is bound to a body of death. This is why we now call upon God to meet us in this place as we now stand at the conflux of the past and future, to give us vision, courage, and faith to meet the new age — a challenge that cannot be evaded or ignored. God changeth not, but the methods by which His servants meet the changing conditions of a changing society must keep pace, change with God's unfolding plans to bring men near to Himself through the procession of ages. We cannot go back to Paul, to Luther and Wesley, to Allen and Turner, to Payne, or even so late a comer as Booker T. Washington. A changed atmosphere envelopes us, changed conditions surround us, new problems confront us. In our bewilderment, we cannot call some Witch of Endor to summon our dead Samuels from the grave. We must furnish our own redeemers and prophets to lead us to go forth and walk with the timeless and ageless God. We must fight not only foes without but the forces of reaction and the obstacles to progress within the borders of our own household of faith.

No institution or custom should be held sacred simply because it is old and comes to us as an inheritance from the past when it can no longer fit into or compete with the life of today. They should be superseded by forms of action and service that will reach our objectives. One steam shovel can accomplish as much in one day as the labor of a hundred men. An automobile can cover more distance in an hour than a horse and buggy can make in one day. Why the backwardness of Africa and China today? They are shackled and bound to the traditions and customs of the past. Why the power and mastery of Japan? The Japanese have overtaken and caught steps with the development and methods of modern civilization and progress.

No man, however respected or revered, however large the contribution of his service in the past, should be permitted to turn back the hands of the clock or to control improved machinery of which he has little knowledge and in the operation of which he has no skill. We need not overturn our idols or banish our gods. We should better put them upon pedestals of honor that men of a new day may look up to them and be inspired to meet their problems with equal wisdom, courage, and fortitude.

Doubtless, before many days have passed, within the walls of this building where we now sit, will be raised the cry: "They are trying to wreck, or destroy, the Church. Let everything remain as it is. Let us pass minor legislation, elect the necessary officers, and adjourn." Certainly, this will be the case if we seriously attempt the things that cry for attention.

Most of our schools and colleges were established when they served a real need and furnished almost the only door of opportunity. But today, the state is increasingly serving that need. To meet present-day standards and requirements in education, we are not able to support more than two or three colleges and one theological seminary. I boldly make the statement and defy a challenge by declaring that in the work of religious education we occupy almost the lowest rung of the ladder.

We are trying to operate the work of our foreign missionary enterprises by methods used forty years ago, but which are unsuited to present-day conditions. The Christian nations of Europe have torn Africa apart; and today, like ravening wolves, they snap and snarl, ready to fly at each other's throats over the division of the spoils.

Italy, under the passionate urge of Mussolini, has wantonly invaded the ancient kingdom of Ethiopia with the avowed purpose of taking it by force to become a colony of Italy. Africa knows now that the white nations who send her missionaries are really there to subjugate her people and to exploit the land. Since we are a kindred people, the problem is not simple as to how our church can best heed the cry and answer the call of Africa. Is our present missionary equal to the task?

Eight years ago, there was much talk on all sides of the union of the three great bodies of Negro Methodists. It has now become almost a dead issue. Will this General Conference revive it and pursue it until it becomes an accomplished fact? Where we are weak, all of us together might be strong. It is more than an ecclesiastical and/or religious question. It lies at the very roots of the economic, political, and social welfare of the millions of our people. If we cannot achieve denominational union, the day of united action along business, commercial, civic, and political lines seems far distant.

The representatives of the Methodist Episcopal Church, Methodist Episcopal Church South, and the Methodist Protestant Church have finally agreed upon a basis of union of these great Methodist bodies which, when ratified, will make them the largest body of Protestant Christians in the world. The name they have agreed upon is simply the "Methodist Church." Shall we still remain separate and divided over questions of official title and minor details, while the strength of our people continues to be weakened under the weight of burdens too heavy to be borne because of our separation? The A.M.E. Church in this General Conference should lead the way to unite all Negro Methodism so that the church and race which support it should have full benefit of the combined strength and influence of its leadership.

As a denomination, we have behind us a hundred and twenty years of organized life. In the beginning, we were simply seeking to achieve freedom and independence. What are our aims and objectives today? Have we a program that appeals to youth? Are our objectives such as will arouse and stir them to volunteer to enlist under our banner? Does anyone court or fear the weight of our influence?

Shall the exploiters and oppressors of our people be challenged here by our united voices? We want work, we want bread, we desire to occupy our proper place in the body of politics. Shall we dedicate ourselves to fight on every front where the battle lines are drawn for freedom and opportunity, and against industrial exploitation and discrimination? Shall we in the presidential campaign this year display enough intelligent political sagacity to take advantage of the main issue on which the two great parties are divided; namely, on the one hand that the policies of the New Deal violate the Constitution which should be upheld as handed down to us, and on the other that the Constitution should be liberalized by judicial interpretation, or otherwise in the interest of the present economic and social condition of the people of this country as a whole?

Let those who would defend the sacredness of the Constitution be faced with the fact that the Fifteenth Amendment is being flagrantly nullified and flouted. Let them be challenged to put a plank in their platform to come to the rescue of our voteless people in this country of American democracy.

Some who hear me speak here doubtless already said within

themselves, "What has all this to do with religion and the church?"
Amaziah, the priest of Bethel, felt the same way about the prophet
Amos when he told Jeroboam that "Amos hath conspired against
thee in the midst of the house of Israel...." All of this because
Amos denounced "the king of Bashan which oppress the poor,
which crush the needy!" "Ye who turn to wormwood and leave off
righteousness in the earth...." "Hear this O ye that swell up the
needy, even to make the poor of the land to fall, and that we may
buy the poor for silver and needy for a pair of shoes...." "Woe to
them that are at ease in Zion...." thus saith the Lord God; "take
away from me the noise of the songs, but let judgment run down
as waters and righteousness as a mighty stream...."

"Seek Him that maketh the seven stars and Orion, and turneth
the Shadow of Death into morning. The Lord is His Name." While
Heaven is our final goal, our chief present concern is with life on
this planet and human relations in our present society, to the end
that the Kingdom of God may be established among men. I see
little hope for the survival of the A.M.E. Church, or any other distinctly religious Negro denomination, if we do not so apply the
gospel of Christ as to make it a vital force in the life of society.
While the National Association for the Advancement of Colored
People and the Urban League may argue, petition, protest, and
appeal, we are clothed with authority to declare, "Thus saith the
Lord."

The world has little interest in us or concern about us as to what
we do and what we say here. To them, we are just a group of
Negroes here legislating and voting on matters that concern our
church. But once let us take up, in the name of a just and righteous God, the conditions that confront our people in this country,
and the newspapers and every other public influence will immediately spring to attention. The sharecroppers of the South whose
present conditions are but little removed from slavery are among
the members of our church who pay a large part of our dollar
money from which our denomination derives support. What have
we done, what will we do, to help them to secure industrial and
economic justice?

The most flourishing domain of lynchers and mobs is found
in communities that are the greatest devotees of religion and the
church. We should turn the searchlight of the gospel of Jesus Christ
upon them and keep it centered there. If he thought about it at all,
Senator Borah knew he was running little risk of repudiation at
the ballot box by the great bulk of Negro voters when he frankly

stated that, if elected president, he would veto a federal law against lynching. No political party would nominate him or any other man out of sympathy with our people if it knew that every Negro pulpit in the country would thunder against him as from Heaven until its blast resounded throughout the nation.

While the weapons of our welfare are not carnal, we should make them mighty through God to the tearing down of the strongholds of the wicked. The church, as organized by St. Paul, would not be able to recognize the church of the Middle Ages. The church in the days of Martin Luther, of John Calvin, and even the church of Jonathan Edwards and Lyman Beecher would not be able to recognize the church as it stands today. The church is constantly changing from age to age so far as the expression of its spiritual and outward activities is concerned. What, then, is "the church that shall survive?" It is evident that in Paul's phrase, it should "become all things to all men," in the sense of being flexible enough to minister to the actual conditions that confront it at a given time. Few things in the church's history are more pathetic and distressing than the manner in which the church functioned during the world war, unless it is the manner in which it is behaving in the face of the social, political, economic, and spiritual crisis that menaces the civilized world today.

Through accommodating it to the philosophy and organization of our materialistic and commercial age, we look almost in vain for the life and manifestation of the spirit radiating from the altars of religion. While none of the white races, either in Europe or America, have ever given to the world a religion, they have taken the simple story of the cross of Christ and so twisted, distorted, and submerged it to accommodate their political and economic practices that most of the beauty and power of God's dear Son have been crushed out of it. The only religion left among the white races today that has vitality is communism, practiced in Russia. Communism, with all its cruelties, actually tries to practice what it preaches. We say this without either approving it or condemning it. We simply state a fact. Let English Christianity in India and South Africa, or American Christianity in the United States, practice what it preaches but for a single day, and its cruel features would be wreathed in smiles, its ruthless spirit would be so transformed as to envelop the world in the folds of a mantle of goodwill.

How may the Negro church survive as a thing apart? It is already a thing apart in management and control. But there is small hope for its survival if it continues to copy and follow the programs and practices of fellow Christians.

The church that shall survive must know neither race, color, nor nationality nor recognize distinctions of wealth, class, or station, but only the dignity and sacredness of our common humanity. The church that shall survive cannot rest secure upon the foundation of wealth or learning or temporal prosperity and power. Like Abraham, it must forever look for a city which "hath foundations... whose builder and maker is God." It must "follow peace with all men and holiness without which no man shall see the Lord," and have the abiding witness that God hath delivered it from the power of darkness and translated it into the Kingdom of His dear Son, who is the head of the church and first born from the dead. We, having been reconciled to God in the body of His flesh through death, shall find that time is only the gate to eternity where our life shall be hid with Christ in God.

The bishops and ministers that lead this church must have their call and commission from God, and the geniuses of their credentials and the divine authority with which they are clothed must be witnessed by their power and faith to proclaim and uphold the gospel message in an evil time. It must be a prophetic church, not only beholding the Lord and lifting up, while the cherubin cry "Holy, Holy, Holy" round His throne; but while the church is marching through the wilderness, they must point to the realm of hope and promise that lies just beyond. They must proclaim liberty to the captives — those that are socially, economically, and politically disinherited — with authority of a divine justice that will not rest until every fetter of injustice and oppression is broken. The church that shall survive has power to call down consuming fire from heaven upon all the altars of Baal. It is supported by the angels and all the hosts of Heaven led on by the Son of God.

I salute you as both pilgrims and pioneers of the Negro race in self-confidence, administration, and control. I admit we are still marching through the wilderness; we still make our tents among the mountains or in valleys dark and bare where violent men assail us. Only a few have lacked faith and confidence and deserted from our fold while others bade us carry on while they changed their armor for robes of white as they ascended into the skies.

We have been out for four years, some tending the flock of Christ, others following their shepherds. We come from lonely missions and circuits out in far-flung islands, the heat of Africa's burning sun, the snows of Canada and our northern lakes, as well as from more favored paths in towns and cities where we were daily put to the test amid clash and struggle of the forces of sin against the cause of moral and spiritual salvation.

For just a few days, we shall tarry here in labor and fellowship to return again to the tasks that await us. Some of us have already heard faint strains of celestial music occasionally wafted down to us from paradise. These tell us we are drawing near to the City of God and may not return to behold the Joshuas and Calebs that are preparing in our midst to arise and come to lead our people forth, out of the wilderness, over the mountains and across the Jordan to slay the giants that confront us and to level the Jerichos that are walled up against us. But those of us who have joined the cloud of witnesses on the thrones of light where stand Allen, Quinn, Payne and Turner, Arnett and Grant, with Coppin and Johnson, Brooks and Parks, will give an answering shout from heaven to your triumphant song of victory for the survival of a church that through faith in Christ has moved mountains, "subdued Kingdoms, obtained promises and wrought righteousness" — wherefore God shall not be ashamed to be called our God.

Emancipation Day Address

Ransom points out during this speech the importance of the Old Court House based upon its connection to Dred Scott's lawsuit (1856). * *It was this case that fostered the Supreme Court's famous refusal to recognize any rights for African Americans that must be respected. Ransom recounts that, through the workings of God, African Americans have made great strides since this unfortunate court decision. Yet, there is more for African Americans to gain.*

•

When the discovery of Christopher Columbus snatched the Western Hemisphere from the uncharted sea, there was set in motion

---

Address delivered in the Old Court House, St. Louis, Missouri, under the auspices of the Cooperative Civic Association, January 1, 1940, housed in the Reverdy C. Ransom Collection, Payne Theological Seminary, Wilberforce, Ohio. Reprinted by permission of Mrs. Ruth L. Ransom and her son, Louis A. Ransom, Jr.

*Dred Scott was a slave taken by his master to live in Illinois, a free state. Upon their return to Missouri, Scott sued for his freedom. He argued that living in a free state released him from slavery. The Court decided against Scott. –Ed.

the greatest influence that has ever touched the life of civilized man upon this planet.

The first European settlers here found a vast continent of untamed wilderness, wild beasts, undeveloped men, unbridged rivers, an inviting climate, and a fertile soil. The native Indian refused to work with them for its development, and the task was far beyond their numbers or their strength; that is why they cast their eyes upon the myriad millions of their brothers on the continent of Africa and brought them here by force, to assist in the physical subjugation and development of our boundless natural resources.

The wave on wave of the black millions brought from Africa were held "to service and labor" — slavery. Both the church and the state held that they were "naturally and inherently inferior," incapable of intellectual development, and in matters of religion "unconvertible."

Out of the backwardness of their African inheritance, out of the depths of the degradation of the American system of slavery, faced with the denial of the most elementary human rights and opportunity, scorned and oppressed: there is nothing in the history of any people to equal the surpassing epic of the development and progress made by Americans of African descent in the past three hundred and twenty-five years of their residence on American soil.

But we are met here today to celebrate the seventy-sixth anniversary of Abraham Lincoln's immortal Proclamation of Emancipation. But the freedom it proclaimed did not free the slaves in Missouri, because the state of Missouri was not in rebellion against the government of the United States. They were later freed by act of the legislature of Missouri.

There are certain places that hold historic value because of far-reaching events that there occurred. State Street, Boston, where Crispus Attucks fell to offer the first blood to consecrate American freedom; Bunker Hill, where the true aim of Peter Salem's rifle helped stem the tide in favor of American independence; Harpers Ferry, where John Brown's martyrdom lighted the campfires of the northern armies; and this Old Court House, here in St. Louis where the trial of Dred Scott, the escaping slave was held, which trial resulted in the opinion by Judge Taney of the United States Supreme Court that "the Negro has no rights a white man is bound to respect." This decision was one of the deciding influences in arousing the forces of freedom to strike for the destruction of slavery. This decision made a potential slave catcher out of every white man and woman in the North.

In an opening clause in his decision, Judge Roger B. Taney said, "The question simply is this: Can a Negro, whose ancestors were imported into this country and sold as slaves, become a member of the political community formed and brought into existence by the Constitution of the United States, and as such become entitled to all the rights and privileges and immunities guaranteed by that instrument to the citizen?"

Judge Taney handed down his decision in 185[7]. What hath God wrought? In less than eighty-four years after Dred Scott was tried here in this building, we have by grace of the Democratic Party a Negro judge, in the person of the Honorable Frank S. Bledsoe, presiding here, and the constable here is a Negro, in the person of Mr. Jordan W. Chambers.

This is a perfect yardstick to measure the distance traveled by Americans of African descent from Judge Taney's opinion up to now, and we have just fairly started on our way.

From January 1, 1864, to January 1, 1940, in a few outstanding fields, Americans of African descent have achieved as follows:

The Negro churches have approximately six million members. These are served by more than forty thousand ministers. These churches support colleges for American youth, which have equipment, plants, and grounds valued at about forty million dollars.

The colored people have contributed about four million dollars toward their own education exclusive of the amount of taxes they have paid as citizens for the support of public schools. There are 120 institutions of learning for Negroes with approximately forty thousand students enrolled with about five thousand graduates. Twenty-five hundred attend leading white universities and colleges in the North. About thirty thousand Negroes have graduated from college.

There are 315 recognized Negro newspapers; 124 of these claim a joint circulation of 1,206,787; estimating that six persons read each paper, we have a total of more than six million people who read Negro newspapers. The combined real estate and machinery of twenty of the larger newspapers have a value of two million dollars.

Negroes own twenty million acres of land, an area about equal to the states of New Hampshire, Vermont, Massachusetts, Connecticut, and Rhode Island. Negroes own eight hundred thousand homes, operate eight hundred and eighty thousand farms, conduct seventy thousand businesses, have accumulated two and a half billion dollars of wealth.

There are twenty-three Negro banks, capitalized at about $2,000,000 and doing an annual business of about $50,000,000. There are thirty Negro insurance companies...with premium income [of] $18,475,389. These companies employ about nine thousand Negroes, several of whom are qualified actuaries.

Negroes are active in many fields. There are about 4,100 physicians and surgeons; 300 employed in the United States government social service agencies; 1,246 lawyers; 2,732 male actors and 1,398 female actors; 1,500 policemen and 50 policewomen, and 4,601 soldiers.

Marvelous as has been our progress and achievement in the past seventy-six years of freedom, this is no time to stop and rejoice over the victories we have won. The walls of Jericho that confront us have not yet fallen down. Why look back along the road we have traveled while some of the filth and mire of the slave pen still cling to us? There are bloodhounds still on our trail. The wounds to our flesh caused by the slave driver's lash may have healed, but the wounds to our minds and spirits bleed afresh every day. The voices of our would-be masters still sell us down the river into peonage, economic and industrial bondage. The overseers will ride among us this year of 1940 to recapture and drive us back into political bondage. The Judge Taneys of today will be handing down decisions that tear to shreds the Fifteenth Amendment and deny us the protection of the law; public sentiment is ceaselessly vigilant to "make the Negro know his place and keep it." Slavish Negroes, some of whom are in high places, continue to betray us to our enemies and oppressors. The fleshpots still tempt many to turn back to the Egypt of intellectual, political, and social bondage. The spirit of slavery is not dead. It stalks abroad to inspire intimidation and fear and with sepulchral voice to speak against us in the hotel lobbies and drawing rooms of the North, while the bony fingers of its skeleton hands spread the virus of race and color prejudice in the citadel of civic life and social contact. We must lay that ghost. Abraham Lincoln pronounced the death sentence upon slavery seventy-six years ago. General Grant met General Lee at Appomattox, where both sheathed their swords and pronounced slavery dead.

Americans of African descent must gird themselves anew to remove, or circumvent, the barriers that are thrown across their path and courageously meet each enemy that challenges our advancement. We must never give place to fear, and above all we must cling to the abiding faith in God which upheld our fathers in a darker day than this. We must firmly resolve that it is our goal to attain the full and equal enjoyment of everything America has to offer, in every department of its life. We must be free to make our contribution to all the things that will make our country a better place in which to live.

The question before us is not what kind of Negroes the white people want us to be, but what kind of Americans and men do we ourselves intend to be. Our goal should not be Negro education, but just education. We should insist on nothing less than an equal share in the money provided for public school education, the same equipment and facilities. State-supported colleges, universities, and professional schools must be opened to us on terms of equal freedom and opportunity. We must ceaselessly agitate and work for the repeal of every law upon the statute books of the state or nation that in any way discriminates against American citizens on the grounds of race, color, or religion; any public convenience, recreation, amusement, or necessity that is labeled "for Negroes," we should reject as an insult to our American citizenship and manhood.

If our country is to become involved in the war now spreading across the continent of Europe, we should now, as always in the past, defend it with our blood and with our treasure, but only on one condition — that we fight on absolutely the same conditions as our white fellow citizens in every branch of the armed services of the United States, whether it be on land, on sea, or in the air. If we are to sacrifice, to suffer, and to die, black Americans must be able to wrap about them the flag of their country with same dignity and honor that await [their] fellow Americans.

Let no one deceive you. Those who have charge of government, whether city, county, state, or nation, hold the reins of power. They have small respect for any group that cannot, or will not, hold them politically responsible. The ballot is our most potent weapon for protection and defense, in civic, social, or political affairs. Regardless of political labels and party lines, we should use it fearlessly to punish our enemies and sustain our friends.

It has been said of us that we are an alien and unassimilable race. But we are not alien in language, religion, ideals, customs, or patriotic devotion to our country and our flag. We are not alien in birth and have no hyphenated allegiance. We are not unassimilable; we have already assimilated everything American, even to the fading color of our skins and the texture of our hair. Here we are born, here we have lived for more than three hundred years, and come whatever fate, here shall our children and our children's children be buried. No one but white men and black men developed, built, and defended this country. It is our common heritage. With America today becoming almost the last refuge of liberty and the spirit of democracy, Americans of African descent must put the climax on the perpetuity of our nation by filling it with the spirit of brotherly cooperation and kindness, with freedom and justice for all, without regard to race, class, color, or creed.

Let us take the chains that bound our fathers to the prison pen and the auction block and weld them into a ladder of ascension upon which we and our children after us shall climb, round by round, above the clouds of prejudice and oppression, into the clear sunlight of equal freedom and equality.

The Paraclete of God the Only Hope for Brotherhood and Peace

The creation of humanity by God entails the equality of all human beings — the human race. Hence, people should be free to marry as they please because they all stem from one family, created in the image of God. This basic principle of freedom and equality is outlined in the Declaration of Independence, but the United States has often failed to live by its outlined principles, which are in essence in keeping with the divine plan of creation. The progress of African Americans in the United States is necessary in order to bring about the truth of the declaration and its connection to Scripture.

•

We have reached the place in human relations where the subject of the creation of man needs to be explored and restated. The world is filled with man-made progress and expedients as a formula for peaceful relations among men in human society throughout the world.

This is an effort to state the primary source and bedrock upon which the entire family of the human race was built and must stand forevermore. In the Book of Genesis it is written, 2:7, "The Lord

Typed manuscript housed in the Reverdy C. Ransom Collection, Payne Theological Seminary, Wilberforce, Ohio. Reprinted by permission of Mrs. Ruth L. Ransom and her son, Louis A. Ransom, Jr.

God formed man of the dust of the ground, and breathed into his nostrils the breath of life; and man became a living soil." And in Genesis 5:1–2 it is written, "This is the book of the generations of Adam. In the day that God created man, in the likeness of God made He him; Male and Female created He them; blessed them, and called their names Adam, in the day when they were created."

The first unit or link in the diversified chain of humanity is the marriage of one man to one woman. There is no distinction, or discrimination, as to color of skin, texture of hair, or other accidents of birth — just one man and one woman. From the marriage of one man to one woman stem families, tribes, nations, states, and empires. But these do not invalidate the fact that "all men are created equal," equal in the sense of having a common origin and fatherhood by the creative act of God. There is but one race, the human race. It follows then, there can be no such thing as "mixed marriages." More than that, they are endowed with certain unalienable rights, among which are "life, liberty and the pursuit of happiness."

Our American Declaration of Independence makes clear the object and purpose of the founding of this republic as follows:

> We hold these truths to be self-evident; that all men are created equal; that they are endowed by their Creator with certain unalienable rights; that among these are life, liberty and the pursuit of happiness. That to secure these rights, governments are instituted among men, deriving their just powers from the consent of the governed.

Thomas Jefferson was inspired in his choice of words when he said, "created equal." This was an act of the Creator — God. Now this does not mean equal in the sense of equally wise, equally endowed, or equally powerful and resourceful.

Our chief weapon is that we have here in America a "classless" society. There is neither Jew, Gentile, white, black, consumer, producer, farmer, labor, or capitalist but because he is a man and possesses the personal God-given integrity of each free man in the American "classless" society.

For added emphasis I declare that God created all men free to develop, achieve, and pursue any line of human activity [they] may desire. No human law is valid that seeks to divide or to segregate mankind into "classes," "minority groups," "labor," "industry," "white," or "black."

In the Eighth Psalm [4–6], it is declared: "What is man, that

Thou art mindful of him? And the son of man, that Thou visitest him? For Thou hast made him a little lower than the angels, and hast crowned him with glory and honor. Thou madest him to have dominion over the works of Thy hands; Thou hast put all things under his feet." This is the crown, the robe of dignity and honor, God has given to every man born into the world.

The Republic of the United States of America is the first nation ever born with the Bible in its hands. This is a religious nation. The constitution of each one of the forty-eight states except one recognizes its faith in and dependence upon the guidance of God.

This nation was founded, defended, and developed by every variety of the race of man. Our present concern and emphasis relates to Americans of African descent. The different varieties of the human race were one people until they were scattered abroad at the building of the tower of Babel in the plains of Shinar.

Thousands of years passed before they met again on the continent of the New World notwithstanding the fact that through the ages many artificial differences had developed such as language, color of skin, texture of hair, customs, habits, traditions, and religion.

Here in this New World they have worked together for four hundred years to establish an ideal society or nation based on the freedom and equality of man.

It is one of the mysteries of the providence of God in bringing to these shores thousands upon thousands of Negroes [from] the continent of Africa to serve as slave labor in developing and establishing on these shores of the Republic of the United States of America.

Whether in war or in peace there never has been a turning point in the history of this nation without the aid and the presence of Americans of African descent. Alexander Hamilton, one of the founders of this nation, was a man of Negro ancestry.

Victory through Resistance

Unlike the Europeans who came to these shores, Negroes brought here from Africa had no traditions of the religious, social, political, and economic struggles for freedom that had plagued Europeans for a thousand years.

In mind and spirit, the Africans subject to slavery here were virgin soil for the seed of freedom and equality. They absorbed the teachings of our Founding Fathers; without question, they accepted the Bible as the Word of God; they believed that the preacher was divinely sent to preach the gospel of Jesus Christ. Unlike the American Indian, the Negro did not overthrow slavery and oppression by violence. They tried to achieve gentleness of spirit and kindness of heart. The Negro spirituals tell us more about the hopes and aspirations, the attitude of mind and spirit of Negroes than could be learned from volumes of literature on the subject.

Despite ignorance and poverty, the Negro has thrown off his handicaps as he advanced; there are no footprints backward. He placed his faith in God and the brotherhood of man set forth in the principles of American democracy.

He constitutes one-tenth of the population of the United States today. He is the best housed, the best fed, the most intelligent, the best educated, and enjoys more freedom in the United States of America than any other group of Negroes on the face of the earth.

Nonresistance to injustice and oppression, love of country, and goodwill to his fellowman shall still continue to be his chief weapon of defense for his survival, the welfare of his country, and the peace of mankind. We have it in our power to be foremost in the rank of the men and women who are the salt of the earth and the light of the world for all men everywhere who strive for peace on earth and goodwill among men.

While nations are drafting men and organizing armies to fight for the preservation of "Our Way of Life," and preservation of "Free Men," we call for the mobilization of our spiritual and moral strength in our churches, pulpits, schools, and newspapers to speak without compromise and firmly stand for the destruction of all artificial barriers between man and his fellowman.

We know that the Negro soldier has a far heavier load to carry than his military equipment, greater hunger and thirst to bear, and deeper wounds to his mind and spirit than his white comrades in arms.

Even while he fights, he must bear these things while wearing the uniform of his country, only to return home to face denial and inequality.

But it is assuring to recall that George Washington, in a speech in Boston, on Patriots Day, cited among the heroes of the American Revolution, Negroes who fought in the battle of Bunker Hill and thus paved the way for establishing the government of the United States of America.

The Negro destroyed over three million slave chains on the battlefields of the Civil War and returned home to freedom and citizenship. After fighting through two world wars, Negroes find social, political, and economic boundaries immensely widened.

The Negro, who is "the poor, blind Samson in our land," is growing new locks; not to destroy, but to build better and stronger temples of freedom and goodwill whose doors swing wide to welcome all mankind to enter and dwell together in absolute equality in the bonds of brotherhood and peace. This faith is as strong as the right hand of God.

Golden Candlesticks Shall Illuminate Darkest Africa

Ransom maintains his notion of history as teleological, moving from the silence of Africa on the world scene to its full blossoming as a major contributor to world civilization in economic (i.e., gold, diamonds, iron, tin) and other ways through the efforts of Africans in the United States. History's development along these lines is overtly presented in Scripture — Abraham, for example. Even the pain involved in these developments, such as the enslavement of Africans, points to the mysterious workings of God in bringing about the divine will.

•

Asleep. Asleep for more than five thousand years of the long, long night that enveloped the black man's Africa. Nowhere throughout the [long, long] night has history contributed a single line to break the silence, nor has it left any tell-tale hieroglyphics upon the broken ruins of pyramids, or columns of marble or stone. Age upon age of silence and the long, long sleep of Africa has been undisturbed by any of the great history-making events that have occurred or history-making personalities that have appeared through five thousand years of recorded history.

Egypt, Babylon, Persia, Greece, and Rome arose, ruled, flourished, and passed away. The black man's Africa knew it not. The new world of North and South America was discovered. Jesus

August 24, 1951, typed manuscript, housed in the Reverdy C. Ransom Collection, Payne Theological Seminary, Wilberforce, Ohio. Bishop Ransom made handwritten corrections, indicated here with brackets. Reprinted by permission of Mrs. Ruth L. Ransom and her son, Louis A. Ransom, Jr.

Christ was born, preached His gospel, was crucified, dead, buried, and ascended into heaven; but the black man's Africa slept undisturbed as one chapter after another of world history was written through the multiplying centuries.

The ways of God are strange and past finding out by mortal men. The patriarch, Abraham, who was called the "Friend of God," had his faith rudely tested over the question of the destruction by fire of the wicked people of Sodom and Gomorrah for the preservation of which he was pleading to the angels of God who had been sent to execute the work. In desperation Abraham cried, "Will not the judge of all the earth do right?"

So, we were tested in the great crisis of slavery, oppression, denial, and the power of the strong against the weak in the most vital forms of human relations. Some have felt that the God who created man had left him to his own device and declined to intervene in the tide of human affairs.

The greatest gift that God has bestowed upon man is freedom of choice, freedom of the will. This gift may prove to be either his salvation or his doom. God has not created for man a world of chance, but life in a world of complete harmony in nature, and human society making a complete pattern. [This pattern is made] to fit the plan that God has made [has designed] for the life of man, in this life and in the life to come [in this world and in the world to come]. But, this plan depends absolutely upon man's willingness to cooperate with God, [in this life and conduct of this world that God has created for man]. God is always seeking and calling for human cooperation. The choice of man not to cooperate produces the human discords that ensue, but God keeps the door open, always calling upon man to return and again keep step with God as He comes to work in cooperation with man in building that form of human life, or human society, on earth that has been the golden dream of mankind from the creation of the world.

The footprints of God across the various phases of the development and growth of human society are clearly marked upon the different pages of the many chapters of the development and growth of human society among different peoples of the world. We know now that Asia had developed a high state of civilization when cavemen clad in the skins of wild animals occupied Europe, but these uncivilized Europeans through the ages were developed into the dominating people of what we call modern civilization for the past five thousand years. For ages the Western Hemisphere knew nothing of this, until the discoveries of Christopher Columbus snatched them from the sea and made a highway for European civilization to cross over to this [the Western] Hemisphere.

They found the American Indians here in an undeveloped state of civilization, scattered into various tribes across North and South America and the adjoining islands of the Caribbean Sea. They had before them the task of conquering the wilderness [up to] of a vast continent; they needed manpower to supplement the labors of the little bands of colonists who had taken upon themselves the super-human task of building a new nation on these shores. They sought to avail themselves of the use of the American Indians who were close at hand, but the Indians refused to engage in enforced labor or submit to coercion or slavery in any form. They refused to ac-cept the white man's religion, or to become a part of his way of life; as a result countless tribal wars ensued. In desperation they sought to recruit labor until a door of relief was found among the inhabitants of equatorial Africa.

Beginning with the year 1627 a trickle of Africans began to be imported for slave labor; this soon grew to a mighty tide of slave labor secured from Africa. Unlike the Indians, the Africans submit-ted to enforced labor, accepted the white man's religion, customs, and his way of life. In a short time they had lost the language, cus-toms, and traditions of Africa, and were completely absorbed into the spirit and customs of the American colonies.

They learned from practice the industrial arts of civilization; without being able to read, they learned about the God of the Bible and accepted the Christian religion with a consuming fervor un-known since the early days of the planting of Christianity, so that, by the time of the American Revolution they were completely in-tegrated into all the currents of American life. It is thus that God made the institution of American slavery fit into His long-range plan for making Africa and the Africans His last reinforcements to building all humanity into a cooperative society where all vari-eties of the human race would live as one family on the different continents of this planet.

God reserved the Americas to be the nursery and the school for the training and development of the backward people. [God planted the African and his descendants here to go to school; the Europeans in every phase of European society became the formula for his education.] "God Sent the African Here to Go to School"; his training was the most thorough and severe to be found in his-tory. He started from scratch; there were no legends, no traditions, no inherited moral, social, political, or religious forms behind them. They had to learn the hard way under the lash, through physical pain, oppression, and suppression in every form of human suffering the institution of slavery could devise. God permitted the transplanted African to descend to the lowest depth of degradation of the human mind and spirit; the reason he permitted him to sink so low in the midst of the most highly developed civilization the world has ever known is because God intended to lift him up to a higher plane of development than the depth from which he came.*

In an inspired moment, David the psalmist, catching a glimpse of the future of his people, burst into song by declaring, "Though you have lain among pots, yet shall you become like a dove whose breast is covered with silver and its feathers with yellow gold." The past history of mankind reveals that the chief objectives have been for complete national domination and subjugation of their surrounding group for personal aggrandizement and power. The present world picture reveals that we are now engaged in the repetition of this age-long struggle that brought destruction to each one of the aggressors who have sought to unseat and bring into subjection their fellowmen. At the present time we are engaged in an international or worldwide contest between two opposing ideologies, communism and democracy. The spirit and objectives of these ideologies arise from opposing conceptions concerning the nature of man and the place of different groups in human society. The spirit of communism is Godless; it knows but one deity, "the state," but a state that is dominated and controlled by a small group of individuals, protected and defended by armed might to enforce its decisions over the defenseless majority. American democracy represents the slow and laborious progress of mankind from the overthrow of despotic kings, emperors, czars, and warlords to the increasing sovereignty of mankind in the realm of human relations. Our American democracy is founded upon the Bible; its chief cornerstone rests upon the fact that God is the common father of all mankind. All men are brothers; if brothers, then all men are equal. This is the very foundation upon which American democracy stands. Upon this conception we have established our American democracy. We do not seek by force of arms to dominate the world, but to give equal opportunity and freedom to each and all. To achieve without limit legal handicaps, to the extent

---

*This explanation of the enslavement of Africans is often referred to as "Redemptive Suffering." For additional information on this see Wilson Jeremiah Moses, *The Wings of Ethiopia* (Ames: Iowa State University Press, 1990), chap. 9. –Ed.

[limit of the boundaries] of their capacity and ability. Our democracy is not based upon race, creed, color, wealth, or nationality, but upon cooperation in the spirit of brotherhood.

The question of survival has been faced by every group, whether tribal, national, or racial, from the beginning of history up to now; none have been able to survive the bitter contest and rivalries that have in successive tides dominated the world for ages past. The present contest between communism and democracy, let us hope, may be the last to sweep this continent and the world. We are faced today with an entirely new dilemma; now it may not be so much a question of victor and vanquished, but rather that of the survival of humanity itself under the explosive power of the atomic bomb and other instruments of annihilation; we have no alternate choice but one: humanity must either cooperate on the basis of human brotherhood or face destruction in the resultant realm of human chaos, where social, economic, moral, and spiritual values have no place.

After more than 350 years of training in the ways of modern civilization, Americans of African descent have advanced no farther than the "grammar school" in their social, economic, civic, and political preparation. In the present era God is stepping up the tempo of their development for the worldwide part they shall play in the unified and peaceful cooperation of all members of the human family. This is the objective and goal of the Kingdom of God. Two "world wars," with another one primed to explode at any moment, shall furnish knowledge and experience for the stellar role they are to play with the continent of Africa as the stage of the Iliad of human relations on this planet. It shall take at least another century of "high school, college, and university" training in human relations before Americans of African descent shall be ready to come forth and banish the darkness as did the golden candlesticks in the seven churches of Asia Minor as described by John in the Book of Revelation.

In its reserves of natural resources, Africa is the richest continent on the earth. Its nearest rival is South America. Today Africa furnishes 90 percent of all the diamonds in the world and 70 percent of all the gold in the world. It has untouched reserves of iron ore, copper, and tin. We have hardly touched the surface of its potentials in reserve of rubber, coffee, cocoa, oils, and almost every variety of the fruits and vegetables in the world. The commercial materials of Africa contain the reserves upon which inhabitants of the other continents shall be compelled to draw for the next thousand years. It has an inexhaustible reserve of manpower to assist in its material development, but this manpower is untrained in the field of business, commerce, and trade; its leaders and teachers should consist of men who are not there to exploit and subjugate its manpower, or to loot its material resources for the selfish ends of predatory nations or great corporations upheld by armed might of military power.

A hundred years from now, Americans of African descent in the United States will number more than twenty-five million souls. They should furnish the sympathetic leadership for the black millions of Africans in the rich fields of human cooperation. Americans of African descent are the only dark-skinned people in the world who have looked the white man in the face for over two hundred years and lived. This achievement certainly was not the result of the white man's fear, for that he considered this dark-skinned group a menace to his unchallenged domination. The dark-skinned Americans on this continent had a technique and a [finesse] that arose from the inward spirit of brotherly kindness, non-resistance, and an attitude not of challenge but a will to cooperate peacefully in the pursuit of happiness for all. Europe and America have been the leaders of human progress for the past three thousand years in the realm of religion, morals, invention, and discoveries, in the realm of arts and sciences. Without controversy, the genius of this group has easily created what is known to us as modern civilization.

I believe that the great and outstanding contributions of Africa and the people of African descent to civilization shall not be scientific, material, philosophical, or intellectual, but emotional and spiritual. England, Europe, and the Americas have the endowments and the spirit for world leadership in these fields. Africa and the people of African descent have endowments in a realm that is distinct and apart from the material, economic, political rivalries of history. Today the modern world is "One World." The telegraph, steam, airplane, radio, and television have made it so, but these things have brought neither brotherhood, nor peace on earth, because these things are not the works of man. It is the dead body of human achievement at its best. It will remain a dead body until God through human agencies breathes into it the breath of life, and causes it to arise and become a living soul.

God seems to have set apart some of the families of the human race to make known and keep alive the true purpose of the creation of man, and the divine purpose, or reason, for man's existence. I do not consider this to be a controversial question. Some of the most highly civilized people that have ever lived were the most pagan and idolatrous the world had ever known. I have in mind the Egyptians, the Greeks, and the Romans.

God choose Abraham of Ur, of the Chaldees to establish and uphold the being and nature of God. "Hear O Israel, the Lord is one God." The Jewish people for the past three thousand years have borne witness to this doctrine to every people throughout Europe, North Africa...the islands of the western world.

The Jews scattered among the nations of the earth, despite persecution, still continue separate and apart to proclaim and uphold the "One God Doctrine." Since all the families of the earth are now one through their daily contacts upon the land, sea, and the air, they are in a position now to receive and accept the "One Blood Doctrine," as a final link in a chain that not only reveals the sovereignty of God, but also unites all the peoples of the earth by affirmation of the "One Blood Doctrine," which means the brotherhood, freedom, and equality of all mankind.

Until World War III or as many more such wars as may be required to convince a prostrate world of the utter futility of achieving world domination by any nation on behalf of rival ideologies, until that day arrives Africa will continue its grim and age-long silence while Americans of African descent complete their training to carry the "golden candlesticks" that shall be a light upon the paths to show her the way of active participation in the stream of modern civilization.

The Sixtieth Anniversary of the Founding of the A.M.E. Church in West Africa

The Americas and the Caribbean islands mark the location of the final phase of God's relationship to humanity. In the way that during the Diaspora the Jews developed skills that helped with the final establishment of Israel, African Americans during their time in the Western world have developed skills that will help them bring about the redemption of Africa — beginning with Liberia. (Readers will note Ran-

Typed document, n.d., housed in the Reverdy C. Ransom Collection, Payne Theological Seminary, Wilberforce, Ohio. Reprinted by permission of Mrs. Ruth L. Ransom and her son, Louis A. Ransom, Jr.

som's Eurocentrism with respect to depictions of Africans and Native Americans as uncivilized.) This endeavor has great promise because the strong spirituality of Africans puts them in an ideal position from which to revive Christianity.

•

More than three hundred years ago our fathers' fathers were brought in captivity and sold as slaves on the continents and adjoining islands of North and South America. This was God's way of launching the people of equatorial Africa into the current of modern civilization. God through the ages had reserved the Western Hemisphere from contacts with other parts of the world which had risen, flourished, and passed away.

He reserved it to let the nations learn, all the way down from [Nineveh], Egypt, Babylon, and Rome, what the mind and spirit of man could achieve by their own devices.

In the providence of God, the new world was reserved for the realization of the final phase of man's relation to his fellowman and the revelation of his relation to God.

The Republic of Liberia is the first attempt in history to establish a nation and government of their own upon the soil of West Africa. The men who pioneered this effort were not Africans but Americans of African descent, who, like Israel in Egypt, brought back to Africa all the learning [and] skills they had acquired in America and from Europeans.

For three thousand years the Jewish people have been scattered abroad among the nations of the world [by] whom they have been enslaved and cruelly oppressed. But through all those centuries their minds and hearts have returned to Jerusalem and the reestablishment of the Jewish people in the land of their forefathers.

In our own day and time we have lived to see the aspirations and hopes and age-long desire of the Jews fulfilled, and the reestablishment of a Jewish nation on the soil of Israel. In the providence of God, Israel could not undertake this venture until it had undergirded itself with financial strength and material influence and power.

Now that it is back upon the soil of its homeland, Israel has men who know how to build highways and throw bridges across its rivers and streams; it has men skilled in the knowledge of minerals, the best adaptable use of the soil, men who know how to apply electricity, steam, and the construction and navigation of airplanes.

It has the ability to bring water into its desert places and to drain its swamps so that Israel shall be made fruitful, prosperous, strong, and free. A miracle like this must come not only to Liberia but to all parts of Africa numerously inhabited by black people.

Africa must become aware and first remove the barriers that separate the Africans because of the hundreds of different languages and dialects and the different tribal customs and traditions that have kept the tribesmen separated and divided for thousands of years. Within the Republic of Liberia we have no such barriers to remove. The Republic of Liberia stands as a beacon light for [the] 150,000,000 black inhabitants of the continent of Africa.

The celebration of the sixtieth anniversary of the organization of the A.M.E. Church in Liberia and Sierra Leone is an era that belongs to history. In the Republic of Liberia we have a free and independent church established in a free and independent nation under the government and control of its citizens and its church members, all of whom are Africans or Americans of African descent.

Here at least the stage is being set for the development and power of leadership for Africans by Africans, in a manner similar to that which is taking place among the Jews in Palestine.

The pattern of the political government of Liberia was drawn along the lines of the Constitution of the United States of America with the absence of a background similar to the lines of the Constitution of the United States of America, but it did stand firmly upon the grounds of freedom, equality, and brotherhood.

Liberia was like America, a land rich and undeveloped in natural resources. Also like the United States [it] was surrounded by uncivilized Africans, even as the pioneers of America were surrounded by uncivilized Indians. American colonization has driven the Indians ever farther backward into the most undesirable portions of the land and threatens them with virtual [extinction]. The American Liberians are surrounded by a native population outnumbering them more than ten to one, yet they are living together on terms of friendship and peace.

Americans are not here to despoil, or to take material, political, or economic advantage of the people of this vast continent. They are here to give freely from the accumulation of wisdom, knowledge, and understanding learned in the school of both oppression and freedom.

The major religious denominations are represented here by the Methodist Church, the Episcopal Church, the Baptist Church, and other religious agencies along with the A.M.E. Church. As Protestants, we each present the same Bible and the same message of salvation from sin through Jesus Christ our Lord.

But African Methodism has something distinctive about it. It represents a distinctive form of ecclesiastical government under the auspices of black men and women. This church presents nothing that is new and original as a contribution to religious faith. When it withdrew from the Methodist Church, it took the doctrine and polity of that church along with it and has added nothing to it in the last 160 years.

Ours is not a church that is born out of the heat of theological controversy, but stands upon the doctrine that all men everywhere are of one blood and that in the church there should be neither nationality, race, nor color, but all meeting together on a plain of absolute freedom and equality. Upon that foundation, we firmly stand today even as the Republic of Liberia stands forth as a national government administered by black men, so the A.M.E. Church is here representing an ecclesiastical government administered by black men.

We have no authority over us except those of our own choosing. It is for us to demonstrate that in the church we have organized, there shall be absolutely no discrimination between any of our members in regard to nationality, race, color, or social and economic position, but we are all one in Jesus Christ our Lord.

The Spiritual Future of Man

The spiritual future of mankind may well be in the hands of the continent of Africa and the Africans, who have occupied it from prehistoric times. We are not prepared to say that God has favorites among the different nations and peoples on the earth. But history abundantly sustains the fact that God did recognize a certain group as "His Chosen People."

There are national groups that possess certain aptitudes, traits, and characteristics that make them distinctive. The different groups and nations that have inhabited Europe since the dawn of history have never produced one of the great religions. The white people have never at any time or in any place produced a religion.

The Indians, who were the aboriginal inhabitants of the Western Hemisphere, produced none of the great religions of the world. God chose the Hebrew people as the vehicle or instrumentality through which He would make a revelation of Himself to man.

He chose this people as His schoolmaster to teach all nations His divine will and purpose in regard to the spiritual life. This was but preparation for the revelation that was to come through Jesus Christ concerning sin and salvation. We have already said that the future spiritual history of mankind may well lie in the hands of the people of Africa.

Of one thing we may be certain: if the Africans will revive and exemplify the teachings of Jesus, they will find no national rivals who are seeking to establish the Kingdom of God on earth. Jesus declared, "My Kingdom is not of this world." It has nothing to do with philosophy, worldly knowledge, or material things. It is not something that belongs to literature; it is not in any book; it is a divine, supernatural union of the spirit of man with the spirit of God.

None will deny the fact that the Africans are the most emotionally and spiritually endowed people in the world. They are in the best position of any people on earth to come to the rescue of Christianity from the power of materialism, and the social, political, economic, and ethical devices that men are trying to substitute for the divine revelation of love, brotherhood, and peace which God intends to establish among men, "From the river to the ends of the Earth."

Men cannot shoot their way to peace with guns and tanks, or blast the path of its progress with atom bombs, nor can they bring it forth from the skies above on the swift wings of airplanes dropping death-dealing missiles from above.

From a cross on a lonely hill, a man with a wounded side and pierced hands still looks down upon us for the fulfillment of his word: "And I, if I be lifted up, from the earth will draw all men unto Me."

Part Two

Articles and Pamphlets

RACE PRIDE

"Find a man who has no pride and you have one whose past
    is inglorious and whose future is without hope.
It is pride that leads man to adventure, pride that steels him
    to endure, pride that brings him an ultimate triumph."
THERE IS PRIDE OF RACE, which vaunts itself upon the color
    of its skin, or, ruthless might, from seats of power;
A PRIDE OF RACE in blood unmingled with the warmth of
    equatorial suns;
A PRIDE OF RACE, the gifted spirits of whose group have
    borne the sword of conflict on the field blood,
Or who, in the vast empire of the mind,
Have won a crown of fadeless immortality.

BUT THE PRIDE OF RACE which breeds exclusiveness,
    intolerance, contempt,
For those who, struggling upward, seek freedom to express
The soul of a people in its higher forms,
Shall like a withered leaf, shrink, fade, and die,
Amid the decaying glories of its vanished power.

Whence from our youth shall spring
A PRIDE OF RACE to clothe their life with dignity, confidence,
    and the sense of power?
Honor and freedom of personality must be, along with
    reverence for one's own soul.

PRIDE IS NO SIN, but a sense of obligation and a pledge, to
    express the sanctities of personality,
And to realize the aims of manhood's highest strivings.
HEROIC SELF-ASSERTION clothes with strength dark-visaged
    men,

Reprinted by permission of the *A.M.E. Church Review.*

Who, according to their limitations and their powers,
Refuse to be denied free access to the passionate urge of
    living-life unbounded.

WE COUNT NOT PRIDE OF RACE, but personality, not color,
    but individuality.
Upon this lofty altitude the race-soul stands secure,
Beyond the reach of hands to do violence.
THIS PRIDE becomes the highest form of meekness which
    inherits the earth and the heaven, too.
Conscious of the divinity that dwells within, we may have
    peers, but no superiors
In a world which slowly, more and more, revolves from
    darkness into light.

                         — REVERDY C. RANSOM

The Negro and Socialism

Ransom is one of the few A.M.E. ministers to openly advo-cate socialism as the answer to the nation's socioeconomic and political problems in general and the African Ameri-can's problems in particular. The advances of the nineteenth century have resulted in material prosperity for some and a larger self-consciousness for all. This self-consciousness has created, among those who have worked hard without mate-rial benefit, a severe discontent. According to Ransom, it is only natural that the poor will see the material treasures of the rich and want compensation. Ransom continues by saying that socialism provides an important way of making societal adjustments that will result in equality. It does this by pro-moting altruism and democracy as well as the advancement of each person's capabilities in ways individualism cannot. Ransom concludes this essay with an apologetic outlining of socialism's characteristics and objectives, and puts all of this in line with God's call for justice through the Christ event.

•

The substantial wealth of man consists in the earth he cul-tivates, with its pleasant or serviceable animals and plants, and in the rightly produced work of his own hands. The material wealth of any country is the portion of its posses-sions which feeds and educates good men and women in it. In fact, it may be discovered that the true veins of wealth are purple — and not in rock, but in flesh — perhaps that even the final outcome and consummation of all wealth is the producing as many as possible full-breathed, bright-eyed and happy-hearted human creatures.

— Ruskin*

First published in the *A.M.E. Church Review*, 13, 1896–97. Reprinted in Philip S. Foner, editor, *Black Socialist Preacher* (San Francisco: Synthesis Publications, 1983), 282–89. Reprinted by permission of the *A.M.E. Church Review*.

*John Ruskin was a nineteenth-century critic of capitalism. Thomas Henry Huxley was a nineteenth-century biologist who supported Darwinism. Benjamin Kidd was a social philosopher of the late nineteenth and twentieth centuries who sought to bring into harmony religion and evolution. And Richard Ely was a college instructor and socialist of the late nineteenth and twentieth centuries whose book (*The Labor Movement in America*) was known to Ransom.

That the closing years of the nineteenth century are pregnant of great changes must be apparent even to the least observant. The minds of men are moving toward new goals; new battle cries are upon their lips. Men have come to regard the close of a century as the end of an epoch, and the beginning of a century as the commencement of a new era. The last century was an epoch of revolt against political despotism. The message of the eighteenth century to man was, "Thou shalt cease to be the slave of nobles and despots who oppress thee; thou art free and sovereign." The dawn of the nineteenth century opened an epoch of human progress unexampled in the history of the world. Universal education, universal suffrage, and the freedom of the slave are included in the long catalogue of splendid achievements. Since the beginning of the century applied science has transformed the world. The industrial revolution has given man such large dominion over the realm of nature, through the application of steam and electricity on an immense scale to machinery, that we stand in the midst of a new heaven and a new earth. With the acquisition of political power and the splendid conquests of science in the domain of nature, a larger self-consciousness has come to the masses.

"Since the middle of the century there has sprung up and spread [well] nigh throughout Christendom a deep discontent on the part of the workingmen. To give to the poor like tastes with the rich is to create an inevitable demand for substantial equality of condition and to stimulate discontent until such equality is secured." One of the clearest and profoundest writers on social and industrial questions has recently stated with what feelings the wage-earning class regards the immense conquests and progress of the century.

"What avails it that the waste places of the earth have been turned into highways of commerce, if the many still work and want, and only a few have leisure and grow rich? What does it profit the worker that knowledge grows, if all appliances of science are not to lighten his labor? Wealth may accumulate, and public and private magnificence may have reached a point never before attained in the history of the world: but wherein is society better, if the Nemesis of poverty still sits like a hollow-eyed spectre at the feast?"

Professor Huxley thus expresses his dissatisfaction with the existing state of things: "If it is true that the increase of knowledge, the winning of a greater domain over nature which is its consequence, and the wealth which follows upon that domain are to make no difference in the extent and the intensity of want with its concomitant physical and moral degeneration amongst the masses of the people, I should hail the advent of some kindly comet which would sweep the whole affair away as a desirable consummation." To the opinions of these thinkers, each one of whom is regarded as an authority in his department of inquiry, we have to add that standing over against huge monopolies and aggregations of capital are also gigantic labor organizations — "trade unions," "federations," while the "captains of industry" and "money kings" are confronted by labor leaders, "agitators," and "grand master workmen." Out of these conditions modern socialism has been born. This new movement has stirred the heart and touched the brain of every civilized land. Its presence is recognized by men of every school. Its powerful effect upon modern thought can be seen in politics, theology, philosophy, and literature. Socialism aims to bring about a readjustment of the relation between man and his brother man, and thus presents to the opening hours of the twentieth century problems surpassing in magnitude any with which civilization has had to deal. "It has ceased to be a theory," says Mr. Kidd, "it has begun to be a kind of religion." There is much vagueness of definition and misapprehension in regard to the true meaning of socialism.

It has been attempted to make it cover every scheme of social, political, or industrial reform. Socialism in a broad and general sense rejects the doctrine of selfishness which rules the present social order and affirms that altruism is a principle sufficient to govern the relations of men in the sense that it is opposed to individualism and does not regard society as composed of an army of warring atoms, but believes that social system to be the best in which the interests of the individual are made subordinate to the interests of society, while allowing freedom for the highest development of his own personality. Dr. Westcott, bishop of Durham, distinguishes individualism from socialism in the following words: "Individualism regards humanity as made up of disconnected atoms. Socialism regards it as an organic whole. The aim of socialism is the fulfillment of service; the aim of individualism the attainment of some personal advantage — riches, place, or fame. Socialism seeks such an organization of life as shall secure everyone the most complete development of his powers; individualism seeks primarily, the satisfaction of the particular wants of each one, in the hope that the pursuit of private interests will, in the end, secure public welfare." Socialism is not a form of anarchy; on the other hand it is a bitter foe. Socialists believe in a republican from of government — a democratic state. They do not believe in the abolition of government, the destruction of the state. They are, however, opposed to the centralization of government or political power. They seek not the overthrow of government, but to gain their ends through existing governments. Socialism is not a scheme of plunder. It aims not at an equal division of all property and wealth. Professor Richard T. Ely, who is a profound student of sociological science and social reform, defines socialism as follows: "Socialism is that contemplated system of industrial society which proposes the abolition of private property in the great material instruments of production and the substitution therefore of collective management of production, together with the distribution of social income by society and private property in the larger proportion of this social income."

By the material instruments of production is meant land, the forests, the mines, the tools. By gaining control of the instruments of production, it is proposed to put an end to the struggle for existence, by permitting all people to hold, manage, and distribute the surplus wealth which is now held and distributed by the few. In his great work on social evolution, Mr. Benjamin Kidd says: "True socialism has always one definite object in view, up to which all its proposals directly or indirectly lead. This is the final suspension of that personal struggle for existence which has been waged, not from the beginning of society, but, in one form or another, from the beginning of life."

We have gone as far as the limitations of a magazine article will permit in attempting to show the interpretation which leading exponents of sociology and social reform place upon the spirit of unrest which pervades almost every avenue of life and is the distinguishing mark of the present age. The present social order, with its poverty and vast reserve army of unemployed, cannot be accepted as final, as the ultimate goal for which the ages have been in travail. If man is the child of God, the present social order is not divine. God, who does not withhold from men their eternal heritage, [or] condemn them to an eternity of misery without giving to each an equal chance, has never sanctioned as by divine right a social order into which the vast majority must be born only to find "no trespass" posted upon every portion of the domain of nature, which is their heritage, and to lead a life of privation and suffering in a struggle to maintain an existence, which the bounteous storehouse of nature is able to sustain in comfort at the touch of toil and skill.

> The proudest now is but my peer,
> The highest not more high;
> Today of all the weary years,
> A king of men am I.

Socialism places its chief value upon man. Socialism, like the inspired Carpenter of Nazareth, places more value upon man than it does upon riches. It believes that the rights of man are more sacred than the rights of property, believes indeed, that the only sacred thing on earth is a human being. Socialism would bring all the people to participate in the rivalry of life upon a footing of equality, allowing to each individual the widest possible range for the development of his powers and personality, with freedom to follow wherever his abilities may lead him.

Socialism and industrial reform is not a question of race: it is not confined to the boundaries of any nation or continent; it is the question of man. The claims of society upon each individual, the bond of union and dependence of nation upon nation and man upon man, are becoming so strong as to sound forever the death knell of the domination of one race over another. The days of race domination are ended, the solidarity of the human race is coming to be admitted by all. It cannot but transpire, because of his past and present situation, that the program of socialism will in time powerfully appeal to the American Negro. The American Negro belongs almost wholly to the proletarian or industrial class. He constitutes a large and important factor in the development of this country and the production of its wealth. No question affecting our social and industrial future can be considered settled until he has rendered his judgment and cast his vote. The Negro by his valor assisted in establishing the American nation and he was present at its birth. By his patriotism and courage he helped to save the Union from destruction. During the days of slavery the effect of his unpaid labor was to debauch or reduce to serfdom the poor whites of the South, while it bound fetters upon free toilers of the North.

Since emancipation the Negro has been busy fighting for the recognition of his manhood, his political and social rights, and slaking his age-long thirst at the fountains of knowledge. But a generation ago, penniless, homeless, ignorant, and despised, he could have little thought beyond securing for himself the most elementary condition of civilized life. He has had little either for reflection, or for grappling with the deep questions that concern the destiny of nations or the welfare of mankind. But a new generation has been born under new conditions. A generation little influenced by the traditions of the past; a generation whose political faith will neither be a heritage nor a sentiment; a generation who will play an active part in every phase of the nation's life; a generation who, struggling from the depths of poverty and oppression, will not lend unwilling ears to a scheme which proposes such a readjustment of the social and industrial relations among men, as to permit all to stand upon an equal plane and each to have an equal chance in the race of life. The great army of toilers who have been crying out against our present social and industrial conditions have steadily refused to recognize the cause of the Negro workmen as one with theirs. This penniless freedman has had to contend against the frown and active opposition of organized labor for a chance to win his bread. In the great hives of industrial activity, the Negro finds almost every door leading to the skilled trades closed against him. In the South, where Negro labor is the main dependence, both their wages and the consideration with which they are treated [is] vastly inferior to [that] bestowed upon white laborers doing similar work.

It has been attempted to proscribe the Negro's sphere in the realm of industry, and to feel that it is an impertinence when he aspires beyond the limitations which have been set for him. The sphere of a Negro is not to be a barber, waiter, or a porter, any more than that of a Chinaman is to keep a laundry, or that [of] an Italian is to be a vendor of fruit, or that of a Jew to be a peddler. The great "labor unions" and "brotherhoods" of this country have, by introducing the word "white" into their constitutions, excluded the Negro from membership. Of course there are exceptions; many of the unions admit colored men. The Federation of Labor draws no color line, and the American Railway Union has submitted the question of striking the word "white" from their constitutions to a vote in all its branches. But when the Negro is admitted to membership in a labor union it is difficult to obtain work, and if he is successful in obtaining employment, it is by no means an infrequent occurrence for white laborers to refuse to work with him. This refusal is based not upon the ground of the Negro's inferiority as a workman, but on the ground of color. If, then, the Negro has little sympathy with, and takes little interest in, the cause of organized labor, his attitude is easily explained. It thus transpires that in the uprising and unrest against present social, economic, and industrial conditions, the Negro has been mostly a silent spectator. He has felt that it was not his fight. Indeed, the disasters and defeats which organized labor has suffered while battling for what it believed to be its rights have mostly accrued to the Negro's material benefit. They have been the lever which opened the doors of factories, mills, and mines, which organized labor had barred against his entrance. When once the strikers' places have been filled by Negroes, if they are permitted to return to work, they are compelled to take their places at the Negro's side.

There are more than a million Negro toilers in this land; they are citizens; they are here to stay. Their destiny is bound up with the destiny of the Republic, with the destiny of man. The Negro will not continue silent; even now there are signs that he is growing articulate. He will be a conspicuous figure on the stage of the twentieth century, in those days when social reform will be the burning question of the hour. In these days the old political parties are crying, "Rally! Rally!" but the people are demanding, "To what cry?" The old rallying cries no longer stir men's hearts. The forces that impelled men to action in the past are mostly spent forces. New issues have arisen, new causes stir men's hearts, among which socialism is the mightiest. The old relations of men, entrenched behind centuries of custom, will not be able to beat back the rising tide. The battles of socialism are not be fought by white men, for the benefit of white men. It is not, as we have said, a question of race, it is the question of man. So far as America is concerned, this question cannot be settled without the Negro's aid. The cause of labor, of the industrial army, is one. Our present social condition, which is organized not upon a basis of equal cooperation but of selfishness, will not give way until this army can present an organized, united, and unbroken front. While one class of toilers is outraged and oppressed, no man is free. When millions of toilers are degraded, labor is degraded, man is degraded. That the Negro will enthusiastically espouse the cause of socialism we cannot doubt. Social and industrial oppression have been his portion for centuries. When he comes to realize that socialism offers him freedom of opportunity to cooperate with all men upon terms of equality in every avenue of life, he will not be slow to accept his social emancipation. The day is not far distant when, with clearer eyes, through the smoke of battle, we shall see the steeples of a new civilization rising. A civilization which shall neither be Anglo-Saxon, Asiatic, nor African; but one which, recognizing the unity of the race and the brotherhood of man, will accord to each individual the full reward which the free exercise of his powers has won, and the right to stand upon an equal plane and share all of the blessings of our common heritage.

A Program for the Negro

*In this essay, Ransom, hinting at the effects of the social
gospel upon notions of democratic practice, explores the
growing role of the African American in the further development of the United States. Theologically, he asserts that
a proper relationship with God is premised upon proper
dealings with other humans. Hence, religious rationales for
oppressive behavior are destroyed. Ransom's platform also
requires a sense of responsibility on the part of African
Americans, who must take some initiative in outlining a
program for their development as citizens. He concludes by
presenting several programs advocated within African American communities, Booker T. Washington's program, among
others.*

•

Since the days when privilege, opportunity, and power were lodged
in the hands of a few, the boundaries of liberty, equality, and opportunity have been immensely widened. The vanished gods of
antiquity all had one defect in common: they bore upon themselves
the stamp of country and of race. Christianity created a new humanity and has revolutionized the conception of man's relation to
his fellowman; it knows neither race nor class.

This planet was built for the growth of manhood. Everything
on earth and in the sea, above, beneath, like the geist in Goethe's
Faust, plies at the whizzing loom of time to weave for humanity
the garments of nobler manhood. No man can degrade the manhood of another without doing violence to his Maker. No man can
surrender his manhood to another without dishonoring God. To
know this is to know the meaning of life and the world.

Under the influence of Christianity, the general diffusion of
knowledge, and the growth of democratic ideas in the state, both
in Europe and America, the more advanced members of society are
trying to lift the lower, if not to the political, industrial, and social heights whereon they stand, at least to a higher plane of life;
while the millions who have not attained equality and freedom of
opportunity are seeking to level up by removing every intervening
barrier.

First published in the *A.M.E. Church Review,* April 1900, 423–30. Reprinted by
permission of the *A.M.E. Church Review.*

Welcome each rebuff
That turns earth's smoothness rough,
Each sting that bids not sit nor stand, but go!
Be our joys three parts pain!
Strive and hold cheap the strain;
Learn nor account the pang; dare, never grudge the three.

Let us not always say,
"Spite of this flesh today
I strove, made head, gained ground upon the whole!"
As the bird wings and sings,
Let us cry, "All good things
Are ours, nor soul helps flesh more than flesh helps soul!"*

Oppressed people have not sought to throw off the yoke and gain rights, privileges, opportunities, by inertly waiting for fortuitous circumstances to transpire. They have sought to attain them by formulating and following out a policy or a program.

Many remedies have been proposed by deliverers and leaders of the people in various countries, to overcome the denial of social equality, class and race hatred, and tyranny. Giuseppe Mazzini, the Italian patriot who strove through a long and stormy career for Italian liberty, sought the elevation and deliverance of his oppressed fellow countrymen by urging them to fulfill their duties to their fellowman rather than to clamor for rights. His program is fully outlined and discussed in his priceless little treatise entitled *Duties of Man.* His watchwords were, "Duties and not rights, self-sacrifice and not self-seeking, association and not competition, humanity and not the individual, God and not the opinions of mankind." The essence of his teachings may be outlined in the following paragraph taken from his *Duties of Man.*

Working men, brothers! When Christ came and changed the face of the world, He spoke not of rights to the rich, who needed not to achieve them; not to the poor, who would doubtless have abused them, in imitation of the rich; He spoke not of utility, nor of interest, to a people whom interest and utility had corrupted; He spoke of duty, He spoke of love, of sacrifice, and of faith; and He said that they should be first among all who had contributed most by their labor to the good of all. And the word of Christ breathed in the ear of

---

*Robert Browning's "Rabbi Ben Ezra."

a society in which all true life was extinct, recalled it to existence, conquered the millions, conquered the word, caused the education of the human race to ascend one degree on the scale of progress.

Count Tolstoi, the great Russian novelist and reformer, would secure to his countrymen their rights, and place all men upon an equal plane by having them follow the teachings of Jesus as contained in the Golden Rule and in St. Matthew [5:38–39]: "You have heard that it hath been said, An eye for an eye, and a tooth for a tooth; But I say unto you that you resist not evil." "The simple meaning of these words suddenly flashed full upon me. I accepted the fact that Christ meant exactly what He said, and though I had found nothing new, all that had hitherto obscured the truth arose before me in all its solemn importance."* He maintains in his book entitled *Life* that a man should renounce the individual aims of his life and devote his life in love to his fellow creatures, thus finding his life in doing God's will and abstaining entirely from violence.

Parnell, the Irish patriot, sought the liberation and elevation of his long-oppressed people through home rule, believing that the affairs of the Irish in Ireland in the hands of Irishmen would be so managed as to overcome the evils suffered under British rule.

It might be interesting in this connection to cite a brief quotation from Henry George, who sought to establish right relations and equal opportunities for all men by advocating a single tax upon land value.

> In seeking to restore all men to their equal and natural rights, we do not seek the benefit of any class, but of all. For we both know by faith and see by fact that injustice can profit no one and that justice must benefit all.
>
> We do not seek to better God's work; we only seek to do His will. The equality we would bring about is not the equality of fortune, but the equality of natural opportunity; the equality that reason and religion alike proclaim; the equality in usufruct of all His children to the bounty of Our Father who art in Heaven.

The examples cited above show us what peoples among civilized nations who have been denied equality of privilege and opportunity have done to overcome the opposition to their progress. We

---

*Tolstoi, *My Religion*, 10.

are not now to discuss what has been done for the Negro by others to assist him in attaining equality and in maintaining the rights which have been conferred upon him, but to discover what the Negro is doing for himself; to see if the race has adopted any policy or has attempted to formulate a program.

Within the last year assemblies composed of the best heart and brain, the foremost representatives of Negro manhood and womanhood, have attempted to formulate a program for the race by means of which they hope to solve the so-called unhappy Negro problem in this land, and put the race on the highway to a future which will assure the same liberty and opportunity that is accorded to all.

At the Tuskegee conference held at Tuskegee, Alabama, February 22, 1899, Professor Booker T. Washington, president, the following declaration was promulgated:

1. Notwithstanding the experience of the past year, we urge our people not to forget that in most of the essential things which now, to the Negro, are homes, property, employment, business, education, and development of moral and Christian character, we have never had greater opportunities.

2. Since the interests of both races are one, we should cultivate, in every honorable way, the most friendly relations with our white neighbors and, in turn, expect them to do all in their power for our elevation, as what lifts up one lifts up the other.

3. At least 5,000,000 Negroes in the South are still unable to read or write. In some southern states the race is increasing faster than it is being educated, yet the amount given per year for the education of each colored child is less than one dollar. These serious facts should lead us to make every possible sacrifice for education.

4. We urge our young people to look more on the serious side of life, that they may be kept from idleness and encouraged to cultivate habits of saving instead of spending so much on outward show, and we would impress all with the fact that profitable employment can only be had as we prove ourselves steady and reliable.

5. It is most important that a larger number of our educated young men and women settle among the people in the country, and teach them by precept and example, not only in education and religion, but also farming, dairying, poultry, stock, and fruit raising and buying land. With prosperous and pleasant homes, the present tendency to the cities will be restrained.

6. We urge our people to put down denominational prejudices

as they relate to public schools, to cooperate along business and educational lines, without regard to church affiliations.

7. We must use well the forces in hand. These will lay the foundation for securing higher privileges and opportunities.

In addition to this, it was proposed to deliver lectures throughout the year to local Negro conferences on the following subjects:

1. How to raise pigs; 2. What crops pay best; 3. How to raise poultry; 4. How to plant a garden; 5. How to begin buying a home; 6. The value of a diversified crop; 7. How the wife can assist the husband; 8. How the husband can assist the wife; 9. The right kind of minister and teacher; 10. How to make the house and yard beautiful; 11. How to live at home instead [of] out of the store; 12. Importance of keeping the children busy in school and out of school.

It will be seen from this that Mr. Washington and his associates hope to lift up their race through preparing them for industrial opportunities, by thrift, education, and the moral and religious forces. Nothing is said about politics, no reference is made to political action, which has been thought for so long by many to be the lever by which the race would be lifted to the enjoyment of its rights.

The National Association of Colored Women, which met in Chicago, Illinois, August 14–16, 1899, was presided over by Mrs. Mollie Terrell, a highly educated and cultured woman, with whom were associated women from every section of the United States, representing the best brains of the womanhood of the race. Their program considers the need of their race under the following themes:

1. Why the National Association of Colored Women Should Devise Means for Establishing Kindergartens.

2. Social Necessity of an Equal Moral Standard for Men and Women.

3. One Phase of the Labor Question.

4. Convict Lease System as It Affects Child Nature.

5. Lynch Law.

6. Prison Work.

7. The Temperance Reform in the Twentieth Century.

8. The Future Club Work of Our Women.

9. Jim Crow Car Law.

10. Racial Literature.

The National Afro-American Council, which met in Chicago, Illinois, August 17–19, 1899, was composed of the foremost representatives of the colored race: bishops, ministers, lawyers, doctors, college professors, editors, legislators, authors, mechanics, etc. The objects of the Afro-American Council are set forth as follows:

1. To investigate and make an impartial report of all lynchings and other outrages perpetrated upon American citizens.

2. To assist in testing the constitutionality of laws which are made for the express purpose of oppressing the Afro-American.

3. To promote the work of securing legislation which in the individual state shall secure to all citizens the rights guaranteed them by the Thirteenth, Fourteenth, and Fifteenth Amendments to the Constitution of the United States.

4. To work in the aid of prison reform.

5. To recommend a healthy migration from terror-ridden sections of our land to states where law is respected and maintained.

6. To encourage both industrial and higher education.

7. To promote business enterprises among the people.

8. To educate sentiment on all lines that specially affect our race.

9. To inaugurate and promote plans for the moral elevation of the Afro-American people.

10. To urge the appropriation for a school fund by the federal government to provide education for citizens who are denied school privileges by discriminating state Laws.

These objects set forth above may be said to clearly represent both the policy and program. While in session they deliberated upon the following subjects:

1. Business Enterprises of the Race and How to Foster Them.

2. Report of Emigration Bureau.

3. Best System of Education Needed for the Race.

4. Best System of Moral Training — Its Needs and Methods.

5. Report of Legislative Bureau.

6. Disfranchisement.

7. Separate Coach Law.

8. Convict Lease System.

9. Lynch Law in America.

10. The Lynching Excuse.

11. Hardships of Colored Laborers Who Are Transported from the South to Work in Northern Mines.

The Hampton Negro Conference, which convened at Hampton, Virginia, July 19, 1899, discussed the following subjects as those most important in their view to the Negro, his progress, and well-being:

1. A Few Hints to the Southern Farmer.

2. Modern Industrialism and the Negro of the United States Historically Considered.

3. The Negro Pulpit and Its Responsibilities.

4. The Burden of the Educated Negro Woman.

5. The Place of Race Consciousness in the Life of the People.

6. The Various Phases of Woman's Work.

7. The African in the Aryan World.

8. The Possibilities for the Negro in Industrial Pursuits.

9. The Negro in Fiction as Portrayed and as Portrayer.

By these programs we are able to read the minds of the leaders of thought among the colored people of the United States. No more does the Negro turn to the declaration of national conventions of the great parties, to state legislatures, or to congressional action for equal opportunities and a recognition of his rights. He seeks to elevate the home and raise the domestic standards. He believes more in the efficiency of the moral forces and the educational advantages and opportunities. The world, at least so far as the United States is concerned, knows both the place and plan which the majority of the Negro's fellow citizens would have him occupy. That place is always secondary, one of subservience.

Many of the Negro's best friends have mapped out for him many programs, programs which agree with those he would make for himself. But notwithstanding all this goodwill on the part of his friends, an unwritten program is in the heart and mind of the majority of the people of this land which the Negro is relentlessly and pitilessly forced to follow. The goal of his ambitions is beset with difficulties, his aspirations may not rise above the prejudices of his fellow citizens without provoking a hand-to-hand conflict as fierce as the contest of two opposing armies upon a field of battle.

Notwithstanding this, the Negro has lost neither heart nor hope. These programs presented above are the confession of the Negro's faith in himself, faith in his country and faith in the future. There is in them no evidence that the Negro has lost heart and surrendered after a generation of struggle with American civilization. There is in them no evidence that he is turning his back on progress, Christianity, and civilization; there is in them no evidence that patriotism is waning or that he is behind the foremost in his respect for the Constitution of his country and its laws; no evidence that he seeks African emigration or segregation in a separate state to escape from the difficulties that lie in his pathway of progress.

In these programs the best heart and brain of Negro manhood and womanhood addresses itself, not to the unattainable, the commercial, but to the actual facts of his condition. There is no evasion here, no cowardice, no note of terror or of fear, but a splendid courage which, clad in the robes of wisdom, stands majestically in every position taken and moves with unfaltering step up the steep ascent of every highway of progress he has built or is building for his feet to tread. The Negro shows to the world by these programs that he is not seeking to make a current for his life separate and distinct from the currents that bear onward the mighty sweep of the life of his fellow citizens, but to unite and blend his tributary streams with the life currents and activities of his fellow citizens.

Whether there be rocks of disaster ahead and stormy waters, or plain sailing and a prosperous breeze, the Negro will move down the currents of American life aboard the same ship of destiny, filling from the highest to the lowest positions in its crew, and having a share in the cargo of our splendid heritage, which he, in common with others, will seek to deliver in safety both to the generations

of his children and the children of his fellow countrymen in years
to come.

The Institutional Church

*Ransom's Institutional Church, which he developed in Chi-
cago in 1900, marks his attempt to bring the social gospel
into full contact with the A.M.E. Church and the needs of
Chicago's underprivileged citizens. Although he received support from some of Chicago's key figures, such as Clarence
Darrow, some within the A.M.E. Church questioned the
importance and relevance of this Institutional Church and
Social Settlement House. In this short article Ransom defends this church and its work. Through the work of this
church, Ransom believes the best of the Christian gospel is
brought to bear on industrial and social concerns, hence allowing citizens to contribute to the "common good." In this
way, Ransom seeks to bring together the three elements that
make for responsible citizens and society: church, school, and
home.*

•

The Institutional A.M.E. Church of Chicago was not born before
its time. It comes to meet and serve the social conditions and industrial needs of the people, and to give answers and solutions to the
many grave problems which confront our Christianity in the great
centers of population of our people. It is not a dream spun out of
the gossamer web of fancy; it is not an evasion, an abridgment,
or a short-cut method for the realization of Christ and the Christ
life in the life of the people. It is a teaching, ministering nursing-
mother, and seeks through its activities and ministrations to level
the inequalities and bridge the chasms between rich and poor, the
educated and the ignorant, the virtuous and the vicious, the indo-
lent and the thrifty, the vulgar and the refined, and to bring all ages
and classes of the community to contribute to the common good.

The kindergarten has an enrollment of nearly eighty children
from three to six years of age, with six teachers; it is free to
all. The day nursery is open from six in the morning until seven

First published in the *Christian Recorder*, March 7, 1901. Reprinted by permission
of the *AME Christian Recorder*.

in the evening, where children of women who go from home to work by the day are cared for at a cost of five cents per day. The mother's meeting brings together each week the mothers of the children in the kindergarten and nursery, when the problems of child life and the home are discussed, and where that contact is enjoyed which gives courage to battle with adverse circumstances and encouragement and hope to overcome obstacles. The reading room, library, and gymnasium are open day and night to all ages. There are boys' clubs, girls' clubs, men's clubs and women's clubs, and classes formed for recreative, industrial, and educational purposes. Vocal and instrumental music is taught. Classes in sewing, dressmaking, and cooking are carried on at a nominal cost. The pennysaving bank teaches the children to form habits of economy and assists the older ones in saving and accumulating small sums of money which would be otherwise frittered away and worse than wasted.

Good pictures are conspicuously placed to educate the eye. Good music is furnished plentifully at frequent recitals and entertainments, while at least once a week some voice of authority is heard on our lecture platform upon a helpful theme. In the midst of our activities, of which these enumerated are a part, is planted the church and the influence of the home life which is given to the whole scheme by the constant residence of the pastor and his three assistants, who live in the building and are in constant touch with each phase of the work every day and night.

In the Sunday school and church the old hymns and simple gospel songs are sung. The collection table has been discarded. Each person is required to pledge what they will give each week, and at the close of the service while an offertory is being played the collection is taken in a quiet and orderly manner.

African Methodism has a great opportunity here to set an example to the entire connection, that under the inspiration of the gospel, moral and social redemption may come to our people in a practical way.

It is our belief that the days of the old method of church work are numbered, and without [with] our activities broadened everywhere the Holy Ghost will breathe an inspiration for enlarged activities in the souls of those who will see and use the opportunity for service which we, through ignorance, blindness, or prejudice, have neglected or refused. Through the Institutional Church our connection is stripping itself to enter the moral and spiritual race of the twentieth century, with the fleetness of foot and the wisdom of method which will make her equal to the forces she has to combat and the obstacles she must meet and overcome.

> A mightier church shall come whose convenient word
>   Shall be the deed of love. — Not Credo then —
> "Amo" shall be the password through its gates,
> Man shall not ask his brother anymore
> "Believest thou?" but "Lovest thou?" and all
> Shall answer at God's altar, "Lord, I Love."
> For hope may anchor, Faith may stir; but Love,
> Great Love, alone is captain of the soul.

Paul Cuffe

Paul Cuffe (1759–1817), the Boston merchant, was an early figure in the forging of relationships between African Americans in the United States and Africans along economic and religious lines. Using his own resources, Cuffe made possible the movement of some African Americans to Africa as missionaries. He also made an effort to establish trade between the United States and Africa. In this essay, Reverdy Ransom recognizes Cuffe as being as significant for the progress of African Americans as the better-known Frederick Douglass. Ransom points out that Cuffe did great work in the effort to secure the vote for African Americans from his home in Massachusetts.

●

Seagirt, sun-kissed, and fanned by ocean breezes from southwest blowing, the little isle of Cuttyhunk keeps watch and ward over the entrance to stately Buzzards Bay. The billows of old Atlantic ceaseless surge on its southern shore, while on the east its bold bluffs curl back the shining waters of the Vineyard Sound.*

First published in the *A.M.E. Church Review*, January 1905, 223–34. Reprinted by permission of the *A.M.E. Church Review*.

*In the preparation of this sketch we acknowledge our indebtedness to the New Bedford, Mass., *Evening Standard*, to Edwin B. Jourdain, Esq., and Mr. William C. Nell, Patriots of the Revolution. We lay small claim to originality; ours has been the pleasant task of patching and weaving together the researches and investigations which have cost others a vast amount of toil.

But not upon its charming location does the islet depend for its attractiveness. Over a century ago, when all the territory around about was included in the ancient town of Dartmouth, a New Bedford colored man made the first move in Massachusetts looking toward the granting to the Negro of rights of suffrage equal to those enjoyed by whites. He was Paul Cuffe, a native of Cuttyhunk and a resident of Dartmouth; a black man of note who is classed as one of the colored patriots of the Revolution.

In later years the fame of Frederick Douglass, another colored leader who claimed New Bedford as the place of his bringing up, eclipsed that of his predecessor of the Revolution, until nowadays Cuffe is almost forgotten. Without attempting to institute a comparison between the two men, it is only fair to say that Cuffe was as famous in his day as Douglass came to be later and that New Bedford can boast of two of the most prominent leaders the black race has ever produced in this country.

In William C. Nell's "Colored Patriots of the Revolution" Paul Cuffe is credited with having brought about legislative enactment which enfranchised the colored people of the state. The story is supported with a mass of documentary evidence, including among other things the original petition, which was drawn up by Paul and his brother, John Cuffe, signed by a number of Dartmouth colored men, and presented to the general court, setting forth that the blacks were subject to taxation without enjoying in return the right of suffrage, and praying for such relief as was proper.

The story was in brief as follows: Some time subsequent to 1770, and after three months' detention as a prisoner at New York in the hands of the British, Paul Cuffe returned to Westport (Dartmouth) and engaged in farming with his two brothers. He and his brother John, during this period, were called upon by the collector for the district in which they resided for the payment of a personal tax. "It appeared to them" (this is quoted from Nell) "that by the laws and constitution of Massachusetts taxation and the whole rights to citizenship were united. If the laws demanded of them the payment of personal taxes, the same laws must necessarily and constitutionally invest them with the rights of representation and being represented in the state legislature. But they had never been considered as entitled to the privilege of voting at elections, or of being elected to places of trust and honor. Under these circumstances they refused to comply. The collector resorted to the force of the laws; and after many delays and vexations, Paul and his brother deemed it most prudent to silence the suit by payment of the demands, which were only small. But they resolved, if it were possible, to obtain the rights which they believed to be connected with taxation. In pursuance of this resolution, they presented a respectful petition to the state legislature which met with a warm and almost indignant opposition from some in authority. A considerable majority, however, perceiving the propriety and justness of the petition, were favorable to the object, and with an honorable magnanimity, in defiance of the prejudice of the times, a law was enacted by them rendering all free persons of color liable to taxation, according to the ratio established for white men, and granting them all the privileges belonging to other citizens. This was a day equally honorable to the petitioner and the legislature; a day in which justice and humanity triumphed over prejudice and oppression; and a day which ought to be gratefully remembered by every person of color within the boundaries of Massachusetts, and the names "of John and Paul Cuffe should always be united with its recollections."

This is the story as Nell tells it. He copied it from a sketch of Cuffe which appeared years before in the *Liverpool Mercury,* a sketch for which the data was furnished by Cuffe himself at the time of his visit to England, and which was subsequently incorporated, with scarcely any modification, in every life of Cuffe that appeared.

The following document will show conclusively that he knew himself every inch a man and had the spirit of a free man to contend for his manhood rights. His brethren had long paid their tax levy under protest, and now Paul, his brother John, and five others, made this appeal to the general court.

"To the Honorable Council and House of Representatives in General Court Assembled for the State of Massachusetts, in New England:

"The petition of several poor Negroes and mulattoes who are inhabitants of the town of Dartmouth, humbly showeth: That we, being chiefly of African extract, and by reason of long bondage and slavery we have been deprived of enjoying the profits of our labor or advantage of inheriting estates from our parents, as our neighbors, the white people, do; yet of late, contrary to the invariable custom and practice of the country, we have been and now are taxed both in our polls and that small pittance of real estate which, through much hard labor and industry, we have got together to sustain ourselves and families withal.

"We apprehend it, therefore, to be hard usage, and will doubtless (if continued) reduce us to a state of beggary whereby we shall become a burden to others, if not timely prevented by the interposition of your justice and power.

"Your petitioners further show that we apprehend ourselves to be aggrieved, in that while we are not allowed the privilege of freedmen of the state, having no vote or influence in the election of those who tax us, yet many of our color (as is well known) have cheerfully entered the field of battle in the defense of the common cause, and that (as we conceive) against a similar exertion of power (in regard to taxation) too well known to need recital in this place.

"We most humbly request, therefore, that you would take our unhappy case under serious consideration, and, in your wisdom and power grant us relief from taxation, while under depressed circumstances; and your petitioners as in duty bound shall ever pray

> John Cuffe,
> Adventure Child,
> Paul Cuffe
> Sam'l Gray, his X mark,
> Pedro Howland, his X mark,
> Pedro Russel, his X mark,
> Pedro Coggeshall, his X mark,
> Dated at Dartmouth, Feb. 10, 1780."

In the handwriting of John Cuffe appears this memorandum:

This is the copy of the petition which we did deliver unto the Hon. Council and House for relief from taxation in the day of our distress, but ewe received none.

Though unsuccessful, Paul Cuffe and his brother John were not discouraged; that indomitable will was exhibited here as all through his life, and the following year we find the attack renewed in another quarter. This time the appeal for justice was to their neighbors and townsfolks:

To the Selectmen of the town of Dartmouth greeting; We, the subscribers, your humble petitioners, desire that you should in your capacity, put a stroke in your next warrant for calling a town meeting; so that it may be legally laid before said town, by way of vote, to know the mind of said town, whether all free Negroes or mulattoes shall have the same privileges in the said town of Dartmouth as the white people have respecting places of profit, choosing offices and the like, together with all other privileges in all cases that shall or may happen to be brought in this our said town of Dartmouth. We, your petitioners, as in duty bound, shall ever pray.

> John Cuffe
> Paul Cuffe
> Dated at Dartmouth, 4th mo., 22d, 1781.

History says not what was the result of this petition. But it was just about this period that the courts of our commonwealth decided that under the noble bill of rights and constitution adopted by our state, slavery could not exist in Massachusetts, and acknowledge the equality of man, before the law, we might be warranted in assuming that their petition prevailed.

It remained for Mr. James B. Congdon, of New Bedford, in 1868 to seek to prove, after an exhaustive investigation conducted at the request of George H. Moore, librarian of the New-York Historical Society, that Nell's story was inaccurate. Mr. Congdon's investigation led him to the conclusions that the memorandum (of John Cuffe), while genuine, was erroneous. There is no record of the petition ever having reached the general court, furthermore, there was no need of its being presented. "In the year of 1778," wrote Mr. Congdon, "in papers which have never been published," a constitution was framed by Massachusetts by the general court of that year, sitting as a convention. The provision in relation to voting was as follows:

"Article V. Every male inhabitant of any town in this state, being free and 21 years of age, excepting Negroes, Indians and Mulattoes, shall be entitled to vote, etc."

This constitution was rejected by the people. A convention elected by the people met in September 1779. They had [by] March 2, 1780, finished their work; [in] October 1780, the new constitution went into effect. In this the dequalification of the Negroes and others was removed. The fundamental law, which up to that time had deprived these people of the right to vote, clearly set forth in the legislative form of government which had been rejected, now placed them, in this respect, in the same condition as the whites.

Whether Mr. Congdon's view is correct or not, this does not alter the fact that Paul Cuffe's petition was the first suggestion on record that the blacks be granted the same rights as the whites. The colored man of Dartmouth, with his brother, protested against being taxed without representation. The justice of the protest was established by the subsequent action of the constitutional convention.

Paul Cuffe was born, poor and lowly, in the year 1759. His father, John Cuffe, was a native of Africa, who had been held in slavery by one Slocum of the town of Dartmouth, but having inborn the soul and aspiration of a man, he learned the English language, labored long and wearily over hours, and at last was enabled to purchase himself, and stood before man as well as God a free man.

He married Ruth Moses, an Indian woman, thus linking in heart and hand two races already joined in misfortune. He died when Paul was only fourteen years of age and when he had no opportunity to acquire any sort of an education. He seems, however, to have been remarkably diligent and persevering; in spite of the necessity he was under to support his father's family, he attained some proficiency in arithmetic and such skill in navigation as to enable him to command vessels in voyages to all parts of the world.

At twenty-five years of age he married a descendant of his mother's tribe. Paul was one of the earliest to go from his community to the Grand Banks fishing, and so profitable did it prove that many of his neighbors in Westport engaged in [Grand] Banks fishing.

He now formed a connection with Michael Wainer, his brother-in-law, who had several sons well qualified for sea service, four of whom afterward became captains and first mates. They built a twenty-five-ton vessel for trading purposes and quickly succeeded it with a forty-two-ton whaler. In 1795 they built the *Ranger*, of sixty-nine tons, out of profits of their whaling venture.

The other boats were now sold and with a cargo worth two thousand dollars, they sailed for a trading voyage to the eastern shore of Maryland. The appearance of this vessel, manned and commanded by a crew of Negroes, was a source of surprise and alarm to the inhabitants, who feared the sight would inspire their slaves to rise in revolt. As Captain Paul's papers were correct, the customs officials could not prevent his entry, and his unassuming manner and quiet dignity, coupled with the exemplary conduct of his crew, soon dispelled the people's fears and changed them from their prejudices, and, to make amends, they extended the strangers openhanded hospitality. As a result Paul found no difficulty in disposing of his cargo to excellent advantage, and securing at very profitable rates a return cargo; arriving home he sold his cargo of corn and cleared one thousand dollars on the round trip.

After several prosperous voyages, he purchased a homestead and farm adjoining in Westport. We find from the land records of Bristol County that this was in 1799, and that for the homestead of forty acres he paid one thousand dollars and for the farm of one hundred acres, he paid two thousand five hundred dollars.

This farm was on the west shore of the east branch of the Accoaxet River, about four miles below Hix bridge, in Westport. The house of Paul Cuffe is standing today, as are the remains of his wharf and storehouse, while hard by dwell some of his descendants, living on acres which have been owned by their family for generations and which belonged to one branch of their common ancestry before the first pilgrim landed on Plymouth Rock or Columbus discovered the new world.

Captain Paul continued to prosper and the land records show his numerous transactions in real estate, buying and selling farm lands, and loaning money to his fellow townsmen on mortgages and securities. He had, however, a commercial "turn of mind" and his predilection for the sea. In 1800 he built a brig of 162 tons burthen [burden] and placed his nephew, Captain Thomas Wainer, in command. In 1806 in company with Wainer, he built the ship *Alpha,* and commanded her on a voyage to Savannah, Wilmington, Gottenburg [Gothenburg, Sweden], and back again to Philadelphia. About the year 1810 he and Wainer built the brig *Traveler,* of 109 tons burthen. This was in many respects his most notable vessel, the vessel in which he sailed later on his great mission of humanity. It was this vessel that, on one of her voyages, brought from Spain merino sheep, the second lot ever landed in America.

By every natural instinct Captain Paul Cuffe was a philanthropist, and from William Armstead's valuable book, we gather the following interesting event: Captain Paul experienced keenly the disadvantages of his own necessarily limited education, and he determined that his children should not suffer for a like cause. There was no school in his vicinity, and so he called a meeting of his neighbors to discuss plans for providing school facilities. All agreed as to the necessity of a school, but it seemed impossible to agree as to details, and no action resulted. Paul, taking matters into his own hands, erected a schoolhouse on his own land, at his personal expense, and threw it open for the use of the neighborhood.

What an example of magnanimous, noble manhood. This scion of two wronged and suffering races, extending with open hand the lamp of knowledge to all alike, regardless of race or color, as well as to the offspring of the oppressed.

Most especially did Paul Cuffe's big sympathetic heart go out to his brethren in bondage and his benighted race in the dark continent. The conditions surrounding slavery in America left little chance to aid the slave, and so in 1811, in his own brig, *Traveler,* with his Negro crew, he sailed to Sierra Leone, to study the people, their needs, and how best to elevate them. He labored among them a while, established a Society of Friends, and then sailed to England with a cargo of native products, and taking with him a native to educate in England.

He arrived in Liverpool in August 1811; it was an event worthy of notice, as the following press comments show, viz: *Edinburgh Review,* August 1811: "On the first of the present month a vessel arrived at Liverpool with a cargo from Sierra Leone, the owner, master, mate and whole crew of which are free Negroes. The master, who is also the owner, is the son of an American slave and is said to be very well skilled, both in navigation and trade, as well as to be of a very pious and moral character.

"It must have been a very strange and animating spectacle to see this free and enlightened African entering as independent trader with his black crew into that port, which was so lately the nidus of the slave trade."

Paul Cuffe remained in England two months and was very well received by men of business and of letters. Twice he visited London, the second time on the express invitation of the Board of Africa Institutions, which had become greatly interested in his plans of uplifting his race and whose admiration and assistance he completely won. He bore highly complimentary letters of introduction from American merchants, and was the guest of one of the directors of the above society during his sojourn in London.

So far as known, Captain Paul Cuffe was the first American Negro to visit England and appeal to Englishmen [on] behalf of his benighted and oppressed people; indeed, he was one of the earliest, black or white, to go forth on such a mission.

Certainly no man, not excepting our own peerless Douglass, presented in himself a stronger argument for the cause he sought to further, than this son of the African slave, who went forth on his mission in his own vessel, commanded by himself, manned by an efficient Negro crew and both vessel and the funds with which he so thoroughly equipped his expedition being the product of his own industry, backed only by the ennobling aspirations of his inherent manhood and his persistent, courageous will. His scheme of carrying a number of intelligent American Negroes to Sierra Leone to instruct the natives in the arts of civilization was interrupted by the war of 1812; but at the cessation of hostilities he sailed again with thirty-eight picked men for Sierra Leone, and at an expense of four thousand dollars from his own private purse, in addition to the funds contributed by the English society, he established his colony, equipped most thoroughly with everything necessary to aid them in teaching the natives how to cultivate their country and better their condition.

A race that has produced such a man has no right to despair. The historian tells us that he was a man of noble appearance; tall, well formed; his countenance blending gravity with modesty, and firmness with gentleness and humanity; his whole exterior indicating the man of respectability and piety. He was a devout member of the Society of Friends, and in speech and manner plain and unostentatious.

Ill health prevented further active efforts [on] behalf of his noble enterprise, but his heartfelt interest he maintained until his death in 1817. The end was peaceful and serene; with family and neighbors around his bedside, he exhorted them to pure and holy lives, calmly bade them good-bye, and sank to well-earned repose.

His remains were buried in the little cemetery at the Friends meetinghouse at Central village, Westport, and a simple slab of slate marks the spot beneath the solemn pines where rests all that is mortal of one of nature's noblemen.

The Mission of the Religious Press

Ransom argues here that the printing press played a vital role in the development of this nation — morally, religiously, politically, technologically. The importance of the printed word has a long history, including Moses' receiving of the Ten

May 16, 1912, Kansas City (n.p., n.d.), housed in the Reverdy C. Ransom Collection, Payne Theological Seminary, Wilberforce, Ohio. Reprinted by permission of Mrs. Ruth L. Ransom and her son, Louis A. Ransom, Jr. The Schomburg also has a copy of this pamphlet.

Commandments. The Christian world also owes much to the printed word. The religious press, not used here to refer to early or apostolic teachings, emerged with the Reformation. Currently, the press has moved beyond its early polemical tone and is now more concerned, not with orthodoxy, but rather general Christian ideals and principles. These principles, within the press, should be brought into fruitful contact with the actual conditions of life in an effort to educate and guide. In this task it must be unbiased. In conclusion, Ransom applies this framework to the publications of the A.M.E. Church.

•

The snowflakes that fall from heaven do not descend upon us in greater volume than the output of the ever-multiplying leaves from the printing press. Printer's ink mixed with brains is fast becoming both the morning and the evening meal of all mankind. It is made palatable alike to all by being seasoned and served to suit the varying and divergent tastes. A thinker harnessed to a printing press is the most powerful and influential force in modern civilization. It is superseding armies and navies as a means of national defense. By this subtle alchemy the modern world has become fluid, flowing into every current of human life. It has taken the best that the heart has felt and the highest that the mind has thought and rarefied it until it has become in our nostrils the very breath of life to humanity.

The press is the servant of every cause and purpose under the sun. It is employed by the statesman to unfold his policies of government; trades and commerce use it to exploit their schemes and display their wares; it portrays the artist's vision and sings the poet's song; the scientist and philosopher make it the vehicle of their thoughts, while the religious teacher and thinker make it a lever for the moral and spiritual elevation of the world.

The pen has always been at the service of religion. The hieroglyphics traced upon the broken columns that have lain for ages buried among the ruins of Babylon and Egypt testify to the gropings of the ancients after God, before the dawn of history. The poets and sages of Greece and Rome struck their noblest strains by invoking the immortal gods. When Jehovah would communicate His commandments to Israel, He let down His throne on Mount Sinai in the midst of thunders, lightnings, thick clouds of smoke, and the voice of a trumpet exceeding loud, and delivered to Moses the Ten Commandments written upon tablets of stone with a pen of iron.

Christianity is not in a book. It is not the result of a literary propaganda. Elijah, the greatest of the prophets and one of the most influential personalities in the world's religious history, wrote nothing; John the Baptist wrote nothing: and Jesus Christ, the founder of our faith, wrote nothing. He was the bearer of a divine light and life that has unloosed human tongues, given to thousands "the pen of a ready writer," and set the printing presses of the world to revolving night and day with the work of sending forth messages more far-reaching than the flying roll which the prophet Zechariah saw speeding across the heavens. Jesus Christ stands at the center of human life. He is the hub around which the course of history must resolve from Eden to Calvary and from the snow-clad heights of Mount Hermon to the gates of Paradise. St. John concludes his gospel by saying that "There are also many other things which Jesus did, if they should be written every one, I suppose that even the world itself could not contain the books that should be written."

While He wrote nothing Himself, there is a sense in which we may say, with reverence, that the Holy Ghost acted as the press agent of Jesus Christ. Under the inspiration of the Spirit the Gospels were written; under His direction the epistles were written by the apostles to primitive Christians.

What the future of Christianity, Christian civilization, and the Christian institutions that have sprung from it would have been without the written or printed page transcends the bounds of the most extravagant imagination. The debt that theology owes to the writings of the apostle Paul is incalculable. On a certain morning in the spring of the year 58 A.D., there stood on one of the wharves of the city of Corinth a middle-aged woman about to take ship to sail across the fair waters of the Gulf of Corinth for Rome. That woman was Phoebe, the deaconess of the church at Cenchreae and Paul's sister in the Lord. To her Paul entrusted a roll of manuscript which was the epistle written from Corinth to the church which was in Rome. This epistle was of such consummate importance to the future of Christianity that Renan makes the startling statement that Phoebe, as she sailed away from Corinth, "carried beneath the folds of her robe the whole future of Christian theology."

We hear a great deal today about Pauline Christianity, with the implication that he was the inventor of what may be called evangelical Christianity. There are in the New Testament, broadly speaking, three sets of teaching — the Pauline, Petrine, and Johannine — and you cannot find between these three any difference as to the fundamental contents of the gospel; for if Paul rings out, "God commendeth His love toward us in that while we were sinners Christ died for us," Peter declares, "Who His own self bore our sins in His own body on the tree," and John from his island solitude sends across the waters the hymn of praise "Unto Him that loved us and washed us from our sins in his own blood." So the proud declaration of the apostle is warranted when he says, "Therefore, whether it were I or they, so we preach."

We would not be understood as so far misconceiving the phrase "religious press" as to apply the term to the age of hieroglyphics or papyrus, nor yet to the writings of the apostles or the church gathers. But as standing nearest to Christ, in point of time, they give us in literary form, authoritative data for the guidance of modern religious thought. Out of the darkness of the Middle Ages there flashed that flaming meteor, Savonarola, the immortal Florentine, who thundered his denunciations against the moral and religious corruption of the de Medici. Savonarola was the precursor of that brilliant galaxy of religious publicists among whom Erasmus and Melancthon shone as stars of the first magnitude. But it was not until the sound of the hammer that nailed Christ to the cross on the lonely hill of Calvary was echoed back by the sound of the hammer in the hands of Martin Luther as he nailed his theses to the door of his obscure Wittenberg church, that the introduction to the religious press was written. However the historian may date the beginnings of modern progress from the Renaissance, we hold that it was out of the fires of the Reformation that the religious press forged for itself white wings with which to carry the world forward through the successive stages of its spiritual and moral progress.

The victorious armies of Napoleon, which brought all Europe to his feet, until the sun of that mighty Corsican went down at Waterloo, and the thundering hoofs of Cromwell's Invincible Ironsides that overturned the British throne, were no more belligerent than was the tone of the religious press in the sixteenth and seventeenth centuries. Its utterances censored, its voice often muffled or suppressed, the heroes and martyrs in this cause take first rank among those who have won for us those foundation stones of democracy — freedom of the press and freedom of religious belief.

The mission of the religious press is no longer polemical. The armor of controversy has been discarded for the peaceful robes of tolerance. It has exchanged the sword of bigotry for the torch of fraternity and cooperation. It is not so much concerned about the character of a man's doxy as it is about the quality and worth of his service.

The religious, or denominational press, like the denominational school, has a field and a mission distinctively its own. Its aims are not simply utilitarian. The secular schools and colleges are employed in the production of intelligent American citizens; their training may be vocational or cultural. The religious or denominational schools may give this training no better than others. Our literary inheritance and the truths of science and philosophy remain the same whether taught at Girard College or a Methodist seminary. The raison d'être of the denominational school does not consist in the fact that it makes new contributions to knowledge, but in the application of education to life, in sanctifying scholarship on the altar of character and dedicating the whole of the service to humanity. Its culture is not simply literary, scientific, or utilitarian, but moral and spiritual, releasing for service the highest and best capacities of the mind and spirit. Its aim is godliness; it places upon culture the stamp of Christ. It seeks not only to make intelligent citizens, but to prepare men for the duties and responsibilities of Christian citizenship.

Now, the religious press is not religious in the sense of teaching a particular form of religious belief, or of devoting its columns exclusively to the dissemination of religious intelligence. It is neither a mouthpiece nor an organ, limited to the narrow confines of denominational boundaries. While not a competitor of the secular press in the sense of being a moving picture screen for the daily life of the people, its field is the world. It should seek to uphold the loftiest Christian ideals, and apply the principles of Christianity to the actual conditions or events arising out of the life of the people. The newspaper and periodical press are too often the hired servant of partisan politics and politicians, of business or moneyed interests, of industrial and commercial schemes.

First of all, the religious press must be free and incorruptible and, so far as human frailty will permit, unbiased. It should be prophet and seer, preacher and teacher, philosopher and guide. It should have the power of Elijah to call down sheets of flame upon unrighteousness in high places; it should have the vision of Isaiah to behold upon the mountaintops the hastening feet of Him who is building a highway for redeemed humanity; it should have the boldness of John the Baptist and make itself a voice, crying out loud enough to awaken our valleys of unrighteousness, shake our mountains of prejudice and pride, and stir up our pleasure-loving and wealth — seeking Jerusalems to behold the Light of the world, who will make straight their paths; it should have the zeal and fire of the apostle Paul, to bear witness everywhere, to Jew and Gentile, rich and poor, black and white, to the great moral principle necessary for the salvation of society as well as the individual.

The religious press should be absolutely divorced from partisan politics, dealing with principles rather than parties, and giving its influence to those men and measures that make for the most enlightened and beneficent statesmanship and policies of government. The political millennium, like other millenniums, is not something made to order that will be bestowed upon us, being handed down by God from heaven. It is something that must be won, worked for, achieved. We do not believe, therefore, in a journalism that is inconsequential, supine, colorless; but one that has backbone, conviction, principle, on all the great questions of government which so vitally affect the moral, intellectual, social, and industrial welfare of the people.

The religious journal should aim to be more than the mouthpiece of public opinion, following in the wake of public sentiment. It should seek to educate, influence, and guide public opinion in the right direction. High moral ground is its place and plane. It should turn the light on evildoers and demagogues in church and state, expose rascality and corruption in religion, politics, or business. It should know no race or country, defending the weak and oppressed, assailing tyrants and tyranny, injustice, and wrong. It should stand for temperance, for law and order, for political and social justice, and righteousness.

The editor of the religious journal should be like the man in Ezekiel's vision, who was "clothed with linen, and had a writer's ink horn by his side," and go through the midst of Jerusalem and set a mark upon the foreheads of the men that uphold the abominations that be done in the midst thereof.

The religious press should deal with the great international and world questions of peace and war, arbitration, colonization, and the exploitation and government of the backward peoples of the earth. The moral and religious aspects of the protectorate of France over Morocco, of Italy over Tripoli, and the struggle of the Chinese masses to overthrow the Manchu dynasty, come legitimately within its view, as do such questions as the high cost of living through the control of the necessities of life in the hands of a few, the freedom of the Panama Canal to the ships of all nations, the use of the aeroplane in war, and the colonial policy of this democratic republic in dealing with Hawaii, [Puerto Rico,] and the Philippines. It should deal as courageously with the moral aspects of stealing Africa from the Africans in the day of freedom as it did with the question of stealing Africans from Africa in the days of slavery.

No matter what path we take, whether it leads across the battle-fields of the nation from Bunker Hill to Appomattox, from the Declaration of Independence to the War Amendments to the Con-stitution, or from the establishment of Methodism in this country to the discovery of the North Pole, we can turn to no important page of American history without finding that the Negro and the Negro question require special treatment. This holds true when we touch the field of journalism, particularly as it relates to the A.M.E. Church. The African M.E. Church was the first Protestant church born on American soil. It was not a protest against the assump-tions of the papacy, or against theological doctrine or dogma. It was founded on Mar's Hill doctrine, as propounded by St. Paul, and on belief in the spirit of Christian unity that fell upon the church on the day of Pentecost. Our pulpit and our press have a distinct mission, and a special message for the Negro in particu-lar, and generally for the dark-skinned races of mankind, namely, this — that the Negro has a soul and that Christ has not prepared for him an inferior brand of redemption; that the Negro is not only a man, but also a man of Christ Jesus; that he will submit to no discrimination at the altars of religion; and that he claims the right to enjoy freely every privilege and opportunity that the church af-fords. Those Negroes who will submit to be held in tutelage to religious denominations and be a kind of a bond servant, occupy-ing an inferior place in the household of faith, whatever else they may be, they are not African Methodist. While others have worked along similar lines, we make bold to say that no single influence has contributed so powerfully to the production of manhood and character and to the demonstration of the Negro's capacity for self-government as the A.M.E. Church.

The Coming Vision

In this address, delivered at the General Conference of 1920, Ransom outlines the manner in which the A.M.E. Church must continue to commit itself to an understanding of religion and worship as open to all, without discrimination. The A.M.E. Church, according to Ransom, must never compromise its concern for the total welfare and liberty of African Americans. Ransom believes that as God worked through history to bring about the welfare of other groups, African Americans now stand squarely within a new phase of human history being written by God. Slavery and racism do not disprove the work of God; rather God made use of African Americans' pain to prepare them for greatness.

•

The Monroe Doctrine forms no part of the Constitution of the United States of America. Yet it is the most zealously guarded and sacredly cherished of all the principles that relate our government to the other nations of the earth.

The African Methodist Episcopal Church has its Monroe Doctrine which is no less sacredly held. Our ecclesiastical Monroe Doctrine rests upon the spirit and principles of Richard Allen, the founder of our denomination.

It stands for absolute equality of all men at [the] altars of the Christian religion. It will neither discriminate nor permit discrimination in the church of Christ on account of nationality, of color, or of race. It will form no alliance nor enter into any compromise by which these principles would be invaded.

As the American people, despite the seductiveness of the alluring covenant of the League of Nations, stand aloof from involving the Western Hemisphere with the monarchical doctrines of the old world, so the A.M.E. Church will remain distinct and independent of all alliances and programs that would invade or compromise the Negro's religious liberty, equality, and manhood.

In responding to the gracious words of welcome which have been extended to our General Conference on this historic occasion, I shall voice the spirit of the thing for which the A.M.E. Church

First published in the *A.M.E. Church Review,* January 1921, 135–39. Reprinted by permission of the *A.M.E. Church Review.*

stands, by taking as the subject of my response "The Coming Vision."

Throughout the ages the prophets of righteousness have been one in spirit. There has been no break in the line of succession. The unfolding fold of their vision has illuminated the path of progress, while their message has rung clear with the voice and authority of the Most High God.

Six hundred years before the birth of Christ, the prophet Habakkuk wrestled with God over great moral and social problems similar to those that confront us today. "O Jehovah, how long shall I cry, and Thou wilt not hear? I cry unto Thee of violence, and Thou wilt not save. Why dost Thou show me iniquity and look upon perverseness? For destruction and violence are before me, and there is strife, and contention riseth up. The law is slackened and justice doth never go forth, for the wicked doth compass about the righteous, therefore justice goeth forth perverted."

This cry of Habakkuk ringing across the centuries finds echo in the cries of pain, bewilderment, and doubt that are on the lips of the black men in America today. In this dark hour for the prophet and his people, Jehovah counseled faith with patience, saying, "I am working a work in your days which you will not believe though it were told you." For reassurance, He gave the prophet a brief glimpse behind the scenes, that he might behold the violent Chaldeans whom He was preparing as the swift and bitter instruments of deliverance.

So, many myriad million hands are working to weave for God the majestic garments He wears in all his goings forth, so many sabers are flashing while screaming shells are bursting upon the battlefields to proclaim his will, we, like Habakkuk, would not believe if it were told us, "the work that God is working our day."

John Brown was hung upon a scaffold; St. Paul was cast into a Roman dungeon; the Galilean was crucified upon a cross; but scaffold and cross and dungeon have become the mightiest thrones of power in the modern world.

The ancients have told us what God did for Israel in the land of Egypt; we have read of His presence at the river Jordan, before the walls of Jericho; we have heard of His power and wonders in the old apostolic days. But what is God doing today?

Alas, the cry — "violence, iniquity, destruction, strife, contention; the law is slackened and justice doth never go forth. O Lord, how long shall I cry and thou wilt not hear."

The nation seethes with unrest and violence; there are sufferings and want in a land of plenty; the course of history is flowing into new channels; old foundations are being loosened; events stupendous and unprecedented are filling the spirits of men with the dim awakening of a world consciousness. While God is resenting [resetting] the stage in the midst of this world upheaval, our statesmanship is halting and confused, and our prophets have no vision. We are caught in the sweep of world-stirring events, which are the strange hieroglyphics out of which God is writing a new chapter of human history.

No man holds the key to their translation. But standing without fear in the midst of alarms across the storms of passion, and above the noise of battles, we join St. Paul and Martin Luther by piercing the skies with the cry of Habakkuk — "The just shall live by faith." While science, philosophy, and statesmanship welter in confusion, calmly confident in the strength of the Everlasting Arm, I leave the low valleys of doubt and despair and go with the prophet "to stand upon my watch, and set me upon the tower, to watch and see what God will say to me." Today, as of old, the voice of the Infinite speaks to the watcher who stands and waits in his watchtower.

The voice of majesty rings clear with both assurance and command, to "write the vision, and make it plain upon tablets, that he may run that readeth it. The vision is yet for an appointed time, but at the end it shall speak, and not lie; though it tarry, wait for it; because it will surely come, it will not delay."

Is there a plan in history? Looking back across the centuries we are able to unite the links of this unending chain. Looking outward through the unfolding years, we watch and wait, we walk and work, with faith in the coming vision.

For centuries down in Egypt, Israel cried unto Jehovah while bondage became more intolerable. Then Jehovah got up from His throne and, speaking out of the heavens, said, "Surely I have seen the affliction of my people which were in Egypt and have heard their cry, and have come down to deliver them."

Up from slavery, and out from wandering in the wilderness, with hope deferred for forty years, Moses ascended the top of Pisgah, the mount of vision, and saw before him his golden dreams. There lay "all the land of Gilead unto Dan, and all the land of Judah, unto the western sea, and the plain of the valley of Jericho, the city of Palm trees unto Zoar."

When every prop had been knocked from under him and he lay prostrate in [the] dust, down in the land of Ur, Job cried with confidence, "I know that my Redeemer liveth." In every age men must forge wings to rise above the barriers that shut out the bright vision of the coming days. Down in the land of Moab, when power and might could not awe him, after flattery and bribes had failed to seduce him, Baalam flung his defiance in the face of the king. "How shall I curse whom God hath not cursed? How shall I defy whom Jehovah hath not defiled? From the top of the rocks I see him. And from the hills I behold him. Who can count the dust of Jacob, or number the fourth part of Israel? Let me die the death of the righteous and let my last end be like his."

Out of the slow unfolding centuries at last appeared a brilliant star, the guide to inquiring wise men from the East; a choir of angels came sweeping down the stairway of the skies to fill with awe some simple shepherds in the plain; a manger-born babe appeared in a stable in Bethlehem, whose feet were to walk the journey of life without sin, whose lips were to speak the word of salvation and life, and whose hands were to plant for every man the flower of immortality above the gates of death. Now let faithful Abraham, long dead, rejoice; while the prophecy spoken ages ago by Moses is fulfilled — "The Lord our God will raise up a Prophet from among your brethren, him shall you hear."

"The vision is yet for an appointed time; though it tarry, wait for it." We cannot hasten God's appointed hour; we cannot set forward the hands upon the dial plate of God's great clock of the ages.

Men dreamed and watched while they awaited; the fulfillment of the vision, God had an appointment with Pharaoh down by the banks of the Red Sea. He kept it to the very hour amid the rushing waters that submerged the wreckage of broken chariots of war. He had an appointment with Nebuchadnezzar in Babylon; God kept His appointment by writing with invisible hands his doom upon the palace walls. Many centuries before the time, God told His servant Daniel that He had an appointment with Rome in the plains of Italy. He kept it by opening the floodgates and sending hordes of Huns into the palaces of the caesars. He has left standing there by the banks of the Tiber, the broken walls of the ruins of the Colosseum as a silent witness to the fact [that] the stone hewn out of the mountains without hands had eclipsed her glory and overwhelmed her might.

God had an appointment with the American slave power. It took Him two hundred and fifty years to arrive upon the scene. He had set it for Gettysburg and Appomattox. When He passed by with fire and sword, He left as His pledge of faithfulness four millions of broken fetters, scattered across this continent from the mountains to the sea.

Somewhere back in the centuries, God made an appointment with decadent and faithless Christian civilization to meet it on the battlefields of France and Flanders, and march with it from the Black Sea to the Bosporus, and from the banks of the Marne to the valley of the Jordan and the Nile. Today, we are standing in the midst of broken scepters and shattered thrones, while the four horsemen of the Apocalypse still ride through the nations to execute the decrees of God at the appointed time. Somewhere out in the jungles of Africa, God made an appointment with a group of black children of the tropics to meet Him here upon the shores of the American continent. They came bound in chains to be driven forth to servitude under the lash of hard taskmasters. They looked everywhere for His presence, in cane brakes, in thickets, and in swamps. They listened for His voice in the moaning wind and in the roaring thunder. They sought Him in the cotton fields, in the chimney corner, and around the cabin door. "The vision was for an appointed time."

These were the days for their apprenticeship for leadership in one of the great world tasks of all ages. Their preparation and their training lay through the paths that led by way of the slave pen and the auction block, in fugitive wanderings under the dim North Star where baying bloodhounds lurked. In pain and agony they came through Ku Klux Klans, through the lynchers' ruthless violence of wanton murder and fiendish orgies of burning at the stake while upon all these barbarities were heaped the dehumanizing programs of American Jim Crowism.

"If the vision tarry, wait for it." But waiting does not mean inaction, to do nothing, to stand still. Those who wait upon God work ceaselessly for the fulfillment of the vision toward which they strive. So these Americans of African descent, while waiting, have been serving their apprenticeship in preparation for the great role they are to play in the consummation of God's plans, by establishing the church, the home, and the school, by acquiring knowledge in all the arts and sciences of the modern world.

God must have people that are prepared to go with Him in spirit, as well as in the things of the mind, in carrying out His divinely ordered program for humanity. Through every moment of the long years of injustice and persecution, God is leading us forward just as fast as we are prepared to follow Him to possession of that inheritance which has been the goal of our highest strivings.

Neither the domination of individual races, nor the supremacy of favored nations, has a place in God's plan. His dominion shall be from the river unto the ends of the earth, and the dominant people in it shall be composed of every race whose supremacy shall be based on uprightness of character, meekness of spirit, and the sense of human brotherhood based on love.

"Though it tarry, wait for it, because it will surely come." In the presence of the great ruling nations of the earth, who by power and might, by huge aggregations of wealth, by control of the sea and other avenues of intercommunication and trade, weaker peoples find themselves dominated and coerced by commercial weapons if not by the sword. Many such people desiring peaceful possession of their native lands are offered the pious fraud of "self-determination" for the priceless boon of their independence and sovereignty.

Shall coalition, treaties, and covenants continue to be the dissolving bonds between nations? Or may we not look for the peoples of the earth to find higher and holier bonds, uniting them as a family of nations, each cooperating for the common good of all?

The cries of oppressed peoples within the great nations of the earth have rung down the ages, from the days of Israel's captivity in Babylon, to those days of British coercion in Ireland and American oppression of Negroes in the United States. Shall the freedom of Ireland fade like an iridescent dream? Shall the complete equality. and freedom of Negroes in the United States prove to be a deceptive will-o'-the-wisp to lure aspiring souls into the quagmires of political and civil despair?

"The vision is yet for an appointed time, at the end it shall speak and not lie." These words have stood through the ages, while the sun of mighty empires has gone down in night. Alas! men say, "how beautiful the vision, how golden the dream of a land where all are free to preserve untarnished the crown of their manhood and womanhood, where neither class, nor blood, nor race shall separate man from his brother man; but how impossible of fulfillment. How can your weakness prevail over the mighty forces that oppose? With what weapons can you fight against such overwhelming odds?" With every confidence we reply, our strength is in God, and our unconquerable weapon is faith in the triumph of righteousness and justice among all men.

There are questions so deep-rooted in the life and interests of mankind that they cannot be settled by financial credits or the strength of armies and navies. They may be denied in India, seethe in Russia, or be overruled by the Supreme Court of the United States, but they will continue to come up and plead for settlement until the righteous judge of all the earth hands down a decision from which there can be no appeal.

The vision of a unified Christianity is one born of the baptismal fires of the day of Pentecost. A unified Christianity which is so evangelical in spirit, aggressive and militant in action that it aims not only at the conquest of Rome and Corinth and Europe, but all the continents and islands of the sea. A union of the bodies of independent Negro Methodists, of the M.E. Church and the M.E. Church South, and of the different bodies of Baptists and Presbyterians, is indeed desirable as a step in the right direction. But if Christianity is to prevail in winning the world, we must have a larger vision. The lines of the kingdom of heaven are not narrow and circumscribed. Its mission is not to save black men, or white men, or yellow men — [but] all men everywhere.

There are too many conflicting and discordant war cries under the divided cross of Christ. Against this stands the solid and united front of paganism, ignorance, and sin. Throughout the different sects of Christendom, the aims and purposes of each must be the same: there must be undivided councils and but one plan of battle if a decisive victory is to be won for the cross of Christ.

Intolerance and pride, the bigotry of privilege and authority, the narrowness of doctrines, and all the fine strategy for the promotion of ecclesiastical dominion must disappear under a united Christendom whose only head is Christ, whose creed is love, and whose life is one of service in the cause of universal peace and righteousness.

As they are now divided, no single religious denomination could ever bring this disordered world back to God; nor can all the religious bodies of Christendom, each working along its separate line, restore to the great Shepherd His sheep who have wandered from the fold. The Oriental faiths and the Occidental skepticism, like Goliath of old, fling their defiant challenge in the face of the divided forces of the Christian world.

Would Africa be safe in the hands of American Christianity? Why should it exchange its physical nakedness for [the] corruption of the moral and economic robes of our civilization? Here must we sanctify ourselves and then go forth with healing to restore the nations that sit in regions of darkness and in the shadow of death.

Out of the multitude of councils, conventions, synods, and conferences the world is awaiting the convocation of all the forces of unified Christianity to move in one solid phalanx against the forces of ignorance and sin.

"The vision is for an appointed time; it will surely come; it will not delay." I see forces of the Christian church uniting with greater power and resources than those which the Allies hurled against the might of Germany. I see a new heaven and a new earth where God has come to make His dwelling place with men, and God Himself shall be with them and be their God.

But our highest goal is not a unified church, but a unified humanity in the bonds of brotherhood. The wise men from the East were guided by a star, but wiser men of our unfolding, coming from the four corners of the earth, are guided by a higher vision. They seek not a manger, but a cross where all men stand with equal footing on common ground. It is the final stand of humanity's last retreat. All other meeting places have failed. For all ages men have tried the decisions of the battlefield, the prerogatives of kings, the decisions of courts, the enactments of parliaments, and union of great power seeking to underwrite the peace of the world. All these have left in their trail misery and chaos, division, and strife.

But at the cross one man is lifted up so high above all the causes that divide, and his arms are extended so wide that they enfold in their loving embrace every tribe, kindred, tongue, and nation, to bind them together with his wounded hands in the everlasting bonds of brotherhood and love.

Africa and America, Europe and Asia, with the isles of the sea, forget their differences and boundaries of nationality and race. The mountains are brought low, the valleys are exalted, there is no more sea. We look not up to see victorious banners streaming from the clouds, nor yet the Jerusalem descending from the skies. For no sun, nor moon, nor star, outshines the light of a redeemed earth whose uniformed humanity has restored again its long-lost paradise with all doors open outward up to God.

Daniel Alexander Payne, the Prophet of an Era

In this essay, Ransom pays tribute to Daniel Alexander Payne as one of the great leaders of the A.M.E. Church and the major figure in the formation of Wilberforce University. Ran-

First published in the *A.M.E. Church Review,* April–June 1952. Reprinted by permission of the *A.M.E. Church Review.*

som understands that the evolution of history is marked by the emergence and contribution of central figures such as Payne who help society develop further. He is impressed by Paynes's intellectual ambitions and his confidence in the African American's capabilities when properly educated and trained to hold key roles in society.

•

All the great periods of history revolve around one great man as its center and symbol. In ancient Israel, it was King David; in Rome, it was Julius Caesar; in Greece, it was Aristotle; in Europe, it was Napoleon Bonaparte; in early America, it was George Washington; in the crisis of freedom and slavery in America, it was Abraham Lincoln.

This is paralleled in the A.M.E. Church by the power and influence of Daniel Alexander Payne. First of all, Bishop Payne had character, vision, understanding, and a will of steel to implement his program. Bishop Payne was elected a bishop in the A.M.E. Church in 1852. He came upon the scene at a time when not more than five Negroes out of a hundred could read or write. The race as a whole was 95 percent illiterate. Our churches were few in number, chiefly along the eastern seaboard: Pennsylvania, Maryland, the District of Columbia, New York, and a few scattered points in New England

The moral and social problems he faced were, first, the family. Under slavery there could be no legal marriage, hence, no home, or family, upon anything like a permanent basis. A Negro woman was just a human thing, to be bought and sold on the open market. Children could be taken from her and sold at will.

There were Negro Christians by the thousands. In free states they were just beginning to organize into religious bodies according to the faith they accepted. Only just a little handful of Negro men and women had any education, training, or experience ten years before the emancipation of the slaves.

Bishop Payne had a vision of what should be done by Negroes themselves to meet the challenge confronting this people in the chaotic time at the close of the Civil War. By faith, and without a dollar in hand, he bought and established Wilberforce University, the first colored college ever started by Negroes in the Western Hemisphere.

The objective was to educate and train ministers to teach and lead the people and to educate men and women as schoolteachers to meet the ignorance that existed everywhere. Certainly there was a small group of men and women who supported him, and held up his arms, for all were agreed that ignorance must be banished.

Back in the year 1880 Bishop Payne wrote a little book on domestic education, forced the preachers to buy it, and tried to persuade the ministers wives and others to read it, and learn how to properly keep house, conduct a home, and train children.

Long before he became a bishop, Daniel Payne started on the task of gathering material for writing the history of the A.M.E. Church. He gave up his church and took a year going every place where Richard Allen had been active in any capacity whatsoever, writing down what was told him by those who had been associated with Richard Allen, gathering all facts that were available in relation to the organization and early history of the A.M.E. Church. When Rev. Payne became a bishop he still continued the task of completing this history. I was a student at Wilberforce University and have heard him lament many times that he was praying to God to let him live to finish his history of the A.M.E. Church. Bishop Payne's history is now and shall continue to be the reliable source of information concerning the A.M.E. Church.

I shall relate a few incidents to which I was an eyewitness, showing the forthright manner with which he met testing situations from time to time.

In 1892 our General Conference met in Bethel Church, Philadelphia, Pennsylvania. A certain very popular man had organized and was putting forth every effort to be elected a bishop. In order to defeat his election Bishop Payne arose and addressed the General Conference, saying, "This man is not fit to be a bishop. He is a politician, and he is a thief." He then dropped to his knees and called upon God to move upon the minds of the delegates not to support this man's election.

Many years ago I happened to be present at a session of the Ohio Conference over which Bishop Payne presided. When the committee on Deacon's Orders reported, one man was turned back. But when the class came to the altar for ordination, the rejected man had slipped unnoticed into the ranks of those to be ordained. After Bishop Payne had ordained the class, his attention was called to the fact that the rejected man had slipped into the circle and that Bishop Payne had unwittingly ordained him. Bishop Payne said, "He is a rascal, but I have ordained him, I cannot take it back. But he is a rascal."

When the late Grover Cleveland was president of the United

States one of our prominent pastors by the name of Rev. Wm. H. Heard aspired to be appointed a United States minister to the Republic of Liberia. He wrote Bishop Payne to recommend him to the president for appointment. In reply Bishop Payne told him, "You are now the ambassador of our Lord Jesus Christ. You want to leave the service of the King of kings and Lord of lords to become the representative of an earthly potentate. No, I will not endorse you."

I managed to salvage a large portion of Bishop Payne's diary, written by his own hand, giving detailed account of his life. The dairy is written in French, but I find it not difficult to translate into English. I am hoping someday to publish it. Daniel A. Payne seems to have been born and ordained for the time in which he lived to hold high the torch of education and guide the uncertain steps of a race coming from [the] degradation, ignorance, and abject poverty of slavery to throw light upon the path of their progress.

He was a frail little man, never weighing more than 96 pounds avoirdupois. But the power of his faith, courage, and wisdom were the mightiest influence that directed the development of the A.M.E. Church for two generations. Daniel Alexander Payne was a man sent from God.

Paul Laurence Dunbar

This essay is one of three contained in a collection titled Paul Laurence Dunbar: Poet Laureate of the Negro Race; *the offering below is from the collection of essays as published in the* A.M.E. Church Review. *Ransom's is the last of the three and the shortest. Ransom comments that those of African descent have not, as a whole, contributed greatly to modern civilization. However, he argues that there are notable examples of African Americans whose work in the arts and other fields matches the work of those from any other group. One such example is Dunbar's poetry. Dunbar's work points to the potential of the African American people.*

•

Reprinted from *A.M.E. Church Review,* published by Reverdy C. Ransom, 631 Pine Street, Philadelphia, Pennsylvania. Housed in the collection of the Schomburg Center for Research in Black Culture, New York. Reprinted by permission of the *A.M.E. Church Review.*

Paul Laurence Dunbar was a product of the first generation of freedom. Whatever of talent, endowment, or genius he possessed belonged to the rich, warm blood of his African inheritance. We know that capacity, genius, ability are limited by race or blood; but so universal is the imputation of racial inferiority to the African and his descendants that the achievements of each gifted son or daughter reflect glory upon the entire race. The Negro has contributed very little to what we know as human progress in the terms of modern civilization. This fact is used against him and is made to justify his unequal and degrading treatment. It is only by multiplying examples of the highest achievement that the universal judgment may be reversed. In the United States, Dunbar and Henry O. Tanner are "the seamark of our farthest sail" in letters and in art. These are not freaks or prodigies, but prophecies of the latent powers of the race, the first unfoldings of which have not yet but fairly begun. Like the midnight sun of the North Polar regions, the darkness that has enveloped the African and his descendants has been briefly illuminated here and there through the centuries by some bright Negro intellect in almost every quarter of the earth. However widely the many varieties of the human race may differ in certain physical characteristics, they have a common origin and are of one and the same family. The Creator has not made one branch of the human family inferior to another. History does, however, abundantly prove that the groups into which the human family is divided differ in race traits, characteristics, and in wealth of endowment in certain specific directions. The world is indebted to the Jews for keeping alive and transmitting across the centuries a pure monotheism. The Greeks realized the highest ideal of beauty to which mankind has attained; while the white races of Europe and America have displayed a genius for colonization, commerce, and invention applied to the development of the physical resources of the earth. So large and comprehensive have been the contributions to knowledge that it is felt by many that there is little left of a distinctive character for the black peoples to do. But in the spiritual realm, in the emotions, in music, in kindness, in cheerfulness, and the spirit of brotherhood, the Negro has a wealth of endowment, which, when his hour comes, will put a living soul into the activities of human life which may well be the glory and the crown of that worldwide civilization which makes for peace, for brotherhood, and love.

Dunbar was an interpreter of the life and spirit of his people. Fresh as a breath from the hills, his poems breathe with the atmosphere which surrounds the life of his race. Dunbar's voice is the first note of the bird that sounds the approach of dawn. He fell asleep before his eyes beheld the day which he had ushered in. But the harp whose strings were touched by him with such poetic grace will not remain forever silent. Other hearts that have been warmed by the equatorial sun will be filled with new and higher inspirations; other hands, black tinseled by the subtle alchemy of the tropics, will lift the veil from off the ability and power of his people, that all the world may feast its hollow metallic senses in the banqueting house of mind and spirit where the heart presides.

Dunbar was always a child — a child at play — who passed from us before he came to full maturity of his powers. From the days of his boyhood, intimately and well we knew him, when he was yet unknown beyond a narrow circle in the busy little city where he held a position of the humblest sort. We have ridden with him many times in the car of his elevator, where, scattered about him on loose sheets of paper, were some of the first of his imperishable lines which were to win the admiration of the world. When his first book, *Oak and Ivy,* came from the press, we introduced him to our congregation and assisted him in disposing of copies he had borrowed from the printer to pay the cost of publication. More than once we have dined with him, with chitterlings and hot cornpone as the pièce de résistance. He has come to us in the late hours of the night, when the muses were singing at the windows of his soul, in search of a word that might better convey the delicate shades of thought or feeling they brought before his vision. The late John Bigelow said of a visit to Alexandre Dumas that Dumas showed him a story that he had just completed, and in reply to a question, remarked that he never rewrote his manuscripts, but let the first draft stand. This, Bigelow gratuitously remarks, was "characteristic of his race." This was not true of Dunbar, who was three-fourths more Negro than Dumas. When the song had spent itself, he carefully corrected and revised. May we not add that this was "characteristic of his race"? Dunbar was the spoiled child of the agreeable men and winsome women of every city where he went. He was not retiring or exclusive; where beauty, pleasure, and music met, he made a feast. He was his own best interpreter of his works. To hear Dunbar read from Dunbar's works, with his rich baritone voice, with every action suited to the word, was to see him at his best and to hold forever afterward a pleasant memory that cannot fade.

A spirit so highly strung and sensitive as his was not without its tragedies. He has come to our study wearing a look of almost hopeless dejection and begged us to come upon our knees alone with him, in the presence of the Alone, to pray for strength and heaven's gracious favor. We have it told elsewhere how he wrought and what, up to now, is the world's estimate of his genius, and we have here, too, an intimate sketch from one who for the first time breaks her silence to speak of him who first won her hand and linked her name forever with his fame.

Phillis Wheatley and Dunbar, each of the pure African type, were the first to enter the enchanted ground of poesy and song. Up there among "the choir invisible," with Elizabeth Barrett Browning, with Burns and Keats, with Shelley and with Poe, may they not await with confidence the day when the gifted children of their people will hold the [rapt] attention of the world, while they flood it with their ravishing strains of music and of song?

Part Three

Book Chapters

The New Negro

HE IS NEW, he is as old as the forests primeval
Stark in their nakedness of limb,
His forebears roamed in the jungle and led the chase.
Crystalized by the heat of the Oriental suns,
God made him a rock of undecaying power,
To become at last the nations' cornerstone.
Rough hewn from the jungle and the desert's sands,
Slavery was the chisel that fashioned him to form,
And gave him all the arts and sciences had won.
The lyncher, mob, and stake have his emery wheel,
TO MAKE A POLISHED MAN of strength and power.
In him, the latest birth of freedom,
God hath again made all things new.
Europe and Asia with ebbing tides recede,
America's unfinished arch of freedom waits,
Till, he the cornerstone of strength,
Is lifted into place and power.
Behold him! dauntless and unafraid he stands.
He comes with laden arms,
Bearing rich gifts to science, religion, poetry, and song.
Labor and capital through him shall find
The equal heritage of common brotherhood,
And statesmanship shall keep the stewardship
Of justice with equal rights and privileges for all.
HE KNOWS HIS PLACE, to keep it
As a sacred trust and heritage for all,
To wear God's image in the ranks of men
And walk as princes of the royal blood divine,
ON EQUAL FOOTING everywhere with all mankind.

Reprinted by permission of Mrs. Ruth L. Ransom and her son, Louis A. Ransom, Jr.

With ever-fading color on these shores,
The Oriental sunshine in his blood
Shall give the warming touch of brotherhood
And love, to all the fused races in our land,
He is the last reserve of God on earth,
Who, in the goodly fellowship of love,
Will rule the world with peace.

— REVERDY C. RANSOM

The Reno Prizefight

In writing about the fight between Jack Johnson and James Jackson Jeffries, Ransom argues that this type of brutality is a movement against social evolution. But through this event, he argues, one gains a sense of the U.S. psychological profile. For example, in pitting the white boxer against the black, the racial debate is given expression. Many whites saw this as an opportunity to reassert white supremacy through athletics, and blacks saw it as an opportunity to assert their worth through athletics. Although he is against this "sport," Ransom argues that the victory of the African American should have ramifications. The development of African Americans in athletics and other areas should precipitate access to all areas of life and endeavor.

•

From pagan Rome and the multitude applauding the gladiators in the arena of the Coliseum, the scenes have shifted through the centuries to be staged at last in the midst of the greatest exponent, and perhaps the highest expression, of Christian civilization on the Western Hemisphere. The place was Reno, Nevada, U.S.A. A place made famous by many whose names stand high in social registers and blue books throughout the country, who resort thither for the purpose of divorcing either husband or wife, as the case may be.

The time was on our national Holiday. In other words it was done on the fourth of July, 1910, and of the independence of the United States, the one hundred and thirty-fourth. While the governments of many cities were seeking to regulate the expression of patriotic joy over the birth of the greatest democratic republic in the world, by having a "safe and sane celebration," the mind of the multitude was centered on the gigantic grizzly white gladiator and the sleek, ebony athlete, who were about to join battle for — for what shall we say? Some said for money; most said it was to demonstrate the superiority of the white race over the black race and to regain for that race the unclouded title of "heavyweight champion of the world."

From *The Spirit of Freedom and Justice: Orations and Speeches* (Nashville: A.M.E. Sunday School Union, 1926), housed in the Schomburg Center for Research in Black Culture, New York. Reprinted by permission of the AMEC Publishing House (Sunday School Union).

A leading New York newspaper records the fact that more people assembled in Times Square to read bulletins of the fight at Reno, than assembled in the same place to receive the returns from the last presidential election. The newspapers gave more space to this prizefight than they did the return of former president Roosevelt from his African hunt and triumphal tour of Europe.

Both the man of religion and the man of science have taught us that we had developed beyond our un-God-like image and brute inheritance, and that our evolutionary development was now proceeding along the line of moral, social, and intellectual progress. (The words "our" and "we" just used refer, of course, to the white people, for, when we ascend into higher regions of ethical, civic, or social questions, whoever considers for a moment the many millions of black people present with us here?)

It is now almost twenty centuries since Jesus, but as we behold the spirit of savagery and brutality prevalent among us, may we not inquire, what fellowship with Christ has our Christian civilization?

Be it remembered it was not the ignorant, vicious, or criminal who were foremost in propagating this fight, and working up public interest in it, almost to fever heat; broadly speaking, it was the American people. For months the newspapers have been pouring out tons of matter in regard to it and employing all the arts of the cartoonist to illustrate their views. All of which has been quickly bought up by an eager public. The attitude of the entire country strongly reminds one of the camp of the Philistines, when Goliath of Gath was girding on his armor and threatening to rend to pieces and feed to fowls of heaven the representative of a poor and despised people who had dared assume to come out and fight against him.

To verify our assertion that public opinion encouraged the fight we quote from a lengthy editorial in the *New York Times* of July 5 as follows:

> It is a curious fact, therefore, though an incontestable one, that the public interest in this encounter should have been so eager. It has been looked forward to as a thrilling event not only in sporting circles, which indeed are not very susceptible to thrills, but by society at large. For weeks if not months it has been a foremost topic of conversation among all sorts and conditions of men and women. Its prominence

as a news topic has been enforced by public opinion. The people who most strenuously denounce prize-fighting have closely followed the daily accounts of the preparations for the battering match. They have deplored the publication of the reports and read every word of them. The huge crowd in Times Square yesterday afternoon was thoroughly representative of the population of this city. It was not composed of roughs and sports. Its mute and grave reception of the result of the fight was most significant.

The prizefight at Reno is more instructive as a psychological study of the American people in their attitude toward the Negro than all the outgivings of Edward G. Murphy, Booker T. Washington, Albert Bushnell Hart, W. E. B. Du Bois, Ray Stannard Baker, and their like combined. It teaches more than magazine writers, learned newspaper editors, and special investigators in the study of the Negro Problem have disclosed. A more vivid insight into their real character is given than by some of the brilliant portrayals of De Tocqueville years ago, and more recently by Wm. T. Stead.

The veneer of civilization and Christianity over the nation's character is penetrated by the X ray of its own self-revelation, disclosing a picture as vivid and true to the facts as the moving pictures of the fight at Reno, against which so many cities are protesting. It is the more sad because the latter pictures represent two human beings matching strength and skill, while the former picture shows the semisavage instincts of a very large section of our population, and reveals our national unfairness, hypocrisy, and insincerity.

The power of self-control is one of the greatest and highest of human attainments because it is the severest test of strength of character. This is true of nations as well as individuals. Now, the Negro has been told that among his many weaknesses one of the most glaring was the lack of self-control, that he was swayed not by his reason, but by his emotions.

No sooner did the result of the fight at Reno become known than Negroes were assailed in every section of the country. They were chased and beaten in the streets, dragged from streetcars and assaulted, cut or shot to death for no other reason than that two thousand miles away a pugilist who happened to be a Negro had defeated another pugilist who was a white man.

After all the tension to which the newspapers and public interest generally had wrought the people, the self-control exhibited by the colored people generally stands in admirable contrast. When the depths are stirred things that have long lain hidden, suppressed, or concealed come to the surface. This is true whether it relates to questions civic, social, political, industrial, moral, or religious. A flash of lightning, a powerful searchlight, an electric light, a lamp or a candle may be alike serviceable under given conditions to reveal what otherwise could not be seen. Is Anglo-Saxon character made of such stuff that its strength must yield when its pride is humbled in one of the lowest forms of contest for supremacy if the other contestant is of a despised and inferior race? In his *Ben Hur,* no one who has read it can ever forget the thrilling picture drawn by Gen. Lew Wallace in his description of the chariot race where the contestants were Messala the Roman and Ben Hur the Jew. Wealth, pride, power, prejudice, sympathy, everything was on the side of the Roman; but the Jew won. But the brilliant imagination of Lew Wallace did not conceive of a race conflict even back in the old pagan days because a representative of the Jewish people had outmatched the superiority and humbled the pride of their Roman masters.

The real rulers of the nation are the ministers of the gospel and the churches, the public schools, colleges and universities and the organs of public opinion, as well as the laws under which we live. We have had three hundred years of Puritanism with its ethical and religious codes and standards. When, therefore, ministers of religion, after all their preaching, feel called upon to descend from their pulpits and seek to reform the people by an act of the state legislature instead of by an act of God, when the leading event of public interest on our national holiday has come to be a prizefight, is it not about time to inquire if there is not something wrong with the power and efficacy of its preaching. Twenty centuries from Calvary should lead us to something higher than the roped arena which was set up in Reno, Nev. *From our viewpoint this country has not witnessed for years, if ever, a greater exhibition of mock Christianity, sham morality, and downright hypocrisy than this prizefight has brought to light.*

The chief things which made this fight possible, aside from the streak of savagery remaining in us, were first, money. This phase of it appealed to the sporting and gambling fraternity throughout the country. But back of this was another thing which overshadowed all. "White supremacy" in the world of pugilism must be regained. This, most of our newspapers had been proclaiming for months.

And this is why many only mildly protested, some were openly tolerant, while others were discreetly silent.

Protest there was, but no such widespread and emphatic protest preceded the holding of this "battle of the century" which was to be as has arisen since its conclusion over the exhibition of all such pictures portraying it. Granted that the exhibition of all such pictures serves no good purpose, but rather tends to coarsen and brutalize. More than this, the exhibition of these pictures may in some places intensify race friction. But on the other hand the Rev. Thomas Dixon has written and staged a play called *The Clansman,* which has been played in the leading cities of the country, North and South. This play depicts the Negro as a fiend, a human brute whose prey is white women. The Negroes of Washington, Baltimore, Philadelphia, New York, Providence, Boston, Chicago, and elsewhere have appealed to the authorities to suppress it, but except in two or three cases without success. Yet the avowed aim and purpose of this play is to excite race antagonism. On an average about two Negroes are being lynched each week with one occasionally burned alive at the stake. Yet no word of protest do we hear from these religionists, moralists, and conservators of public virtue. It is announced that these pictures are to be prohibited in the Philippines, India, South Africa, and South America, [not] on the ground of their demoralizing or brutalizing influence. No. They are to be prohibited because the black or darker peoples might go restive and could not be held so firmly in leash after they had witnessed the spectacle of a white man being defeated by a black man in a contest of brute strength, endurance, and skill.

After more than a thousand years of civilization and progress, must a cry go up for "white supremacy" when Anglo-Saxon prestige seems to be menaced in a realm which might well be relegated to the days of the cavemen of Europe? If the Negro should develop in the course of time, as seems likely, into a competitor in the domain of music, of art, of science, of philosophy, of statecraft, of commerce, industry, and trade, must an alarm be sounded reaching from New York to London and Berlin for the preservation of "white supremacy"?

Already the Japanese, belonging to one of the darker races of mankind, have caused grave concern to many nations because of their position in the Far East. What is to become of "white supremacy" when China, India and Africa become competitors, possessing equal ability and strength? Neither an individual, nor a nation conscious of its strength and sure of its ground, has aught to fear. God has appointed no race or nation a trustee to administer the affairs of the earth on behalf of their fellowmen. Christianity teaches that there is neither Greek nor Jew, barbarian, Scythian, bond nor free, but that all men are brothers. The thing most to be desired is not the supremacy of any race but the supremacy of man upon the earth over all of its laws and forces. The ages have been and now are preparing for the day when each shall make his contribution of the highest and best within him, for the common good of all.

The Reno prizefight may at least teach one lesson. Since the field where the Negro might demonstrate his ability has been confined to prizefighting and the various forms of menial service, should he not be given an opportunity to demonstrate his ability in all those fields of activity to which others are freely admitted?

While denouncing this fight and all of the influences connected with it, as a reproach upon our Christianity and civilization, can we not afford to give to the people represented by the victor of the contest an equal opportunity in the race of life to that enjoyed by the people represented by the vanquished? Open wide the gates and let the strength, dexterity, and skill the Negro has shown as a prizefighter be employed in factory and mill, in the arts and every department of industry, commerce, and trade.

He will thus as a productive factor of the nation's wealth add to its strength while becoming at the same time a safer political quantity and a better and stronger citizen to bear and share the burdens and responsibilities of the state.

Lynching and American Public Opinion

In this essay, Ransom argues that lynching is a means of social control that has nothing to do with the maintenance of "law and order." Rather, lynching allows white Americans to maintain an unfair advantage in the major arenas of life. To justify the lynching of African Americans, many in the United States have painted African American males as beasts who seek to ravage white women and social norms. This has been

From *The Spirit of Freedom and Justice: Orations and Speeches* (Nashville: A.M.E. Sunday School Union, 1926), housed in the Schomburg Center for Research in Black Culture, New York. Reprinted by permission of the AMEC Publishing House (Sunday School Union).

effective as one can tell from the relative silence concerning the barbarity of lynching. Ransom admits that African Americans may only save themselves from these barbarities by making use of their political power and through self-defense.

•

When truth desired a hearing and liberty a voice, men have in the past looked to Faneuil Hall. These walls have been articulate with the cry of the oppressed, not only of our country, but throughout the world. No spot on earth is more sacred to the cause of freedom and justice than the ground upon which we stand. While one stone rises above another here, Faneuil Hall will remain a standing challenge to tyrants and tyranny. By the high ideals it has championed, Faneuil Hall doctrine has done more than any other to make this country's history worth recording. The acts of Faneuil Hall audiences have done more to influence American public opinion in the right direction than have the acts of Congress.

With the flight of years a great tribulation has been wrought in public sentiment and the personnel of the audiences assembled here. In the old days white audiences thronged these walls to hear white men, representing the best heart and brain of the nation, plead for liberty and justice for the poor oppressed blacks. Today the burden rests upon black men and women to come here and appeal to a public opinion and a public press, which is, for the most part, indifferent or hostile. Our appeal is for the supremacy of civilization over barbarism and savagery.

We are here not in the spirit of anger or of that discouragement which has abandoned hope. We are here not so much to denounce and assail, as to appeal to this nation to forsake its sins, to cast off its bloody robes of murder, to throw back into the deepest abysmal pit of hell its lyncher's torch and seek that righteousness that exalteth a nation.

The question that confronts us is older than the Declaration of Independence, the Magna Charta, or the laws of Moses upon the table of stone; it goes back to the time when God beheld the blood of Abel crying from the ground. Can this nation, consecrated to freedom, afford to face the future with the mark of Cain branded upon its brow?

Lynching, which is fast becoming a national crime, reaches far beyond the helpless victim who perishes horribly by the fury of the mob. The question that most vitally concerns us is not of race antipathy or sympathy; it concerns our Christianity, democracy, and civilization itself. Some who object to protests of this kind tell us to make our people cease committing crimes against women, then lynching will cease. But in eighty percent of the lynchings this crime is not even alleged.

In approaching a question like that of the freedom with which Negroes may be put to death by mobs, we should seek for causes. We have not far to seek. Primarily, it sprang out of the desire of the former slaveholding states to repress the Negro. The South, in order to justify itself in these barbarities, began by blackening his character, by painting him a monster who menaced the safety of women. By continually dinning this into the ears of this country and of the world, they have finally so quieted the public conscience that now a Negro charged with any crime, and sometimes with no crime at all, may be lynched with impunity anywhere in the South and occasionally in the North. The conscience of the nation has become so seared that it is no longer horrified when [in] the state of Pennsylvania or Georgia a human being is burned to death at [the] stake. The newspaper press does not use its influence to arouse public opinion against this iniquity, while the pulpit, which should be the first to lead in an attempt to purge the nation of this foul blot, is, for the most part, silent.

Negroes themselves are largely to blame for the contempt in which they are held and the impunity with which their liberties and their lives may be invaded. Sheriffs, mayors, courts, governors will not take seriously into account the interests of a people who have lost or surrendered the right to retaliate or call them to account at the ballot box. Mobs do not quail when there is no fear that their wild brutalities will be answered by a volley of bullets.

I am unwillingly, but slowly, coming to the conclusion that the only way for the Negro in particular, and the dark-skinned people in general, to win and hold the respect of white people is to mete out to them a white man's measure in all relations of life.

In at least seven states of this Union the Negro holds the balance of political power. He should use this weapon in an effort to stir the national government against lynching. We are all familiar with the argument that the national government can do nothing to put down lynching in the southern states. The national government can do anything it desires to do when the public welfare or interests demand it. The national government found a way to interfere when the boll weevil was destroying cotton crops in Texas and other southern states. The national government found a way to legislate on the question of marriage in relation to the Mormon

Church, and would immediately take steps to nullify any action the State of Utah might take on this subject contrary to the prevailing public opinion.

Are not the rights of human beings as sacred as the cotton crop? Is not the doctrine of the inviolability of human life more sacred than this nation's attitude toward the doctrines of the Mormon Church?

But the action of this government in abrogating the treaty with Russia furnishes a still more striking example as to how the lynching evil can be combated. The treaty was abrogated because American citizens of the Jewish race visiting Russia did not receive the same treatment accorded to other American citizens. Now, the treaty of the United States with Great Britain contains the clause "the most favored nation."

We would advise that Negro subjects of the British Empire who come to this country numerously from the British West Indies travel freely throughout the southern states and when they are Jim Crowed and otherwise assaulted and degraded, that they appeal to the British government on the ground that their treaty rights have been violated. Let them urge that England abrogate its treaty with the United States, unless the government of the United States guarantees to British subjects of the Negro race the same treatment as it accorded to other subjects.

Why were American public opinion and American statesmen aroused to such heights of indignation on behalf of the Jews? Is it because they are in love with the Jews, or rather is it because of the Jewish vote? One of the reasons why the Negro's cause in this country has in recent years sadly gone from bad to worse is because misguided Negro leaders have counseled them to an attitude of submission, which is both unmanly and un-American. He has largely lost or surrendered his right to vote to the nullification of the Fifteenth Amendment.

To demand the enforcement of the Fifteenth Amendment today is to be branded as "an enemy of both races," "a fanatic," "a mischievous agitator." To all outside interference the South says: Leave the Negro to us. We understand him, and know best how to deal with him, both for his own good and the welfare of the South. President Taft, who has boldly committed himself to the doctrine of race discrimination, pipes his grand diapason in harmony with this sentiment by declaring that the Negro "ought to come and is coming more and more under the guardianship of the South!"

With far more justification, we reply on behalf of the Negro —

Leave the southern white people to us. We have lived among them
for two and a half centuries, we both know and understand them.
We have nursed their children, built their homes, and for more than
two hundred [years] we have fed and clothed them. When they
took up arms to destroy the Union in order to bind us in perpetual chains, we did not fire their cities with the torch, nor rise in
violence against them, but protected their property, their helpless
women and children. Leave them to us. We have imbibed not the
ideals of feudalism, but of democracy; we are Americans filled with
the spirit of the twentieth century. Leave them to us, and we will
make the free public school universal throughout the South and
open alike to all, without regard to race, creed, or color. We will
make free speech as safe in Mississippi as it is in Massachusetts;
we will abolish lynching and usher in a reign of law, of courts
and juries, instead of the shotgun, the faggot, and the mob. We
will abolish peonage, elevate and protect labor, and make capital
secure. Leave them to us; our chivalry shall know no color line,
but our womanhood shall be protected and defended, and our citizens, regardless of race or color, shall be permitted to participate
in the government under which we live. Leave them to us, and we
will make them know their place and keep it, under the Constitution as amended. We will remove the last vestige of Jim Crowism
under the forms of law, and make the places of public necessity,
convenience, recreation, and amusement open alike to all without
respect to race or color. We will make intelligence, character, and
worth, instead of race and color, the sole test of recognition and
preferment for all. Thus as North and South divided over the Negro, so would the Negro unite them in the only bond of union that
can stand the test of time — fraternity, justice, and righteousness.

The Negro Church

*In this essay, Ransom rehearses the religious development
of Africans in North America — from "fetishism" to participation in Christian denominations, and finally the establishment of African American denominations. Ransom, in
the language of social evolution and racial genius, asserts
that African Americans have made original contributions to*

From *The Negro: The Hope or the Despair of Christianity* (Boston: Ruth Hill,
1935), housed in the Schomburg Center for Research in Black Culture, New York.

*"American" religiosity through the spirituals and the depth
of their spirituality. And this profound sense of spirituality
sparked their quest for socioeconomic and political equality.*

•

By the Negro church, I mean churches whose membership is composed of Negroes. The Negro church is not the result of differences of language, doctrine, creed, or polity. The Negro church is based entirely upon race and color. It is not the result of the difference of religious belief. It is purely the result of the unchristian spirit and attitude of American Christianity.

When Negroes were first brought to this country, they held and practiced the age-long beliefs and customs of their fathers. Broadly speaking, their religion was fetishism. Of the revealed religion, which we accept as the standard of our faith, they knew nothing. Never from the days of St. Paul and the other apostles was Christianity ever furnished with such pliant material for transformation into the Christian faith and practice as was furnished by these crude Negroes, fresh from the continent of Africa. But it was first held that they were so low in the scale of human development that they were unconvertible. Since, therefore, they could not comprehend the teachings of Jesus and thus become baptized believers, slaveholding Christians were violating no law of God or man by holding them in involuntary servitude. But almost from the beginning, the teachings of Jesus had a strong appeal to these black men and women fresh from the jungles of Africa. Despite the teachings of priests and ministers and the attitude of the Christian church that embraces Christianity, they were recruited into different religious denominations. Not through any personal conviction in regard to religious doctrine, they entered the religious denomination to which their masters belonged. Thus in the state of Louisiana, we have many Negro Roman Catholics, while in other southern states, there are Baptists and Methodists shading off into other religious denominations, according to the prevailing beliefs of the white people.

Throughout the more than three hundred years of his sojourn in America, the Negro has made no distinctive contribution to religious thought in the realm of doctrine or dogma. He has sampled all of the denominational and theological labels the white people have handed him.

The only theology to which the Negro can lay claim may be found in the upward surge of his spirit, as we find it expressed in that rich and original contribution to the hope and aspiration of the soul, as it is expressed in the Negro spiritual. His belief in reward and punishment in future life was taken literally from the Bible as it was expounded to him. In the same manner, John Milton, in his immortal poem, *Paradise Lost,* expressed the theology and scientific beliefs current in his day. But the Negro has faith and spiritual intuition. There is a double meaning in the words of many of these spirituals. "Didn't Old Pharaoh Get Lost in the Red Sea" meant also that the pharaohs, who were holding them down in chains, would likewise perish. "Didn't God Deliver Daniel; Then Why Not Deliver Me" was also a prayer for freedom. "Joshua Fit the Battle of Jericho and the Walls Came Tumbling Down" meant also that they would finally enter the land of promise which was freedom.

While they seem to accept the teachings of the church as well as the customs of society and the laws and decisions of the courts as to the place they should occupy in the social, economic, and political realm, faith and spiritual intuition led them to believe that these barriers should finally be swept away. They believed in equality, and when opportunity presented itself, they sought to achieve it. Thus, in 1787, Negroes were refused admittance to partake of the holy communion side by side with their white fellow Christians in St. George's Methodist Church in the city of Philadelphia. A small group of Negroes resented this denial of the teachings of Jesus by rising from their knees and withdrawing from that church and laying the foundation of what is now the African Methodist Episcopal Church, which draws no line of color or of race but which for nearly one hundred and twenty years has been an independent religious body under the direction and control of Negroes.

While the Negro has contributed nothing to theological dogma or religious creed in systematic or written form, this is not to his discredit, for it could not be expected from an illiterate people. Even had he been educated and trained, the Negro could not express his religious beliefs, his social and spiritual aspirations in the forms of current, theological doctrines and religious customs and beliefs.

Calvinism and various other austere brands of religious teaching and belief are a frigid blast for the warmth and enthusiasm inherent in the very blood and spirit of the Negro. There are very few black Presbyterians, Congregationalists, and Episcopalians. The spiritual atmosphere out there is too cold and bleak. The warmth and enthusiasm that used to belong to Methodists and Baptists gave him more room to spread his spiritual wings and to express the wealth of emotion that surged within him.

I do not say that the Negroes are hypocrites in the matter of their religious belief, but I have no hesitation in saying that the religious doctrines, forms, and customs have rarely ever penetrated beneath the surface of the real spiritual life of the Negro. When the Negro took over Christianity, he adapted to it religious dances and other outward forms of expression, which they had brought from Africa. Even today, when the Negro submerges himself into the rigid forms of the white man's spiritual expression, his spirit dies. Nothing is left but an empty shell. He becomes colder than the most rigid Presbyterian.

With centuries of civilization behind it, the white race, having deserted its pagan gods among all the religions of the world, cannot point to a single religion to which it has given birth. In the realm of religion, the white race has nothing except that which it has received from the Orient. It Romanized the Christian religion sufficiently to squeeze its pagan forms and philosophy into what really amounts to a much disfigured image of the sweet and gentle picture of Jesus Christ. Its theologians, ministers, philosophers, and statesmen have been able to divide the garments of Christ to make them a cloak to cover any position they choose to take. It is thus that the church was the apologist and defender of slavery. Aside from our recent national legislation in regard to prohibition, it has not led any social reform. Jesus said, "The poor have the gospel preached to them." But so long as the church is the refuge and defense of wealth and great corporations that oppress and grind the poor and turn deaf ears to the condition of the toiling millions, it has no appeal or influence upon the masses as the voice of God speaking to men. Jesus Christ is proclaimed as the Prince of Peace, but the overwhelming influence of the churches that bear his name, both in Europe and America, overwhelmingly supports the sanguinary wars waged by their different states.

Now if by religion we mean the Christian religion, and if by the term Christian religion we mean the teachings of Jesus, the Negro Christians of America are in [a] position to make a rich and redemptive contribution to every phase of American religious life. They have copied, adapted, and complied with outward forms; they have followed the white man afar off in the realm of religion, but when they became sufficiently spiritually emancipated to realize that they own their own souls they can organize their spiritual life in harmony with the teachings of Jesus as well as with the depth of their own emotional nature.

One of the chief influences that has kept the Negro church alive is not religion. Through all the years of its existence, the Negro Church has been and is now the chief center of his social life. The Y.M.C.A., the Y.W.C.A., and similar organizations are not comparable to the influence exerted by the Negro church upon every phase of the social life of its people. Here there are no high and no low, no class distinctions, no rich and poor; but just one big family of brothers and sisters among whom every religious service, whether on Sunday or through the week, is also a family reunion. When the Negro is not trying to act like white people, his church is not formal, staid, decorous. It is noisy with laughter, and warmth of greeting and shouts of praise and moments of sympathy for sorrow, and sobbing with tears for suffering and distress.

In all forms of activity and adventure, the Negro always turns first to his church. The Negro doctor, lawyer, dentist, insurance company, and merchant, in embarking upon their careers, or business, started first with the church to present themselves for inspection, approval, endorsement, and support. However far they may stray from the church and its teachings, most of these through the years that have passed, have received their first recommendation and support from some Negro preacher and his influence with his congregation. This has been largely true also in the political realm.

For fifty years, the politicians have used Negro preachers and the Negro churches to hold the Negro loyal to the Republican Party. Until the last four years, the co-partnership of the Negro church with Republican Party was so strong that a Negro resented disloyalty to the [the] Republican Party more quickly than he would disloyalty to his church. The religious imagination of the race had identified the Republican Party with the glamor of a Heaven-sent agency for the political deliverance of the race. It took more than fifty years of faithlessness and betrayal on the part of the Republican Party to bring what, at this writing, are the beginnings of the Negro's political disillusionment. The Negro is beginning to consider the political values and is gradually turning away from his blind idolatry of a political tradition. His religion and his church should still continue to exert potential influence over his political activities, but his religious imagination will exercise itself upon the higher level of education and discriminating intelligence.

I have said that American Christianity has rarely played a leading part in political and social reform, and this is particularly true as relates to the Negro. In the month of January 1934, a Pastor's Brotherhood of Detroit addressed the following telegram to a number of religious bodies:

> Faith in the integrity of organized Christianity is challenged by the apparent unwillingness of the leaders of unorganized Christianity to speak unequivocally and specifically against wrongs committed upon minority groups in America. Is it left to radical organizations to practice brotherhood under conditions of extreme pressure? Cannot the church say one word upon the Scottsboro case?

The above is a good cross-section of how Negroes generally feel toward the attitude of the white churches of America. It may be true that individual white churches and denominations have not spoken out in regard to the famous Scottsboro case, but truth and justice compel us to say that the Federal Council of the Churches of Christ in America, which represents almost all of the denominations of American Protestant Christianity, has used its influence in the interest of justice in the Scottsboro case just as it has taken no unequivocal stand on the general subject of lynching, but American Christianity does not seem to have enough of the spirit of Christ to lift up its voice and cry aloud for justice for the Negro, or any other oppressed group within the nation.

The powerful appeal, which Negro spirituals have upon all classes, leads me to believe that in the near future the Negro shall make the richest contribution to church music our modern world has yet known. Of course, this cannot come until the Negro emancipates himself from slavish imitation of white composers, and the belief he has held so long, that when a white man speaks, the last word has been said. But we all now know that within the realm of church music, neither the deepest nor the highest note has yet been struck. Hymns and music are wings to the soul. In the realm of church music, we expect the Negro to enrich and deepen religious worship through the contribution he shall make to church music.

There are approximately six million Negro church members in the United States of whom fifty thousand are ministers of the gospel. This formidable religious and spiritual force, when it becomes more courageous and enlightened, should exert a powerful influence in leavening American Christianity with courage to take its stand upon the teachings of Jesus, upon the prayer of our common humanity and brotherhood in the spirit of righteousness and justice for all without the distinction of class, sex, color, or race.

The Future of the Negro in the United States

According to Ransom, nations rise and fall based upon their ability to address changing conditions, and in Europe, Japan, and the United States there is a continuing struggle for relevance and dominance. Ransom perceives within these various claims a common notion that the future of the world rests squarely within the grasp of the white race by whatever name it is called. Yet, the United States — his primary concern here — must recognize that it consists of beautiful diversity, and it must show humility through the recognition that God controls history and calls the world's nations to justice and righteousness. African Americans play a role in this movement, having gained skills and talents through the redemptive suffering they have endured.

•

Europe and Asia have been plowed, cultivated, and harvested in the fields of religion, philosophy, and statecraft. Through the age, many nations and peoples have vanished because the soil grew weak and sterile; they were not revitalized in mind and spirit by ideals capable of meeting the changed conditions of the changing years.

To whom does the future belong? Once Egypt said, "The future belongs to me." Proud Babylon once held the same belief. Rome, that proud and mighty mistress of the world, felt that the key to the future was held securely in her iron grasp. I do not know that any nation of this day claims to hold the key to the future. By their present warlike preparations, they are only striving as nations and peoples to preserve for themselves each a place among other nations and peoples. At the present hour, the struggle to hold a place in the future seems most intense in Europe, in Japan, and in the United States. Perhaps among the peoples of the earth today, none cherishes the dream that the future belongs to England, Germany,

---

From *The Negro: The Hope or the Despair of Christianity* (Boston: Ruth Hill Publishers, 1935), housed in the Schomburg Center for Research in Black Culture, New York.

France, or Japan. The ruling nations and peoples of the earth today find themselves in the center of a current which, despite armaments, diplomacy, religion, and education, is bearing them either resistlessly toward the brink of an abyss, or to a future destination they cannot even predict.

But as to the future, there is one thing upon which the ruling peoples of Europe and America agree; namely this: the future must and shall belong to the white race. Call it Aryan, Nordic, Anglo-Saxon, what you will. The future must belong to those white races, which today dominate and control the whole vast structure of the white man's civilization. The nations are arming against each other with feverish haste, but in greater terror, they would join arms against the future domination, or even the freedom and equality, of other peoples not derived from the soil of Europe. For this, they are willing that their blood shall flow, that the treasures of their wealth shall be sacrificed, rather than permit Asia or Africa to share equally with them in freedom, privilege, and power.

They shudder at the thought that the scepter of world wide domination should be taken from them, and given to the yellow or brown races of mankind; that it should ever, in any distant future, pass to the Blacks of Africa, and their descendants scattered abroad would fill them with terror were not even the thought of such a catastrophe ridiculous and chimerical.

During the world war, often we heard the solemn warning that the destruction of civilization was threatened; that the next step would be to be enveloped by the "Yellow Peril" through the resistless tide of Asia.

Who owns the future? Should it be the possession of nation, color, or race? Is it desirable that the scepter of world domination pass from the white to [the] yellow, brown, or black races of mankind?

Is the hand of God in history? Or is it as Napoleon is attributed to have said, "God is on the side of the heaviest battalions." Perhaps of the present Napoleon would say, "God is on the side of the very strongest navy and the most powerful fleet of battle airplanes."

Regardless of the view we may hold, history has shown repeatedly that the event is often decided by a power outside ourselves. Some call it fate, luck, chance; others call it God.

The source of absolute justice cannot originate with men. We must look beyond the motives and passions that sway us; we must look to one unchanging source. Both rulers and courts of law must look to some "higher source" if they would have others to believe that they are seeking to conform standards absolutely just and righteous. Freedom, justice, righteousness are the very foundation stones of our American democracy. We are attempting to establish here something unique in human society among the nations of the earth.

As a nation, we are not diverse, but a homogeneous people. But our homogeneity does not consist in our being of the same race, color, or national derivation. These are trivial and nonessential attributes. We are homogeneous insofar as we cherish and share the same ideals and aspirations, and count as one of ourselves all who in spirit, in purpose, and in will unite to uphold and achieve our goal as free people. Thus our national household consists of people derived chiefly from Europe, Africa, and Asia. But this nation was established, and has [been] developed and sustained by white men and black men. They cleared its forests, conquered and tilled its soil, built its roads, spanned its rivers, and established its institutions and its homes.

Americans of African descent have been members of our national family since it was first established on American soil. But they have never had a seat at the first table, either in religion, education, economic opportunity, or politics. They have only received that which was left or discarded, after others had been fully served. Indeed, they are often refused even the crumbs that fall from the bounteous provision served at our material, social, and economic feast.

Upon this meager fare, the Negro has sustained himself in health and courage, with laughter, music and song, because he believes in his full achievement of a place at the first table in our national life. We believe God to be not a cruel monster, but a loving Father, training and testing under severe discipline the weakest and most unenlightened of his children. If the Negro survives, it will not be by power and might. Human resources he has none equal to combat the odds that are against him. Through faith in God and fellowship with Jesus Christ, he must make his way. Without this, he can but perish. America is God's proving ground for the possibilities of the Negro's capacity to win with faith and love what others have failed to hold with wealth, privilege, and power.

I have said America is God's proving ground for the Negro. Yea, more, is it not our proving ground for God? The Negro, the last untried human reserve God has at His command, was suddenly thrust from his native jungle and forest and delivered fettered and chained into the severest test that has ever been applied to the teachings of Jesus since Christ was lifted up on a cross. The Negro has been placed at the very center of American life. In home, in church, in school, in business, and in politics, he cannot be entirely ignored. Day and night, on land and water, his ebony presence is there to greet us. God has declared He can take the "things that are weak to confound the mighty." He says He can take "things that are and make them as though they were not." May we not look here for love among all brothers to prove and vindicate the all-fatherhood of God? Shall the Negro live to voice the cry, "There is no God in the affairs of men"? Or shall he and the white man in America prove the cross of Christ superior to differences of color and race?

We have seen God open dungeon and the prison pen; we look now to see Him make enough standing room under the cross of Christ for black and white to stand upon equal footing, without reservation or denial, in full recognition of their abounding good will, each for the other, contributing without hindrance or denial the highest and best there is within them.

In the realm of the mind and spirit, no other people on the face of the earth has contributed such rich, virgin soil for the growth of the teachings of Jesus as have Americans of African descent. Here were minds and spirits free from the philosophies, religions, systems of ethics, and theories of government which for ages had engaged the attention of the choicest spirits among men. These had built and overthrown empires, colonized continents, established laws, written poems, and set their songs to music.

The crude, human material brought to our shores at first was thought to be so low in the human scale as to be incapable of comprehending and developing the achievements of the more highly developed groups of mankind. The Negro came without symbols to express in writing his religious belief or his moral and social creeds. His only history was tradition. His racial and territorial isolation had, for ages, been complete both from Europe and the Americas. Here was the opportunity for which ages had waited, to see what Christianity could accomplish on soil left barren by vanished gods. Here were neither Greek, Mohammedan, nor Jew, tenaciously holding to a Sacred Book believed to be a revelation from God; but a people strongly emotional, pulsating with rich, warm blood, highly imaginative, and trustful as children in things that are spiritual and invisible.

For two hundred and fifty years, though denied access to a

knowledge of the written revelation of God, by contact and association, by religious temperament, and, above all, by faith, they laid hold of God in the darkness and held on until they were lifted up and illuminated by Him who is the Light of the World.

Neither at Jerusalem, Ephesus, Corinth, or Rome, did St. Paul, or other apostles have such plastic material to mold into the spirit and likeness of Jesus Christ, as was, and is presented to American Christians, white and black, teaching how they may live together here in all the relations of organized society. We know the social, economic, spiritual, and political pathway the Negro has traversed in America for the past three hundred years. Bondage, servitude, ignorance, poverty, freedom, citizenship, the home, church, school, restricted industrial and economic opportunities, with disfranchisement, lynching, and burning at the stake, along with almost universal racial segregation and social ostracism, together with flat and open denial of equal industrial and economic opportunity.

In the face of all of this, have Negroes given way to the spirit of defeatism? Have they any thought of surrendering to the artificial social and economic barriers by which they are surrounded? Are they discouraged and cast down in spirit while doors upon every hand are shut in their faces? No; their aspirations were never higher and stronger, and their faith in the future more firm.

The Negro has survived every crisis and met every test with which he has been confronted on American soil. He feels himself to be a child of destiny, an heir to the future, who shall finally inherit the best that America has to bestow. Our fellow citizens, in their security, are deceived by the silent acquiescence and the air of outward submission preserved by the great majority of Negroes in the United States touching equality. In their heart of hearts, all Negroes aspire to attain it. I mean social equality, industrial, economic, and political equality. For them to proclaim it would be the signal for the release of fresh measures of repression and persecution by "Christian America." In their struggle for survival and attainment, no minority group has ever shown a finer technique than that practiced by Negroes in dealing with their white fellow citizens. Whatever they must suffer and endure for the present, they bear with fortitude which is embellished with smiles and laughter. With their eyes fixed upon the future, they are biding their time.

The colonizing, exploring, inventive, and materialistic white man is the chief servant who is preparing the way for the future of the black race. A nation, no more than an individual, can be engrossed in things material for purely selfish, racial, or national ends, and at the same time excel in the higher, finer things of the mind and spirit. Under their thin veneer of religion, they are as gross as the material creations they have woven upon which to base their prosperity, supremacy, and power. The pyramids, the Pantheon, the Colosseum, and remnants of the material arts and sciences are the tombstones of Egypt, Greece, and Rome. They mark the spot where lie the dust of nations and peoples long since passed away. Their mind and spirit live only in the literature and arts that survive them. It remains true of all peoples [that] nothing but the intangible things of the mind and spirit have power of survival. David, Jeremiah, Isaiah, Jesus, Paul, and Socrates have caused Jews and Greeks to make succeeding generations their debtors.

The Negro's natural aptitudes and special endowments do not seem to indicate that he is to make his contribution to humanity in the realm of things material, scientific, or commercial. The pain and travail through which the Negro has passed must produce results worthy of the things he has suffered. He must leave to others to boast past or present prestige and power. His face is toward the future, the control of which lies not in the power of any nation or of any race. It is the domain of literature, the arts, and things spiritual [in which] his future lies. From *Uncle Tom's Cabin* down to some of the latest prizewinning Pulitzer Prize novels, white people have woven their stories about the life of Negroes as they conceived it. But when the Negro explores his rich field of literary material, he shall create classic tales of surpassing purity, beauty, and power.

In music, the sweetest voice shall not be heard, nor all the range of height and depth be reached until his golden voice, unhindered, may be heard on every stage, and his fingers touch the keys and vibrate the strings to the most ravishing strains that have ever captivated the human mind and heart.

If a great American epic poem is ever written, it will be written by a Negro. If a great American symphony is ever composed, it will be composed by a Negro. A really great American grand opera can neither be written nor produced without casting Negroes in some leading roles. I hazard little in saying this, for no one else is capable of sounding the depths and scaling the heights of the emotional and spiritual things from which alone they can be created.

The sable thread of Negro life is woven so firmly into warp and woof of the pattern of American life it cannot be disentangled or unraveled. Our American race problem revolves around the Negro. There are those who see its solution only in immigration of the Negro to Africa, or setting apart in this country a Negro state. It is true that more than five thousand Negroes have been lynched in the United States in the last seventy years. But despite American savagery and barbarism, against which American Christianity has been strangely silent, the nation will never agree upon any of these methods to settle the question of the future of the Negro. All these proposals take no account of the fact that he must have a part by either giving his consent or resisting to the death brute force. But above all, in matters so gravely threatening, the destiny of a people who love and fear Him, it is God Himself who casts the deciding vote. There are more "white Negroes" in the United States today than there were white people in New England when the Declaration of Independence was proclaimed. It is beyond mortal power to take from the veins of America its infusion of Negro blood.

No, the Negro is here to stay. If he were transplanted elsewhere, he would still remain in American folk lore, in the melting melody of the weird, sad music of the spirituals, in the soft, honied sweetness of the voices of the southern people with the musical sounds of their broad pronunciation, which derive from whispering winds across jungle paths and the lazy ripple of streams among the reeds in the valleys of the Congo or the Nile. God took the barbarians and fashioned them upon the anvil of Rome into what we now know as European civilization. God brought naked barbarians from Africa and put them upon the anvil of American Christianity and democracy; under the white heat of denial and persecution, He is fashioning them with sledgehammer blows into a new pattern for American civilization. His mission is to spiritualize it, make it pulsate with emotion until throughout the whole range of our social, economic, and political life it shall level the walls of wealth and privilege, of bigotry and pride, of color and race. Fifty million unborn Americans of African descent shall, a few generations hence, lead America to achieve that brotherhood which transforms the children of men into the spirit and likeness of the children of God.

> The crest and crowning of all good,
> Life's final star is Brotherhood....
> Our hope is in heroic men,
> Star-led to build the world again.
> To this event the ages ran:
> Make way for Brotherhood — make way for Man!

The Institutional Church and Social Settlement

In this chapter of his autobiography, Ransom discusses the sociopolitical, economic, and spiritual motivations for the development of this church structure that concretely presented his sense of the social gospel. It outlines the programs housed in this church and rehearses the support and opposition encountered.

•

After four years continued service as pastor of Bethel A.M.E. Church, Chicago, I resigned in order to devote myself to the organization and service of the Institutional Church and Social Settlement on Dearborn Street near Thirty-ninth Street, Chicago. For several years I had cherished the hope of devoting myself to this form of social service. I meditated and dreamed my dream of several years. I told the dream to Bishop B. W. Arnett, who at that time was my presiding bishop, and he told it to some of his colleagues. He not only told them the dream but sold it to them. I discovered that the "Railroad Chapel," a large building ideally constructed for the purpose of our work, was for sale. I found it could be bought for $34,000. Dr. Phil Hubbard was financial secretary of the A.M.E. Church at that time. Bishop Arnett had previously held this position and was at the time president of the financial board. He induced the financial secretary and board to buy it in the name of the A.M.E. connection. They did so by making a down payment with deferred payments to follow, all of which payments were made by the financial department and the debt cleared within four years. The property was therefore a connectional institution. Aside from the purchase of the property by the financial department, the general church never did anything about it. I have no knowledge of the method or mode of procedure but evidently by some action of the financial board of the A.M.E. Church, title to the property was so changed under the pastorate of Rev. A. J. Carey as to place this property under the control of what is now known as the Chicago Annual Conference. The auditorium of our building had a seating capacity of more than 1,200; it contained seven or eight other commodious rooms besides a dining room,

From *The Pilgrimage of Harriet Ransom's Son* (Nashville: A.M.E. Sunday School Union, 1949), housed in the Schomburg Center for Research in Black Culture, New York. Reprinted by permission of the AMEC Publishing House (Sunday School Union).

kitchen, gymnasium, and other facilities. It was dirty and out of repair from top to bottom.

We did not have a dollar from any outside source with which to begin the work, but we managed to get together enough money to clean and repair it sufficiently to open its doors for service. This occurred on July 24, 1900. We set aside three rooms for my family and used the church dining room and kitchen. We announced our formal opening. We did not have a dollar or a member. I induced Mr. H. P. Jones, then a clerk in the Chicago Post Office, to volunteer as superintendent of our Sunday School, which he did. But he did not have an officer, a teacher, or a Sunday School scholar. I organized a group of teachers and sent them out into the streets and highways, each to recruit a Sunday School class, and have them present on the day [of] our opening. This most of them did. Mrs. Ransom chose to recruit a men's Bible class; among the members of that class were former congressman Oscar Depriest, former alderman Louis B. Anderson, and a group of some of the brightest and most promising young men in the city of Chicago. Some drawn by personal friendship for me and others by curiosity brought us a sizable audience on our opening day. People soon began to join the church by the scores, which eventually hundreds of others registered as members of the different activities of our social settlement that most strongly appealed to their interest and support.

From our initial movement until the end of our connection, we had the active sympathy and cooperation of Miss Jane Addams of Hull House, of Rev. Graham Taylor of Chicago Commons, which he conducted in connection with his church, and of Miss Mary McDowell of the Chicago University Settlement. Knowing that we were taking our first uncertain steps in the work of social service, Jane Addams made haste to come to me. She immediately inquired: "Mr. Ransom, where do you expect to get the money with which to operate your ambitious program?" I told her I was moving forward by faith alone. "You must have some money," she declared. Through her influence a check for $100 was mailed to me from a Mr. Winesap of Los Angeles, California. I cherish the memory of this gift, for it was the first contribution from anyone up to that time. As our community service grew and enlarged, friends and supporters multiplied....

The launching of our Church and Settlement was bitterly fought by some of the leading Negro clergymen of Chicago, particularly those of my own denomination. A few months after we started, Quinn Chapel A.M.E. Church announced, under the leadership of

Rev. A. J. Carey, a program of activities which [paralleled] nearly everything we conducted at the Institutional Church; they did not, in fact, conduct these activities at all, except that for a time they did have a kindergarten and a "Men's Sunday Club." The same year we opened our Church Settlement, Bishop Abram Grant became our presiding bishop, Bishop Arnett having been assigned to another district. The Rev. A. J. Carey and Rev. A. L. Murray persuaded him to believe that because I had such a large following in Bethel Church and throughout the city of Chicago, I should not be permitted to preach at the morning hour on Sunday, because it would affect the attendance at Bethel Church which I had recently left, as well as other churches throughout the city. The bishop therefore directed that I should not preach except on Sunday night or on weekday nights. I complied with this order until Bishop H. M. Turner, then our senior bishop, came to Chicago a few weeks later. He came to see me and said, "I am the senior bishop of the church and regardless of what Bishop Grant says, I order you to preach. Announce your church service at this place for next Sunday morning. I shall be present." I announced the service as directed; the bishop was in the pulpit with me, but he said to me, "I am not going to preach this morning, these people came to hear you — you preach." When I had finished my sermon he arose and said, "Great God!! Just think of anybody trying to silence a voice like that on Sunday morning. My God!! How that man can preach." These forms of speech were characteristic of Bishop Turner's mode of expression, but from that day onward we held Sunday morning services.

Then these opposers of mine shifted their attack in another direction. They announced from their pulpit to their members that the Institutional Church was not really a church and forbade their members to take communion, or to cooperate with any activity of the Institutional Church. They were not permitted to have one of the Sunday School conventions at the Institutional Church. This opposition, instead of doing us an injury, tended to quicken the interest and curiosity of the people in regard to the work of the church. Through the suggestion and influence of Jane Addams of Hull House, we were able to contact several wealthy and influential people of Chicago, who became interested in our work, among them were Mrs. George M. Pullman, widow of the founder of the company that bears his name; Mr. Robert T. Lincoln, the son of President Abraham Lincoln, was the president of the Pullman Company at that time.... Through kindred interest in public social service, Clarence Darrow, the noted criminal lawyer, Rev. Frank W. Gunsaulus, president of Armour Institute, and I were drawn together, but more closely because each of us happen to be sons of Ohio.

During the summer of 1902, we had one of the periodic strikes of employees at the Chicago stockyards. The strikes assumed the proportions of great violence when hundreds of Negroes were brought into many departments there to take the places of the strikers. Many were beaten while others were either knocked or dragged from the great delivery trucks. They went through the usual forms of mediation and police protection without avail to stop the continued outbreaks of violence. The halfhearted intervention of the police force gave little protection to Negro workers. I talked with the superintendent of the Armour packing plant and also with Mr. Lewis Swift of the Swift Company, and finally managed with them to meet some of the leaders of the stockyard. I called my friend Clarence Darrow and others to confer with us on methods of procedure. I decided to go out to the stockyards and personally talk with some of the strike leaders. My friends tried to persuade me not to go for fear of violence, but I went. I talked with several of the leaders and told them colored men had no desire to take their jobs and would be quite willing to join the union if permitted, but colored men were laborers, had families to support, and wanted jobs, but had no desire to take their jobs or deprive others from their bread and butter but that there were enough jobs for all if black and white workers could agree upon some plan of friendly cooperation. I invited them to come to the Institutional Church to meet face-to-face, the Negro and white workers in an effort to compose their differences.... After conversing quite a long time in conference with the manager of the strikers [and] the representatives of the Negro workers, we settled the stockyard strike that day in the Forum of the Institutional Church and Social Settlement. This meeting concerning the strike at the stockyards is typical of many services rendered the city of Chicago by the initiative and leadership of the Institutional Church.

One of the greatest sensations to stir the city of Chicago in many years was the dynamiting of the Institutional Church.... Events leading up to it revolved around the "policy gambling racket." At that time, policy gambling flourished in Chicago unchallenged. It became bold and open, particularly on Chicago's South Side and in other areas thickly populated with the poor and underprivileged....

The nature of our activities in our Social Settlement brought us in daily contact with the less favored people of our group, and our hands were full with the moral, social, and economic problems that confronted them.

It was not until the policy gamblers waxed bold enough to ply their trade among our Negro schoolchildren on Chicago's South Side that we determined to do something about it. We conferred with the alderman, with the police department and other sources thought to be able to bring restraining influences to bear. The police department informed me that it could find no place or places where policy offices were located. I finally got a reporter who knew the location of some of these places to agree to go and take pictures of several of the places from which policy gambling was being operated. While taking these pictures he was physically assaulted in the street, his camera was broken, and he was readily lodged in the Harrison Street police station on a flimsy charge. Since I could get no action from any source, I announced a series of sermons based on the facts ascertained and the evil effects of its operation on our youth and the poor in general. The reply to my challenge was to plant a charge of dynamite in the rear of the building, where my office was located. The force of the explosion cracked walls and large foundation stones, and blew out the windows on that side of the building, tore my books to shreds, and caused general ruin. Fortunately none of us were in that part of the building at the time. . . .

"Moral and Religious Influences" and "Literary Societies"

Although Ransom transferred to Oberlin College from Wilberforce as a result of his dislike for some of Wilberforce's strict policies, he eventually returned and completed his education there. And, when reflecting on that experience, he gave Bishop Daniel Payne and several faculty members credit for much of his religious and theological development. This text provides his reflections on his time at Wilberforce University. It is interesting in that it not only records his personal devel-

From *School Days at Wilberforce* (Springfield, Ohio: New Era Co., Printers, 1890), 32–40, 53–59, housed in the Schomburg Center for Research in Black Culture, New York.

opment but also provides information concerning the nature of education at Wilberforce during the late nineteenth and early twentieth centuries. In the following selection, Ransom discusses his thoughts on the importance of moral and religious influences on education (using Wilberforce as an example) and literary societies. Through the latter, Ransom argues that students are free to develop their sense of literary culture and their oratorical skills, with the encouragement and support of the university. Both the influences on education listed and the societies serve to better prepare students for full participation in the life of the country, and push the country toward a stronger embrace of "truth."

•

I do not wish that my subjects be learned at the cost of religion, nor religious at the cost of learning.
— The King of Bavaria at the founding
of the University of Munich

The preservation and dissemination of knowledge have from of old been largely the work of priests and clergy. In the Christian faith nearly all great colleges and universities have been founded, and by Christians they have been perpetuated and sustained. Outside of academic halls many teachers have arisen who have disciples or scholars in many languages and many lands. Some of them are worthy to be followed, but to many of these "thinkers" is due the intellectual superficiality and moral degeneracy, under scientific nomenclature, that mark our times. The stability and strength of a nation depend largely upon its attitude toward systems of education, especially upon which system. Educational systems purely scientific or philosophic — concerned with intellect alone — may give mental acuteness or intellectual dexterity, but never strength. Under such conditions, affairs of government, questions commercial, and intercourse between man and man will never be matters of "policy" or "expediency" rather than right and wrong. As the highest building, the loftiest pyramid, or tower rests upon the earth as well as the most miserable hut, so the most powerful intellect as well as the weakest must rest upon the moral nature of man. This foundation wanting, the moral vacuity must be filled by the "made ground" of philosophy. The character and quality of action will never rise higher than the moral strength determining action. We see great intellects who, having lost all trace of God within themselves, are trying to reason Him off His throne. But the human mind wandering, like Noah's dove, over the wastes of philosophy finds no place of rest. It is to those trained under correct moral and religious influences that the learned professions must look for men to maintain their high character and properly apply them. Here must government, capital, and labor look for wise laws, just stewards of this world's goods, and honest hands to direct and move the wheels of industry. The idea that a student forms, while at college, of the universe, his relation to it, and his mission in it will greatly influence, perhaps decide, all his future career. For a young person entering college, the ability of professors and the studies of the curriculum are not alone important; the moral principles there instilled, the religious views there held, are subjects of greater moment and concern.

The view of education held by our Christian colleges is that all the powers of the student should be drawn out and trained. But it is of Wilberforce we write, and she proclaims her mission to be Christian education. This she hopes to impart by training the whole man in the principles of religion, knowledge, and virtue. American literature, when it touches on the "Negro problem," proclaims loudly not only the low moral condition of the Negro, but also his low conception of morality. If the Negro is permitted to judge himself by same rule that the Anglo-Saxon employs when passing judgment upon his own race, we will take the Negro at his best, not at his worst. It is from the study of the institutions of a people we may learn what they are or have been. In establishing an institution for the training of his children, we would expect the Negro to give expression to his conception or idea of morality, and to apply that idea in the practical workings of such institution. We could also judge the effect of the moral idea practically applied by the effects produced upon the character and life of those to whom applied. Wilberforce University has proclaimed to the world, for more than a quarter of a century, the Negro's idea of Christian education.

Search where we may among Christian institutions and communities, none can be found where the highest ethics of nineteen centuries of Christianity and civilization are more fully held and practiced than here: none where the morality of the New Testament is more generally revived and obeyed. Within the jurisdiction of the college intoxicating drinks are not allowed; the true moral distinctions in regard to right and wrong in all dealings and associations are recognized and enforced. Immoral books and papers, firearms, cardplaying, games of chance, etc., are expressly prohibited and forbidden. Cleanliness and regular habits must be observed, economy and industry practiced. One may reside in this community for years and never hear a profane word or see an intoxicated person on or about the college grounds.

The high moral tone of the university has attracted around it a community as intelligent, refined, and morally pure as is anywhere to be found. It cannot be said of this community that the presence and influence of "intelligent and Christian whites" are here to educate and restrain "an ignorant and immoral race." The universal intelligence and moral uprightness of the community are due to the teaching and example of professors and residents. Nor have they in the name of "progress" left "optional" or "elective" that ancient morality and religious observance enunciated by the Savior of men, but they are kept steadily before the student's mind. This little community, when viewed in the light of the past and present, becomes a rebuke, a verification, and an inspiration. It is a rebuke to those who in the past have prophesied and at present do declare that the Negro left to himself will not advance, that left to himself he will degenerate rather than maintain a high standard of morality, that his religion is superstition and his morality a sham, and that his presence in a community is a cloud upon its intelligence and a stain upon its morals. This college and community are a verification of the Negro's humanity and manhood. It proves that darkest centuries of heathenism, and other centuries black with crimes against the life of the soul, have not been able to rob the Negro of his humanity or destroy within him the image of God. In the light of what the Negro is today, the fanaticism of John Brown becomes like that of Jesus, Luther, and Paul — sublime confidence in the right of every man to enjoy the freedom of himself and a weapon of mightiest powers against all fetters upon the body, the conscience, or the soul. In less than a generation of freedom the most confident predictions of the great liberators have been fulfilled.

Wilberforce is an inspiration to the Negro to believe in himself. It should encourage others laboring on his behalf. Taking Wilberforce for an example of what the Afro-American has done and is doing in the realm of moral and intellectual culture, he has put to shame all false accusations and sneers; gathering inspiration from the achievements of the past and hope of the present, he will stand with the leaders of the world's progress. The Afro-American has never verified the predictions of his enemies, nor disappointed the hopes of his friends. If those who would aid him in his effort to rise are timid and seek assurance, or, if others are skeptical and seek for proof, we point them to Wilberforce, which now happily stands not alone, but speaks nonetheless eloquently of the Negro's real progress and worth.

We have said elsewhere that before students are admitted here they must present [a] certificate of good character, and as long as they remain a good character must be maintained. While those possessing the above named quality are welcomed, it is the desire of the faculty to induce all to become Christians. They seek to gain to this end by bringing all under Christian influence. The students are required to attend "prayers" in the chapel morning and evening of each day except Monday, that being a holiday. On Sunday they must go to church morning and evening and to "students' prayer meeting" on Monday evenings. The students assemble in the morning for prayers at 7:40. This service, which is usually conducted by the president, consists of singing a hymn, a prayer, and the reading of a portion of Scripture. In the evening at 4 the service is the same, except that the students take no part in the Scripture lesson as in the morning, when they read every alternate verse. In our day each student had a seat assigned him in the chapel, in which he was required to sit at all meetings or services held by the school. But prayers was not to all either a solemn or sacred assembly. While the devout were paying their vows unto the Lord, one not so engaged, if irreverent enough to look around upon the worshipers, would doubtless see some of the young men and women paying their vows to each other in the form [of] little notes passed to and fro. At prayers we were occasionally treated to some student oratory. The death of a prominent man or some event of unusual interest generally furnishing the text. The exhibitions usually came in the morning, just before we marched from the chapel. The orator, having previously obtained permission to present his matter to the school, would arise grandly in his place, and in tones that to us seemed menacing, exclaim, "Mr. President!" when would follow a neat little speech, a preamble, and some resolutions.

On Saturday morning after prayers the roll was called, at which time each student must report with how much fidelity he had kept the rules. As the names were called responses would come back about as follows: "Perfect," "Nothing to report," "Burning light after half past nine," "Off the grounds without permission," "Talking with the opposite sex." All failures reported were recorded by the secretary of the faculty, and the student "black marked" accordingly. When a student received ten black marks he was expelled. But for such failures as those noted above, if a reasonable excuse could be given, the president would excuse the offender, and at roll call he would report "Excused." The preaching on Sunday was usually by the president, the professor of theology, or one of the students in the theological department. When it was one of the latter who arose to face his fellow students and break to them the bread of life, it often happened that his inspiration took wings and fled from him, the result being confusion to him and amusement rather than edification to his hearers. Each year of our stay at Wilberforce the school was visited with stirring revivals of religion. Sometimes the religious feeling would run so high that students would fall down in the classroom and plead with the Lord to pardon their sin, while others would arise and profess faith in Christ, so that for a whole day recitations would be suspended. The percentage of professing Christians among students is always high. One year 99 percent of the students were professors of Christianity. Because of the strong religious sentiment here, the idea has gone abroad in many quarters that they try to make a preacher out of every young man sent to Wilberforce. But this "they" do not try to do. Students, if qualified, are free to pursue any course of study taught in the university, no influence being brought to bear for the purpose of affecting their decision in any way. In fact, the number of students in the theological department has never formed but a small percentage of those enrolled at any one time.

The moral and religious influence of Wilberforce is now being felt by scores of communities in almost every state in the Union. The students who go out from her halls are not religious at the cost of learning, nor learned at the cost of religion, but with intellect and heart well balanced and trained they are going forth to direct and lead their fellowman in paths of true progress and success.

Literary Societies: "Non Scholar sed Vita Discimas"

Wilberforce has no fraternities. But it has excellent literary societies, fitted to qualify their members for our loquacious American life. In our day there were but two literary societies, the Sodalian, composed of young men in the academic and college departments, and the Philomathean, composed of young women in the same departments. In recent years two more have been organized, the Payne and the Dodds, for the benefit of students of lower classification. The Sodalian furnished an excellent school for the cultivation of literary tastes and oratorical skill. The members were merciless critics. Deficiencies and failures were not overlooked and but rarely excused. Many students when they come to college are self-conceited and puffed up. But there is no better place to cure a self-important young man or woman than at college, especially a college literary society. Here they meet persons their equals in every way and many who far excel them. In literary work they find themselves excelled, in parliamentary tactics outgeneraled, in debate defeated, and in oratory surpassed. The mere imitator is ridiculed, the blundering parliamentarian is laughed at, and the literary pirate is treated as a pirate. Everything tends to put one on his mettle and bring out the best that is in him. There is no place where hard work and true merit are so fully and freely recognized as in these societies. If one reads a meritorious paper, its excellence is instantly discovered and commended; if he skillfully carries a point, he is heartily applauded; and if he delivers a good oration or is victorious in debate, many take him by the hand, speaking words of congratulation and praise. In the Sodalian the election of officers was always an exciting event. There were always two factions, each striving to gain for itself the ascendency in the management of affairs. Sometimes these contests became very bitter as the supporters of each ambitious aspirant for honors strove for victory. At times we would have two presidents attempting to occupy the chair, until one side or the other was outgeneraled, when things would move on peacefully for a time. The society had a prosecuting attorney, whose duty it was to bring to trial all offenders against the constitution and bylaws. The accused could either plead his own cause or choose someone to defend him. These trials, always interesting, became sometimes very stormy. The attorney, who was successful in securing many convictions, had great influence in the society, and was sure of promotion to higher honors; while, on the other hand, the one who had established a reputation as a great criminal lawyer, by the number of acquittals he had secured, was always in great demand and the recipient of many favors. Much attention was given to literary composition, but oratory held the first rank and was the thing in which all most desired to excel. Once a month these societies hold a public meeting, the exercises consisting of essays, orations, a debate, preparations for these meetings, and the exercises are usually of a high order. Of the internal workings of the Philomathean, the ladies' society, we have no personal knowledge, as the writer's gender disqualified him from entering its sacred portals. But we have been told that they addressed the chairman as "Miss President," rose to points of order, became unparliamentary, and even noisy at times, just like their brothers. In the Sodalian we had a sergeant at arms, whose duty it was to preserve order. In the exercise of his prerogatives it sometimes became necessary for him [to] eject unruly members from the room. If his authority was resisted, which often happened, he could deputize any number to assist him, in which case the unruly member was seized and carried or dragged bodily from the room. But we were not always successful. In one instance the combined efforts of the whole society were not sufficient to eject an unruly member. He backed himself into a corner, faced, and defied the president, sergeant at arms, and the whole society to put him out. We advanced upon him, and for some moments the scrummage raged; when the smoke of battle cleared there were many trampled feet, furniture had been overthrown, and clothes were torn, but our offending brother held his corner, defiant and unmoved. It must not be inferred from this that such things ever occurred among the Philomatheans; for of course a society of young women could never survive a mortal combat. The public exercises of the young ladies, consisting of essays, orations, select readings, and recitations, were always excellent. But these societies are not the only means of training the students in literary composition and the art of public speaking. The school is divided into rhetorical divisions, to one of which divisions each student is assigned. Over each of these divisions one of the professors presides, criticizing the composition and instructing in the art of oratory. Between the rhetorical divisions and literary societies, with their disputations, orations, essays, declamations, and recitations, no student can pass through the college without much instruction and practice in all these particulars. A few weeks before commencement is a time when many are exercising themselves in composition and oratory. The young men of the graduating class, already burdened with much self-consciousness, become more serious and grave. They are forging oratorical thunderbolts for their commencement orations. (Be it known, to speak in mild figures of speech, that during the senior year one stands with the college under his feet. For there are great oceans of Greek and Latin, mountains of mathematics, and continents of philosophy between other undergraduates and the senior. The senior is held in admiration to a degree not exceeded by that paid to the president of the college.) But we drop our parenthesis and resume. As commencement week draws near we see the pretty brows of the young ladies haunted "by the pale cast of thought." They are meditating pretty sentences to connect the poetical quotations which must find a place in their graduating essays. Indeed, we now see many young men and maidens with knitted brows and thoughtful mien; they are the orators, the disputants, the essayists, preparing to compete for prizes and to represent the literary societies [during] commencement week. The woods become vocal; the orators are practicing their orations. What sermons have been preached, what speeches have been made under the trees round about Wilberforce! They have heard the first sermon of many a young minister; they have been the silent auditors of commencement orations for more than a quarter of a century. Ah, me! could they but give back to us some of the sweet voices, grown silent now, that once mingled with the rustle of their leaves! Each succeeding year the unprotesting trees stand silent as before, while the glorious valedictorian, the graduate, and the representatives of the societies pour forth their thoughts on their deeply pondered themes. But this practice, this exercise, this instruction, has been fruitful.

There are many able writers and orators among us who first discovered their talents and their power in the rhetorical and literary societies of Wilberforce. Among the graduates few poor speakers or writers can be found. No particular style of oratory or writing is taught, but aside from the correction of absolute errors each student is left free to develop in the way most natural to him. After one has passed through the literary societies and rhetorical divisions of Wilberforce, he is able to express with ease what has been learned in the classroom. The toil, the defeats, the humiliations that all must meet who would pass these literary departments, are, after all, but the precursors of victories to come. These departments have sent forth men and women who, with voice and pen, have been and are now potent influences in the diffusion of intelligence and the advancement of truth.

Selected Bibliography

SELECTED ARCHIVE HOLDINGS

Payne Theological Seminary, Wilberforce, Ohio

"The Bad Negro," typed manuscript.

"Brotherhood Through Self-help," typewritten manuscript. (Reverdy C. Ransom?)

"Centennial Oration of Reverdy C. Ransom at Faneuil Hall, Boston, December 11, 1905, on William Lloyd Garrison," with handwritten corrections (Boston: Boston Suffrage League, n.d.).

"Charles Sumner: A Plea for the Civil and Political Rights of Negro Americans," Boston Centennial Oration, January 6, 1911, Park Street Church, Boston, sponsored by the New England Suffrage League and the Massachusetts branch of the National Independent Political League, and the Citizens Auxiliary Committee.

"Christianity, the Church and the Episcopacy: A Factual Statement on the Economic Status of the Negro, the Church Speaks to the World," selection (n.p.: A.M.E. Church, Bureau of Research and Publicity, bulletin no. 3, February 1942).

"Crispus Attucks, a Negro, the First to Die for American Independence: An Address," the Metropolitan Opera House, Philadelphia, March 6, 1930 (Philadelphia: Printed by A.M.E. Book Concern, n.d.).

"The Color Line among Negroes (n.d.), handwritten document. (Reverdy C. Ransom?)

"Deborah and Jael," a sermon to the I.B.W. Woman's Club, at Bethel A.M.E. Church, Chicago, June 6, 1897 (Chicago: Crystal Print, n.d.).

"Ecclesiastical Imperialism" (n.d.), handwritten document. (Reverdy C. Ransom?)

"Emancipation Day Address," Old Court House, St. Louis, Missouri, under the auspices of the Cooperative Civic Association, January 1, 1940.

"Environment," Indianapolis, 1896, handwritten document. (Reverdy C. Ransom?)

Unless otherwise indicated, Reverdy C. Ransom is recognized to be the author of each entry in this bibliography. During my visit to the Payne Theological Seminary, the papers were being reorganized, and as a result the Payne list does not correspond to box numbers.

"Episcopal Saboteurs," January 17, 1946, name of the publication omitted (vol. 59, no. 42).

"Fifteenth Amendment," delivered at the Sixth Annual Lincoln Banquet, Columbus, Ohio, February 14, 1893, typewritten manuscript.

"The Finished Product of American Womanhood," typewritten manuscript with handwritten corrections (n.d.). (Reverdy C. Ransom?)

"The Gate of the Temple Which Is Called Beautiful, Acts 3:2" (n.d.), selection from typewritten manuscript with at least one page missing.

"God's Last Reserves," typed manuscript.

"Golden Candlesticks Shall Illuminate Darkest Africa," August 24, 1951, typewritten with handwritten corrections.

"Grandmother," typewritten manuscript with handwritten corrections, presented to the Grandmothers' Club of Zion Baptist church.

"Hobbies," typewritten manuscript.

"Liberia, West Africa Faces the Rising Sun," selections from typewritten manuscript with some missing material (n.d.).

"Lions by the Way," in *The Disadvantages and Opportunities of the Colored Youth* (Cleveland: Thomas & Mattill, Printers, 1894).

"The Mission of the Religious Press," May 16, 1912, Kansas City (New York: Press of the New York Age, 1912).

"Orators and Oratory."

"Out of the Midnight Sky: A Thanksgiving Address," November 30, 1893, in Mt. Zion Congregational Church, Cleveland, Ohio (Cleveland: Praternal Printing and Publishing, n.d.).

"The Paraclete of God the Only Hope for Brotherhood and Peace," typed manuscript.

"Prophesy," poem.

"A Resolution and Confession" (n.d.).

Lucius Harper's Dustin' Off the News, "Reverdy C. Ransom Has Done the Unusual Thing for a Negro Bishop: He's Written His Life's Story" (n.p., n.d.).

"The Role of Women in the Home and the Church," typed manuscript. This piece includes Ransom's handwritten corrections.

"The Secret of Garfield's Success," handwritten document most likely from Ransom's time at Wilberforce based upon the comments, in another pen, found in the text (n.d.).

"Seeking a Seat in Congress and a Voice in Government," in the *A.M.E. Church Review,* April 1918, typewritten copy.

"The Sixtieth Anniversary of the Founding of the A.M.E. Church in West Africa" (n.d.).

"The Spirit of John Brown: A Speech Delivered by Rev. Reverdy C. Ransom, D.D., of Boston, Massachusetts, before the Second Annual Meeting of the Niagara Movement, Harpers Ferry, West Virginia, August 17, 1906."

"Testimonial by T. M. Green, pastor of St. Paul A.M.E. Church, Washington, Pennsylvania to Bishop R. C. Ransom Celebrating His Sixtieth Anniversary in the Ministry Sponsored by the Third Episcopal District at Allen Temple, Cincinnati, Ohio."

"The Thin Veneer of Christianity on European Civilization," typed manuscript (with handwritten pages).

"Visions and Tasks for Africa, the Americas and the Orient," January 17, 1946, newspaper article (unnamed paper).

"Wendell Phillips: Centennial Oration," November 29, 1911, Plymouth Church, Brooklyn, New York (n.p., n.d.).

Schomburg Center for Research in Black Culture, New York

"Boston Whittier Centennial Oration," Whittier Centenary in Faneuil Hall, Boston, December 17, 1907.

"Charles Sumner: A Plea for the Civil and Political Rights of Negro-Americans."

The Disadvantages and Opportunities of the Colored Youth (Cleveland: Thomas and Mattill, printers, 1894).

Duty and Destiny: A Thanksgiving Address, at the Union Thanksgiving Service in Bethel A.M.E. Church, New Bedford, Massachusetts (New Bedford?, Mass.: L. I. Jenkins, printer, 1904).

"How Should the Christian State Deal with the Race Problem?" an address delivered October 3, 1905, before the National Reform Convention in the Park Street Congregational Church, Boston.

The Mission of the Religious Press (New York: Press of the New York Age, 1912).

The Negro: The Hope or the Despair of Christianity (Boston: Ruth Hill Publisher, 1935).

Paul Laurence Dunbar: Poet Laureate of the Negro Race (Philadelphia?: s.n., 1908?). (With Mrs. Paul Laurence Dunbar and W. S. Scarborough.)

The Pilgrimage of Harriet Ransom's Son (Nashville: A.M.E. Sunday School Union, 1949).

"Richard B. Harrison: A Winsome Personality and Artist of Beauty and Power."

School Days at Wilberforce (Springfield, Ohio: New Era Co., Printers, 1890).

The Spirit of Freedom and Justice: Orations and Speeches (Nashville: A.M.E. Sunday School Union, 1926).

"Wendell Phillips: Centennial Oration," Plymouth Church, November 29, 1911, Brooklyn, New York.

Wilberforce University, Wilberforce, Ohio

Box One, Folder One

"The Fifteenth Amendment."

Box One, Folder Two

Preface to the *History of the A.M.E. Church*, two copies, one with
    handwritten corrections.

Box One, Folder Three

"Ma Tourterelle [My Turtle Dove]," poem.
"Ocean So Wide!" poem.

Box One, Unnumbered Green Folder (possibly Folder Five)

"Buried Treasure."
"Charles Sumner: A Plea for the Civil and Political Rights of Negro-
    Americans" (January 6, 1911).
"The Cream Jug."
"Crispus Attucks: A Negro, the First to Die for American Independence."
"Duty and Destiny," typed copy.
"The Fellowship of Friends."
"The Industrial and Social Conditions of the Negro: A Thanksgiving
    Sermon."
"The Menace of Narrow Minds."
"Mind."
"The Mission of the Religious Press."
"The Negroes Bewildering Political Predicament."
"One Fold and One Shepherd for the United Methodist Episcopal
    Church."
"Prophesy."
"The Spirit of John Brown."
"Wendell Phillips Centennial Oration" (November 29, 1911).
"William Lloyd Garrison, Centennial Oration at Faneuil Hall, Boston,
    December 11, 1905."
"You Cannot Run Away from Your Shadow."

Box One, Folder Six

"The Class of 1886," three copies.
"A Rebroadcast after One Hundred Years."

Box One, Folder Seven

"A Christmas Meditation (1951)."
"Old Men for Counsel, Young Men for War."
"Poem Dedicated to Bishop Reverdy C. Ransom, 1950" (by Matei Mark-
    wei), two copies.
"Prejudice versus Dignity," two drafts.
"Yard-Stick of Values."

Box One, Folder Eight

"All Things Are Yours," several copies.
"Daniel Alexander Payne, the Prophet of an Era."
"Doors," several copies.
"Fear."
"The Great Adventure," several copies.
"The Mature Mind," several copies.
"Rags."
"Solid Rock or Shifting Sand in Human Relations."
"Tid Bits Extracted from Browning in the Field of Literature."
"Tribute to Dr. A. S. Jackson," several copies.
"Weeds."

Box Three, Folder One

"The Social Role of the Negro Minister." (Reverdy C. Ransom?)

Box Four, Folder One

"The Leaf," May 10, 1924, Louisville, Kentucky.
"The New Negro," poem.

Box Four, Green Folder (number uncertain)

"Address by Rev. R. C. Ransom at Joint Hearing before Senate Committee
    on Taxation and Retrenchment and Assembly Excise Committee on
    the Brackett-Gray Local Option Bill, April 14, 1909, Albany, New
    York."

Box Four, Folder Twenty-One

"Ecumenical, What? Ecumenical Where? The Shame of Negro Method-
    ism."
"God's Last Reserve," *Christian Recorder* (July 19, 1957).

Box Five, Folder Nine

"Things Present and Things to Come," *Voice of Missions.*

Box Five, Folder Marked Bishops Council of 1948

"The President's Address to the Bishop's Council," February 18, 1948, Dallas, Texas.

Box Six, Folder One

Photo of Reverdy C. Ransom as editor of the *A.M.E. Church Review.*

Box Thirteen

A.M.E. Year Book, 1918 (Philadelphia: A.M.E. Book Concern, 1918). (With John Hurst and J. R. Hawkins.)
A Handbook of the A.M.E. Church, Compiled and Edited. (Nashville: A.M.E. Sunday School Union, 1916). (With John R. Hawkins.)
"To Rev. R. C. Ransom" (by Thos. Atkins).

Box Fourteen, Folder Sixteen

"Report of Bureau of Research and History to the General Conference of the A.M.E. Church," May 7, 1952, Chicago.

Box Fifteen, Folder One

"Christianity, the Church and the Episcopacy: A Factual Statement on the Economic Status of the Negro, the Church Speaks to the World," February 1942.

Box Fifteen, Folder Six

"Fortune-Telling in History."

Box Fifteen, Folder Eleven

"Paul Laurence Dunbar."

Box Fifteen, Folder Twelve

"Duty and Destiny."
"The Industrial and Social Conditions of the Negro," November 26, 1896.

NONARCHIVE PRIMARY PUBLICATIONS

The Pilgrimage of Harriet Ransom's Son (Nashville: A.M.E. Sunday School Union, 1949).

Preface to the History of the A.M.E. Church (Nashville: A.M.E. Sunday School Union, 1950).

NEWSPAPERS

A.M.E. Church Review (esp. 1912–24)
Christian Recorder (1886–1930; 1942–57)
Crisis (1916–35)
Indianapolis Freeman (1890–1900)
Southern Christian Recorder (1926–28; 1947)
Voice of Mission (1901–7; 1955–59)

SECONDARY RESOURCES*

Aptheker, Herbert, editor. *A Documentary History of the Negro People in the United States,* vol. 6 (New York: Citadel Press Books/Carol Publishing Group, 1993).

Bardolph, Richard. *The Negro Vanguard* (New York: Vintage Books, 1961).

Branley, Benjamin. *The Negro Genius: A New Appraisal of the Achievement of the American Negro in Literature and the Fine Arts* (New York: Biblo and Tannen, 1972).

Drewett, Donald A. "Ransom on Race and Racism: The Racial and Social Thought of Reverdy Cassius Ransom, Preacher, Editor and Bishop in the African Methodist Episcopal Church, 1861–1959," Ph.D. dissertation, Drew University, 1988.

Fullinwider, S. P. *The Mind and Mood of Black America: 20th Century Thought* (Homewood, Ill.: The Dorsey Press, 1969).

Logan, Rayford, and Michael Winston. *Dictionary of American Negro Biography* (New York: Norton, 1982).

Matthews, Geraldine. *Black American Writers, 1773–1949* (Boston: G. K. Hall, 1975).

---

*According to David Wills, Frank Moorer, at Johns Hopkins University, several years ago began a dissertation titled "Reverdy C. Ransom and the Transformation of the A.M.E. Church." I did not find it in my search of the University of Michigan Microfilm service; I assume, therefore, that he is still in the process of completing it.

Meier, August. *Negro Thought in America, 1880–1915: Racial Ideologies in the Age of Booker T. Washington* (Ann Arbor: University of Michigan Press, 1988).

Morris, Calvin S. "Reverdy Ransom, the Social Gospel and Race." *Journal of Religious Thought* 4/1 (October 1984) reprinted in the *A.M.E. Church Review* 102/329 (January–March 1988).

———. *Reverdy C. Ransom: Black Advocate of the Social Gospel* (New York: University Press of America, 1990).

Penn, I. Garland. *The Afro-American Press and Its Editors* (New York: Arno Press and the New York Times, 1969).

Pinn, Anthony B. *Why, Lord? Suffering and Evil in Black Theology* (New York: Continuum, 1995).

Singleton, George A. *The Romance of African Methodism* (New York: Exposition Press, 1952).

Wills, David. "Reverdy C. Ransom: The Making of an A.M.E. Bishop," in *Black Apostles: Afro-American Clergy Confront the Twentieth Century*, ed. Richard Newman and Randall K. Burkett (Boston: G. K. Hall, 1978).

Wright, Richard R., Jr. *The Bishops of the African Methodist Episcopal Church* (Nashville: A.M.E. Sunday School Union, 1963).

Index